RENEWING

Ruth Magdala

for Jim
because of Jesus
from 'Ruth'

RETHINK PRESS

Published in Great Britain 2014
by Rethink Press (www.rethinkpress.com)

FOREWORD

I like books about real people. Most of those who write of their own experiences only let readers in to certain parts, the bits they want us to see, and think will impress. Not this one. Ruth takes us right into her life. She writes in such a colourful, vivid way that when I'd finished reading the characters and incidents were still hanging in my memory as if I'd been there with her. That is exactly what I want a book to do for me. In her journey towards God she uses no pious jargon or clichés. I was also delighted to discover someone else who uses a journal as a way of relating to God; usually her entries are prayers or intimate letters to Him – and not always polite ones. This makes the book real and immediate. Because of this, even the darker side of her story, which Ruth does not gloss over, was strangely cleansing and inspiring. Often we humans can think we have to live a perfect, pure, and rather dull life before God could possibly notice us at all, but Ruth proves that this is certainly not the case. I found this book totally absorbing from the very first page; I recommend you read it too.

Jennifer Rees Larcombe

THANKS

With thanks to all the wonderful people who have joined me on this journey, some briefly, others long-term. Far-flung family and friends as well as those close by; some mentioned here, some not, but each of you firmly embedded in my heart. Several names have been changed for obvious reasons. Special thanks also toLucy, James, Joe and Elaine of Rethink Press for releasing a very small fish into a very big pond.

DEDICATION

Into marvellous light I'm running
Out of darkness, out of shame
By the cross You are the truth
You are the life, You are the way.

INTRODUCTION

Lingering over coffee at the dinner table, enjoying the company of friends, the conversations ran in circles around hopes and plans, childhood memories and past times and future expectations. Someone asked me, 'If you're so fond of your native land why did you leave to go live in the States?' Many people over the years have asked the same, and what did I do, and which country do I prefer, but no single answer could satisfy or explain sufficiently. Perhaps there are things worth recording. Each time I started to write what happened and how I survived it, I kept getting stuck. Progress was only possible with a change of perspective. God has been very present throughout my life whether I chose to acknowledge Him or not, so I had to differentiate between a rambling journey of personal discovery – so fashionable at present – and an account of discovering God. This is His story. He has not kept me out of trouble but He has been with me through it all, and He promises to 'restore the years the locusts have eaten.'

'If I rise on the wings of the dawn, if I settle on the far side of the sea, even there Your hand will guide me, Your right hand will hold me fast' (Psalm 139:9). 'My mouth will tell of Your righteousness, of Your salvation… I will proclaim Your mighty acts, O Sovereign Lord… Even when I am old and grey do not forsake me, O God, till I declare Your power to the next generation' (taken from Psalm 71:15-18).

1

1

On the evening of September 19th 1990, the QE2 was steaming homewards from New York after a calm Atlantic crossing. Passengers were busily enjoying the last night aboard while anticipating the following morning's arrival at Southampton. The great ship offered all kinds of entertainment, shopping, wining and dining, none of which was going to waste.

My table companions and I shared thoughts of the voyage as we finished dinner, before adjourning to watch one of the shows. Being asked to dance was nice and the lively music encouraged a footloose and fancy-free attitude. The vast hall accommodated throngs of dancers, plus plenty of watchers at tables round three sides. The fourth, or top side, was raised to form a stage where a full band was hard at work. There was no sensation of being afloat, and nothing to jar the pleasantries of the evening. Every wish could be attended to simply by beckoning one of the many Redcoat stewards.

Thus lulled by the relaxing ambience of luxury, the shock when it came was even worse. With no warning, everyone and everything began sliding to the left. A few gasps were heard but mostly it went rather quiet. An unreal hesitation, as if with one mind, each person denied that the floor was tipping. The band stepped up the tempo but only briefly as their instruments slid away from them. Then the screams started. One or two at first but gaining strength as a fire does when fanned by wind. Over the screaming was the nightmare noise of glass and china smashing, shards flying amongst us. Tables and chairs fell. The drums rolled away from the drummer and the grand piano became a lethal weapon as it crashed into the wall, firing black and white shrapnel in all directions. The awful tilt continued until it felt as if we must surely be horizontal then, shuddering, the giant vessel groaned, struggling to right herself. Not stopping at the longed for vertical, she leaned the other way, though not quite as far, before easing back to upright.

The cessation of noise was eerie. Slowly releasing my vice-like grip on the pillar I'd fallen against, I stood in shaky amazement, thanking God for my life and for no evidence of water. Titanic thoughts had flourished, but in surveying the chaos, only a mammoth clean up appeared necessary. Soothing words from the captain poured from the loudspeakers, explaining how a freak wave had hit us broadside on as we entered English waters. The ship sustained no structural damage and could, we were assured, have coped with a far greater storm. Few of the passengers could have. Stewards bustled about helping those in need and ushering us out to find places to sit and something to drink. The organised efficiency of the staff was impressive and there was soon a makeshift band trying to erase anxieties and recreate the dancing mood. It seemed incredible to be sitting in the plush velvet armchairs, brightly chatting about what had, minutes ago, felt like disaster. Sleep appealed more, so I made my way down the now familiar decks and staircases to my tiny cabin.

Packed and ready early next morning, I savoured the last leisurely breakfast prior to finding a good spot up on the main deck, out in the open at the very front. Just as I'd stood for several hours at the back, five days ago, to watch New York fade out of my life, perhaps forever, so I wanted to watch Sussex reappear into it. Emotions threatened to engulf reality. What was I expecting? What was I afraid of? The ache of leaving America, my home for nearly twenty-four years, was somewhat soothed by the finalised divorce, but what lay ahead? What was I to do?

Unable to contain the swirling thoughts and feelings, my tears added more salt to the waters below. The huge ship pushed herself importantly between the Isle of Wight and the south coast cliffs, so close to both it seemed as if I only had to reach out to grab a handful of chalk. Was I pushing my returning self into a space apparently too small also? Perhaps I'd been away too long? In movies when ships arrive in port there is great rejoicing and fanfare, champagne and streamers. Was Southampton dock going to be like that? The closer we got the worse I felt. Was I going to glide down a red-carpeted gangplank, waving graciously to a welcoming committee, or slither off a different sort of gangplank and sink into oblivion, guilt and failure?

The impending berthing in England felt somehow connected to an earlier birthing there in 1946.

'What a nice fat little girl.' Not quite the sort of comment one revels in, but well meant I think, as were several other similar remarks made about me in the family. Not due till the end of April, I arrived a month early, a day after Mother fell over. She had hung the washing out, returning to the kitchen with snow on her shoes and slipped, squashing me. Dad drove us in his old Austin 10 to the Surrey nursing home in Croydon, leaving her there for a couple of weeks. Confinement in those days meant exactly that. Quotes from a couple of telegrams: 'Praise God for your baby's safe arrival, may she be blest indeed;' and one that explained the sender's absence this way: 'My children have ringworm. They have been shaved and wear white linen caps. We'll come to visit you very soon.' Let's hope she didn't rush.

My three siblings were breast fed for many months, but at my turn Mother's asthma was bad. She substituted Trufood, liberal doses of Virol, cod liver oil, orange juice and carrot juice. I was not a contented baby (possibly diet related) and cried a great deal, keeping my family and neighbours awake at night. When I was 18 months old Mother bought a blue and white wool romper suit, and noted in my baby book:

Dressed her in it the same afternoon as paternal Nanny and Grandpa were coming to tea. She stood on the drawing room hearthrug, legs apart, and unabashed made a pool. She was of course out of nappies by then; this was an embarrassing mistake. My vigilance must have been relaxed on account of my guests.

The four of us, Alison the eldest, David, me, then Jonathan, grew up near Crawley, in Lowfield Heath. Most of that village has since been demolished to make room for Gatwick Airport. The first home I can remember was the much loved old house, Clyro. We had the freedom to wander safely through its gardens and out into the couple of hundred acres of nursery land. J. Cheal and Sons, our firm of landscape architects, was founded by my father's grandfather, Joseph, in 1871. He came from a long line of ancient Quakers; the first recorded was Thomas Cheal, born in 1625. Six generations later John married Mary Fox from another great old Quaker dynasty, and their firstborn was Joseph in 1848. I wish I'd known earlier and appreciated more about my rich legacy of godly Christian forebears.

Our playgrounds were wide fields of roses and dahlias, greenhouses and ponds, trees, plus the topiary box bushes specially trained and clipped. I used to clamber up onto the trim dark green birds, chessmen and animals, knowing I wasn't supposed to. The haystacks were also great to climb into, as was the ancient high-wheeled wooden cart left to rot. Since the new tractor's arrival there was little work for the shire horses, Ginger and Prince, and none for the cart. I remember a painful moment jumping off that cart, onto a rusty nail, which went right through the crepe sole of my sandal into my foot. I'm sure it was well purpled with gentian violet, or a generous dab of witch-hazel, the mainstays of the medicine cupboard.

We kept bantams called Gert, Daisy and Oddie. They laid two kinds of eggs. The shelled ones we ate for breakfast, but the others were horrible slimy splodges that had to be cleared up, usually by me. We always had dogs too, who also enjoyed the space to roam. I disliked going down the path to visit Mother's Aunt Grace because in summer the bees buzzed out of the lavender around my legs, and in winter Aunt poked her long bony fingers down my neck to show me how cold they were. Her tiny home really was called Aunt's Cottage. At Easter in 1952 she was nice and joined in our egg hunt, and there is a photograph of us four children with her and our eggs. I still have the china mug that one of those eggs came in, plain now, though it did have a picture of Jemima Puddleduck on it.

The sandpit on the south-west side of the house was the scene of many happy hours, and a few altercations too, especially between me and little brother Jonny. There was a rain-butt on the corner, useful for filling moats around castles, but mostly we had to sit on it for haircutting sessions. Mother dipped into it for rinses after shampoos, claiming rainwater made hair shine. Behind the sandpit was the bad part, dark and dank and to be avoided when possible. The outside lavatory was there, opposite the coal and wood sheds, with the dustbins and lots of nettles. The woodshed was where Mother allowed the tramps to sit. Those gentlemen of the road often knocked on our door because there were no other houses close by. We offered sandwiches, tea, and leaflets about Jesus and the Bible. I think the men were as wary of Mother as I was. She had a good heart, in her staunchly Anglican way, but stood no nonsense. I was taken out there sometimes to have my mouth washed out with soap at the basin by the outside loo; an awful punishment. In the kitchen was a drawer where ration books were kept. I don't remember much of post war deprivations, except those little books had to be stamped when we collected orange juice, which was thick and strong, in slim square-shouldered glass bottles with small screw caps. Along with my baby record book I have a red clothing book from 1945-6, still containing some blue and maroon coupons. Our play clothes were mostly knitted or made from old curtains, but we were well nourished, and used to strict routines of early bedtimes with windows open year round, midday rests and plenty of outdoor exercise in all weathers.

Nothing helped me during nocturnal thunderstorms however. I crept into my parents' room to squeeze under Mother's side of the bed (Dad's always had the pot). The dust, the stringy bits hanging down from the hessian covered springs and the cramped, cold misery of it were all preferable to being anywhere else where the lightning could get me. My dislike of the dark has lessened, but not gone. Nor am I happy in small, unlit places. Samuel Whiskers has a lot to answer for. Those whose literary education included the wonderful Beatrix Potter children's stories will know they are mostly wonderful, but one or two need a rating of 18 years and over. Samuel is an enormous rat who displays anti-social behaviour in dark, cramped attic areas.

Sundays were sombre days: we went to church twice, morning and evening, or to the Quaker meeting in the morning sometimes. Alison and I went to Girl Crusaders in the afternoon, but before that there was lunch to get through. I loathed meat and most vegetables, especially brussels sprouts, and picked miserably at my plateful week after week knowing I'd not be allowed to leave the table until it was gone. Watching the fat congeal on the gravy like ice on a mud puddle rendered me unable to swallow even the bile in my throat. I recall being so angry and upset one post-lunch departure that when we got to Crusaders I wet myself, and can hear and feel again the mortification trickling onto the floor. We had plenty of Bible stories, and Bible colouring books because other games were not played on Sunday.

Instead of church some Sunday evenings we went to the Lowfield Mission hall. In 1903 my grandfather received permission to hold a weekly Gospel Service there. During the war it was changed to afternoon to avoid the blackout. There was a rota of speakers, and an ancient organ from which someone coaxed enough notes to sing by. By 1956 enthusiasm had sadly waned and there were no more gatherings. One old soul, Edie, remained and she took up residence in the hall behind a thick, heavy curtain, possibly as a sort of caretaker. She was very old and crippled and needed a lot of help. I used to cycle there and heat up soup for her and feed her cat. There was always a dreadful smell behind that curtain.

Clyro had a large playroom with an old billiards table taking up a lot of space. Endless hours were spent making dolls house furniture with matchboxes, scraps of material and Gripfix, that solid white glue in round tins with little ladles to scoop it out. It smelled wonderful and tasted even better; I would have been quite happy with that for

Sunday lunch. No doubt it was made from unappetising bovine hooves, but I still ate copious amounts of it. I don't remember being ill very much, but whenever we were, it was Lucozade, and Marmite sandwiches to aid recuperation.

In the dining room there was a solid dresser along one wall. Once when feeling particularly unfairly treated, I took a knife and furiously gouged the door. Afterwards I had to work with sandpaper for a long time, then beeswax. The expected punishment for bad behaviour was being sent to my room and forbidden to return until I could remember my manners. I stayed in isolation until either hunger or cold persuaded me, then shuffled back into whichever room they were all in, stood at the door and spat out, insincerely, 'I'm sorry.' After one major row I ran upstairs to the bathroom and locked the door, planning to stay there forever. All the towels from the rack made an adequate bed in the bathtub. There had been several exhortations to come out, but I stayed put, wrapped in misery. Eventually my father came to the rescue, his gentle words filling me with remorse.

There were some funny times too. Mother's sense of humour was great, when she let it out, and Dad was well known for his puns and droll wit. Once, round the dining table at the beginning of school summer holidays, we were waiting for David, who seemed so grown up after another term away, to change out of his uniform and join us so we could eat. Finally he strode in, wearing nothing but one of Dad's large handkerchiefs looped over a string belt, slung dangerously low, and Mum's lipstick daubed in circles round his nipples, and a big grin. It was such a surprise, so out of character and unexpected, that we stared at him in stunned silence before bursting into laughter. Helpless, tear-producing laughter which Dad tried his best to squash, or at least control, but soon was overtaken himself with one of his 'I give in, you lot are hopeless' noises from deep between his tight collar, tie, and double chin.

We went on holiday during several summers to the Isle of Wight with parental friends called Uncle and Auntie. I remember the Dimbola Hotel at Freshwater Bay, Blackgang Chine, the coloured sand at Alum Bay and one of those beaches when a sudden storm came. The only way back was up the steep path between two high cliffs that we had come down earlier when it was dry and rocky. The heavy downpour rendered it nearly impassable, a torrent of wet chalky clay sliding down to meet the hastily incoming tide. Up it we had to go, carrying the day's equipment. Auntie and Uncle were neither young nor fit, Jonny was very young, Alison shrieked as she dropped her prized camera, and we were all soaked. I crawled up pushing or dragging one person after another and some belongings, anchoring them as best I could before sliding back down for the next. A sense of overpowering responsibility felt heavier than everything else.

At times like that I was most aware of my sister's disability and instinctively knew Mother expected twice as much from me, in every respect. Alison was born without her left forearm and hand. I was not supposed to be angry, even when she was often mean to me. I was always told: 'Bear with her dear, she has so much to put up with.' Battles raged in me, not about having a handicapped sister (that word was never mentioned) just an inaccessible one. So my anger, plus great sympathy, and juvenile intuition, had nowhere to go. Difficult topics were never discussed. It was years before I began to understand the real effects on us all.

One of my father's aunts, Auntie Jo, lived nearby. I liked her, but not Sam, her black cat who once got stuck on a roof, requiring rescue. He thanked me in scratches, but she invited me to choose a reward from her curio cabinet. Whenever I polish that tiny silver filigree basket entwined with grapes I think of her. I would love to know the current whereabouts of her other treasures, such as the framed Bible texts. They exhorted one to do good works, resist the devil and pray without ceasing, all of which seemed impossible to me, and only what old people needed to do anyway. I did love the flowers weaving their delicate way around the old-fashioned letters. Auntie Jo's hair was very long and white. Occasionally she'd uncoil it and wash it, then sit quite still at her open window while it dried: a scary sight.

In April 1956 Mother had some professional photographs taken. She and Dad looked the part, she in twinset and pearls, he in his smart tweed tie. Alison, our teenager, was resplendent in a velvet dress and pearls (we won't mention the thick knee socks) David at eleven still in short trousers and six-year-old Jonny with a toothy grin and white shirt and tie. Then there is yours truly, in a royal blue dress, short socks and a ghastly haircut. Mother was convinced the corners of one's fringe must go up, not level or down. We four had best shoes on, no cutout toes, an economy measure sometimes exercised to make room for growing feet. I did complain, although I knew I shouldn't, about having to wear Alison's cast-offs. When asking why we couldn't have something new there would always be the same maternal response: 'We can't afford it, dear', followed by a withering look in Dad's direction. She often sounded unfriendly when talking to him and was not good at hiding her disapproval. I was unaware of the other legacy sitting so heavily on Dad's shoulders. He had inherited the nursery firm when it was no longer the thriving business of the previous century, and constantly struggled with failing finances. The tensions this caused were not pleasant. I loved my dad and tried to stick up for him.

One thing I enjoyed was modelling clay. Pounding and bashing the stuff until it became malleable enough to create something amazing. At one stage I'd finished a large tray full of sculptures, and put them to dry up on the mantelpiece. Later, eagerly showing my work to Dad, his shoulder caught the edge of the tray, bringing the whole lot crashing down. That was a tragedy; not only for the loss of my creations, but the pain that stabbed through my heart as I saw the horror of self reproach on my father's face. I believe that was my first awareness of true forgiveness. Of course I was upset, but I was far more concerned about alleviating his anguish. I could get over the breakages, sculpt some more, but he was broken apart, shattered far worse. I was able then to pour all my crossness into a warm, accepting hug, surprising myself and maybe him too.

2

We began our education in turn at Miss Reynolds' school, and were taught all the basics, including drawing, music and Latin. When the boys each turned seven they were sent to boarding school, and Alison and I moved on to a private school in Horley. Those were grim days for me, as I grew fat and felt disliked. At the end of the first year I was greatly burdened by a real fear of the 'moving-up' business. It clouded my summer, but the relief was huge upon realising the whole class was to move-up. Later the fear reversed as it became far more likely that I alone would not move-up, but have to repeat a year. I just managed to pass the exams, but struggled in most subjects, only enjoying art and needlework. Although a hopeless speller I did love writing and, eventually, reading. Dyslexia was unknown in those days.

We four took an adventurous trip by ourselves in 1958 to the Lake District. Later Mother agreed she had been unwise to let us. Possibly not quite the dangers then that there are today, but I am still convinced the Almighty provided guardian angels around us. The whole thing was masterminded by Alison, and her meticulous preparations kept us on track. We went north by coach to the first overnight stop at a youth hostel and from there we walked and walked. Each of us carried our own belongings in backpacks and we followed, not uncomplainingly, our leader. Sometimes she brought up the rear and a picture comes to mind of part of the Bayeux tapestry. The king is goading his men into battle by prodding them with a large spear from behind, and the caption reads, 'The king encourageth his troops.' We hiked vast distances and one day climbed Helvellen by crossing Striding Edge, to the amazement of the other hostellers who shared our quarters that night. It is a treacherously narrow mountain path with a sheer drop either side, usually only attempted by professional walkers. The hostels were divided, girls one end, boys the other, and when there was no bathroom we washed in painfully cold lakes or streams. At one point Jonny fell, hurting his ankle, and Alison decided he'd pushed his eight-year old muscles far enough so arranged for him to go home on a coach.

The poor chap went through another experience with one of his sisters, and this time it was me. He suffered from asthma and that day he must have been quite bad, needing a suppository. Mother called me in to hold the lamp so she could see what she was doing. Happy to oblige, I removed the lampshade for even better illumination. Thinking of the only television show we were allowed to watch, *The Lone Ranger*, where I'd recently seen some cattle being branded, I became a cowboy. The 'roped calf' was in front of me, the 'branding iron' was in my hand, so of course I had to press naked bulb to naked buttock. The noise and smell of burning skin was dreadful, as was the reaction in the bedroom.

Near our house was an old apple tree in which I made a place to sit. Those apples were the crunchiest, tartest green gems ever grown, and I ate quantities of them without the slightest stomach ache. The cores got collected and fed to the two retired horses, those large lumbering animals I could not ride, but they enjoyed my visits. I did have a friend with a New Forest pony. Many Saturdays I would cycle through the Nurseries to the big white gate at the back, into Poles Lane, at the end of which was Alicia's farm. She let me ride whenever we could catch Honey, and I never tired of it, though frequently fell off. We rode bareback with just a halter rope instead of a bridle.

A younger friend, Penny, lived nearby and we three often played together, not always amicably. On days when we neither rode nor paddled we went further along the lane to the 'dark house'. My memory of it is foreboding, crepuscular even on a sunny day, but an old photo shows a stunning Tudor manor with a well-kept lawn. We only went through the back hedge to use the pool. Whether we asked permission, or simply took it as given I don't know. I don't remember seeing any adults, just the fear that we would. I loathed being 'encouraged' over the edge into the sludge because I knew my feet would slide on the slime at the bottom in a desperate attempt to push up to the surface again. Goodness knows what else lived in that pool; probably originally designed for fish and ornamental lilies, it would have made a perfect setting for a horror story.

Slowly advancing years brought a few benefits, and I was permitted to cycle further afield. One excitement was pedalling to Charlwood's Fish and Chip Shop, where every order was wrapped directly into old newspaper liberally sprinkled with vinegar. To get there meant going the long way round, past the back of the newly opened part of Gatwick Airport. Lovell House, another spooky place, was nearer home, but took even more courage to cycle to. Across the road was the Rolander's windmill, another playground entirely unsuitable for children, yet we were often there. Jill and I were usually plagued by her brother Jack, yet we spent a lot of time together.

I also frequented a local riding stable and worked hard, willingly mucking out stalls, heaving loads of manure and polishing tack, all to earn an infrequent ride. My enthusiasm was perhaps taken advantage of. Once I entered a gymkhana, having slaved for weeks previously, to be able to use one of the horses all day. I believe it was the only time my whole family came to support me and they even brought a picnic to make a day of it. My excitement knew no bounds. Never had a horse been so beautifully groomed, mane braided and beribboned, leathers supple and gleaming and even the rider kitted out in borrowed finery. Into the ring we trotted at the right moment, circled the jumps to check the course, went for the first jump – oops, a refusal. Turned around and tried again, twice. Three refusals earned humiliating disqualification. No longer was I destined for international equestrian events.

In 1960 we moved house, a short distance up the road to Brookfield, another large, rambling brick house. My grandfather had it built early in 1900 when he brought his young bride over from Ireland and they raised their four children there. They had five, but little Ruth died in infancy. Dad lived there most of his young life, then brought his wife and four children to live there. As before, we had large gardens bordering on the Nurseries. There was a grass tennis court in the front next to a wild area full of azalea bushes, an excellent buffer between us and the ever-growing amount of traffic on the main road. Opposite us was a large place known as Hydens. A friend kept her horse there, and during a severely cold winter it escaped from the stable and trotted about the hard frosty ground. Unsuspectingly walking over the edge of the frozen pool, its weight shattered the ice. The noise of the terrified animal screaming and thrashing about amid chunks of thick ice was awful. Firemen were called to the rescue, but they asked me to plunge in astride the horse in an attempt to calm it and guide it to where the ropes could be slung under to hoist it out.

Brookfield also had a rose garden which, at one time had a wooden pergola and trellis. There was a covered veranda where we sat for photos, just as Dad had done in his childhood with his family around him. The kitchen contained a Rayburn (the poor man's Aga) and in the centre was a large scrubbed pine table. The stone-floored larder had stone shelves, fine wire mesh over a tiny north-facing window, and a water-filled earthenware crock on the floor in which to stand the milk. Upstairs, I had a beautiful bedroom to myself. It looked out over the tennis lawn and azaleas. Roses trailed down the wallpaper beside the basin in the corner and, other than freezing up there three-quarters of the year (no heat of any sort) it was great.

Another part of growing up was our individual visits to my godparents. They were good people and I know they loved our whole family. Uncle John and Aunt Maisie had all this life offers, except children. When staying there I was treated to dinners out at fine restaurants, theatres and shows, and my first experience of bed on a cold night being deliciously warm, due to an electric blanket. Their large Surrey bungalow had a wide picture window facing extensive

15

views. Any time Aunt Maisie was busy in the kitchen, her husband would invite me to admire the view from that window. He always stood very close behind me, very close, and began by pointing out places of interest, but gradually his large hands found their way to my budding chest. The fondling was not unpleasant, but I knew it must be wrong, partly because it made me feel so strange, but mostly because he stopped immediately we heard his wife's footsteps returning.

One place Alison and I went to regularly, by bus, was Crawley to do the shopping, all of which had to be carried home. Once or twice we were given just enough extra cash for a fish and chip lunch, and the cinema if there was a Walt Disney nature film. I was often carsick, but I did eventually outgrow the actual vomiting, although the wretched feelings persisted in any moving vehicle. I dreaded family occasions when we drove to the boys' schools to collect my brothers or take them back at the start of a new term. Often there was a cricket match and tea or a concert, but always for me was the car journey to endure.

Having grown up loving animals, this developed in me possibly to the point of obsession. Animals never ridicule, criticise or ostracise. For a while I had thirteen guinea pigs. I loved those little cavies and took great care of them, keeping them clean and well fed. I constructed cages for them out of boxes, bits of wood and wire, and also made large wire mesh enclosures for them to run about in on the grass. Whenever I went near the door of their shed I'd be greeted with a chorus of high-pitched squeals.

3

Great Aunt Ethel, Mother's other aunt, was quite a character, with the air of a slightly naughty past. Never anything but elegant, her trademarks were lace handkerchiefs, and pearls hanging heavily from her throat and ears. She and her handbag were seldom apart, and I discovered why one day at tea. She asked Mother to fetch a little more hot water, and instantly foraged in that bag, producing a miniature bottle of whisky which she then poured into her teacup. A juicy wink at me sealed the secret. She never smelled of anything but eau de cologne and I wasn't aware of her 'having a problem', although one of her well-used phrases was, 'drunk and disorderly, but always a lady.'

Our earliest church experience was divided between the Church of England and the Quaker meetings. The ancient Ifield Meetinghouse was a wonderful place and I loved going there, maybe not for the meditative hour we had to sit silently through, but the peaceful security of it. I liked the giant chestnut tree towering over the uneven roof, making shadows dance through the diamond leaded windows high up near the rafters. In the front yard was the old stone mounting block with well-worn steps to climb up and jump off, and to the side, the gate in the hedge leading to the graveyard where many of my relatives lie buried. Going home from there was fun once we turned into the Nurseries through the big white gate. Jonny and I jumped out to open up for Dad to drive through, then close it, puffing and heaving as it was a heavy gate. Then we were allowed to get up on the running board, one each side and cling on as we bumped home along the track through the fields.

As the years went by we went there less, and more often to the new church in Crawley. When the Queen visited Crawley New Town we saw her on her tour of St Mary's and its new Hall. She planted a Cheal's tree, using the silver spade from my great grandfather's era, with engraved silver bands from other famous users. Many years later my son, when very young, hearing of the royal occasion while reverently holding the spade, asked if the hotness of the Queen's hand was still there. St Mary's church was large, ultra modern and painted duck-egg blue inside. One wall was filled with bright stained-glass pieces providing a marvellous rainbow effect on sunny days. My father sang in the choir, perhaps making up for all the Quaker years of no music, and I sang with him. The youth club was my only social outing. I went by bus and had to go home when Dad arrived to pick me up. He was usually early. I hated leaving before it was quite over. Even with my very pointed cream shoes, green bouclé sweater and bouffant hair, I still didn't look right. That may sound trivial but it wasn't. Without dress-sense or confidence one feels unattractive.

During a notable sermon, the Vicar urged his congregation to come forward to commit hearts and lives to Jesus. Nobody moved. Feeling sorry for him I went forward myself. Merely a formality, surely: wasn't I born a Christian anyway? Due to the Quaker influence none of us had been baptised in infancy, so I agreed to 'be done' as an adult, standing up at the font. Then it was confirmation by the Bishop in a most solemn ceremony. The Vicar and his family were good friends and there were many tea parties with them, and visiting missionaries home on furlough, and other church families. It was always assumed, that I would take the children, so we were excused from the table and it was up to me to look after and amuse whichever little ones were around.

By 1961 I reached the legal school leaving age of fifteen with great relief. I had counted the days till freedom which, in hindsight, is strange because I was directionless, with no particular ambition to be doing anything else. I saw no point in putting much effort into anything to do with school. The comments most frequently heard were not complimentary: 'She'll get by on common sense'; 'Its only puppy fat'; 'Doesn't she drink tea yet?', and 'What are you going to do with her?'

I resented having to wear boned corsets and bra, plus suspenders and stockings. They spoke of womanhood, something I did not look forward to. At a Crusader camp in the New Forest a most appalling affliction struck. Death had to be imminent. Using outdoor latrines was bad enough without menstruation as well. It was as unexpected as unwelcome. I was shocked. I am sure I'd been told the facts and possibly saw a connection between them and my sister being 'unwell' fairly regularly and staying home from school. Truly, I had no idea it would have anything to do with me, or be so nasty.

My first job was at Manor Royal Industrial Estate, in the Mallory Battery factory. Cycling along the wide, new road with its distinctive smell of bad oranges was refreshing after hours of tedious monotony. To earn the meagre pay packet, as countless shiny batteries dashed past I had to grab as many as possible to press on the positive and negative bits at the correct ends.

That autumn I started a two-year domestic science course at Croydon Technical College, though I don't recall participating in the decision to do so. It meant getting the bus to Gatwick, going under the new fly-over up onto the station for the train to East Croydon every morning. I took basic classes to complete my GCEs, plus art, cookery, needlework and health. I did not work hard, and did spend a lot of time in the bakery department full of trainee chefs. Whole new flirtatious vistas were opening up, but I had no idea what to do with them. I did learn to smoke on the train with a friend called Gaynor, then to suck peppermints before getting home. On September 12th my grandfather died. The only memory is the quiet service at Ifield Meetinghouse, and how lovely and peaceful it felt leaving him in the shady cemetery beside all his ancient relatives.

Every year we celebrated Guy Fawkes' night by driving to the boys' school to watch fireworks and eat sausages round the enormous bonfire. Everyone else looked forward to it and thoroughly enjoyed it but I hated it, and not only the car journey. I was afraid. Afraid of the fire itself, plus the gruesome shadows it threw on the surrounding fields and dark woods; and even more afraid of the fireworks and their shrieking whizzes, explosions and choking smell. My only concession was being allowed to stand in the school porch, but it was comfortless there alone, still seeing, hearing and smelling everything, with much teasing later.

On the other hand Christmas was always special, with traditions happily adhered to with minimal expenditure. It started as soon as the boys were home from school, with the four of us going out into the Nurseries with the big old pram to collect evergreens. That pram had an extra compartment under the ancient horsehair mattress and we couldn't go home till it was full and piled high. Then the making of yards and yards of garlands by intertwining trailing ivy and fir branches, red ribbon and wire. A painful job, but gladly done, usually to the accompaniment of scratchy carols on the gramophone records and us singing. We wove the garlands up the banisters, draped them along mantelpieces, filling the house with Christmas smells. Every picture had to have a sprig of holly; red candles into every holder and red ribbons attached to the wall onto which we pinned the cards as they arrived in the post. All the silver, especially the fluted fruit bowl, and copper and brass had to be polished.

The tree was fresh and sticky with resin which increased the wonderful Christmassy aromas. We had few decorations other than the ancient tin candleholders. Those holders lived in a battered blue tin, and I had to scrape out the old wax before inserting the new candles carefully, then not clipping any directly under another branch. It was a long time before I discovered that most people had electric lights on their trees, and even artificial trees. Our candles were only lit on Christmas Eve and Christmas Day while we gathered round the piano for carol singing. There was always a bucket of water strategically hidden close by. We had little contact with our maternal grandfather, but he did send a turkey every December. It would arrive in a hamper, looking blue and very dead. The boys used to argue over the parson's nose and gleefully pull out any remaining feather stalks, while Mum trussed and stuffed the bird. Boxing Day was enforced thank- you- letter writing time and that stands out more clearly than any gifts received or given.

My first proper date was at a dance in aid of the Cheshire Homes. His name escapes me, but after the introductions he asked what I'd like to drink. I assured him I was not thirsty. He repeated the question, twice. I thought he was slightly simple, though I didn't do much better with chitchat myself. Coming from an entirely teetotal family I knew nothing of social drinking, and not much of any other social behaviour, just plain good manners and strict ones at that. The evening was not a success.

The summer I was 16 I joined our church's house-party week in Cromer, Norfolk. Barely back from Cromer, I was soon off again, by myself to stay with German friends. Both Alison and David had done the same trip before me and loved it, as Mother had, many times. On that amazing solo voyage, which turned out to be the first of many, I went by train via the Hook of Holland. It must have been a fearsome crossing, as I wrote home:

It got bad at 2.30am. The chap the other side was snoring worse than Dad. I had to hold the ledge to stay in bed as we went over to the right, up and up for miles, down and down for miles, then over to the left. Glass breaking and people crying; amazingly I wasn't sick but felt vile. On dry land again, found my seat on the Rheingold Express, watched flat Dutch fields and Zees go by. Rotterdam Noord brought Anne Frank's Diary *suddenly alive for me. In Arnhem I saw an old man harvesting with a scythe and binding the sheaves himself, and outside Koln someone was ploughing with a horse.*

I was met at Mannheim and welcomed into the family. Amongst many highlights was Heidelberg Castle, and evening walks into the mountains with fantastic views along the Rhine valley. Life experiences

21

were certainly widened in several spheres. Just the constant use and quantity of wine and cigarettes, plus staying up late playing cards every night, took some getting used to. It was exceptionally hot and I felt unwell a lot. One weekend I was violently ill in Tante Leischen's home and made an awful mess. I shall not forget her cleaning up after me and spraying eau-de-cologne everywhere before calling the doctor in. He thought it was *blinddarm* (appendicitis). I thought sunstroke aided and abetted by alcohol. In Ludwigshafen with Victor and Mechtilde, I had a lot of fun with their four young children, and it was with them I learned a smattering of very colloquial German. In Neustadt there were the six children of Onkel Rudi and Tante Leischen, four of them lovely teenagers. Several evenings we turned out the lights, lit candles, rolled back the carpet and danced. It was fun being fought over.

Travel sickness was a problem and spoiled many day trips, but one I did manage and loved was to Durrenbach and Trefels, with the restorative *kaffe* and ices in the same cafe my mother, sister and brother had been to before. We drove on to the French border, only to be met by barriers and police. No entry for us because someone had just taken a shot at President de Gaulle. From a letter home:

On the way back there was a weinfest on the Weintor so of course we stopped to enjoy it. Beer and wine, bands playing, carousels, stalls, bread rolls and wurst sausages; throngs of noisy, happy people. It was such fun. We drank and ate and danced and danced and I didn't feel at all sick and my sore toe stopped hurting after more wine.

In Bad Durkheim we ate at a huge barrel, sitting on some smaller barrels, again where my family had been before me. Everyone was so kind it made me feel special and important, but Winfried was the dearest. I liked him, despite his terribly bitten nails. I believed all his promises to write regularly, and come to England to visit me. He did neither, and then he died. How very sad. Although the Germans were Roman Catholics they made sure I got to the evangelical church most

Sundays. In Duisburg there was a communion service where the bread was taken standing up and the wine was white. In Koln we took a cable car across the Rhine to the park and back, climbed the 501 steps to the top of the cathedral for spectacular views, and someone had Chris Barber and Acker Bilk music playing. The last week flew by because I went to school with Doris, also 16. I had to stand up and talk about England but they understood perfectly and asked lots of questions.

Returning from Europe, I found I had managed three O level passes in English Language, Literature, and Art, also City and Guilds of London Institute Domestic Cookery. I'd learned to produce nutritious and economical meals and for that I have been thankful many times since. Sadly there was no sense of achievement, only shame in the light of my brainy siblings' successes. There was still more of: 'what are we going to do with her now?'

On September 29th 1963 my parents drove me to Lewes, to be a live-in mother's help in a big house called Owlpen It was a residential home for a few elderly people, plus a small farm. The owners had three young children to be my charges, which in itself would have been enough, but general domestic chores, including endless washing up, bed making, vacuuming, and waiting at tables, kept me busy for at least 12 hours every day. Once they took the children and me to the beach for a treat. Some treat. This is what I wrote at the time:

Everything carried from car to beach, then deciding on a spot and settling, much to other peoples' amused interest. Undressing children, finding bathing things, tying up sand shoes. Five minutes later rescuing lost ball, drowning child, floating shoe, emptying pebbles out of another shoe, applauding one child's efforts at swimming, then another, dragging them from the water, calming quarrels as to which one I dry first, drying and removing sand and salt stickiness, finding respective underwear, doling out the picnic, discovering I'd left the flask of tea in the kitchen, etc, till we returned home exhausted and cross. I had a wretched headache.

At the end of another letter home there is a message to my father:

Yes I am keeping my accounts carefully – not difficult since I haven't been paid anything yet.

It wasn't long before they found out I could ride and almost at once they bought a pony. Not a nice, traffic-safe, kid-proof animal but a semi-wild New Forest, straight from an auction round-up. Breaking her in and teaching the children to ride and look after her became my job also, and I thoroughly enjoyed the whole process, supplementing my little knowledge with books. First getting her used to me in her field, then gently handling her and grooming, getting a halter on her head and leading her about. Then I hopped on and rode bareback, just using the leading rein, doing a bit more with her each day. The saddle went on and off frequently, then bridle, then I rode with both. All the time teaching and repeating commands firmly but gently, and when she was ready, introducing the children to her and teaching them to respect, love, and manage her well and so become confident riders. Eventually some encouraging compliments came. They said I had worked wonders with pony and children.

After some free time I was returning in a taxi whose driver was upset. The date was November 22nd 1963. John F Kennedy had just been shot. Two days later assassin Lee Harvey Oswald was himself shot by Jack Ruby. Americans were not then high on my list of concerns, but even my youthfully limited worldview took in that this was a moment of history that would have far-reaching effects.

Having left Owlpen after Christmas with few regrets and only missing the pony, I moved on to Dorking, Surrey, to another live-in mother's help position with Mr and Mrs B. What a different set-up. I was treated as one of the family instead of a servant, included in everything, and invited to call my employers by their Christian names. The children were beautiful in looks and behaviour. We all got along well, and it was a delight to be in such a happy household. Standards were high, there was a great deal of work and my responsibilities increased. The oldest child was as quiet and thoughtful as her sister was outgoing and imaginative, and the baby was adorable. I dreamed of having a frothy white wedding with him as a pageboy. Unfortunately I became ill and had to go home for a while. Childhood mumps in adults can be unpleasant. I hardly thought of myself as an adult, but for medical purposes then I was and it was unpleasant. Not much in my face, but dreadful stomach pains, mumps in the pancreas, requiring a no-fat diet. What a blessing I could not know then how much that would affect me in future years.

During my weeks with the mumps, I received a long letter from a chap I'd thought of as my boyfriend, who had written reams about his engineering studies in an attempt to cheer me up. We met again shortly after I left the Bs and returned home. He arrived to take me out in his new vehicle, a three-wheeler bubble car, an unnerving experience in every way. We had only held hands before he went away to college, and once walked through a bluebell wood, pushing our bikes and he kissed me by a gate, just a little peck on the cheek. Squashed together in that bubble car, he suddenly kissed me with newly acquired passion and know-how, and quite literally took my breath away, and nearly my life too. I was sure I would drown.

4

A cousin, Sally, returned to England after many years of antipodean life and was living and working in London. That autumn I moved into her Earls Court flat and have strangely few memories, no photographs and no letters, which makes me wonder if anything wildly wicked and exciting happened that I've blocked out. It is more likely that nothing did and we kept hoping it would. We did laugh a lot, and were always running out of electricity and the right coins to feed the meter. I worked at Harrods for some months over Christmas, in the millinery and lingerie department. So unlike me, but having no idea who the real me was, I adapted pretty well, chameleon-like, and just got on with selling elegant things to elegant people in a frightfully elegant manner.

Before leaving I bought myself a black fur hood, long coveted in one of the display cabinets. It cost five pounds, a whole week's salary. It had a soft tartan lining and was large enough to contain my long hair and still do up under my chin. Not only did I wear it for many winters, but years later it kept my daughter's head warm and eventually became part of a Halloween costume then a cat-head in a school play. Five pounds well spent.

In January 1965 we were all saddened by the death of Winston Churchill. Perhaps to prove that even I could be interested in such important happenings, I willingly joined with Sally and Alison to attend the funeral. Along with thousands of others we arrived prepared, the evening before, with sleeping bags, thermos flasks and food. Sleeping alone on a London street in January must be awful, but *en masse* it was quite exciting, with bodies strewn everywhere. That was long before London's post-war bombings began. In the morning it was overwhelming when the cortege went slowly past. All men removed their hats and those carrying flags dipped them low. An emotional hush could be heard and felt all around.

March arrived too quickly and saw me dragging my feet towards Wellgarth Nursery Training College, Golders Green, North London, to start my studies again. The college was a peculiar collection of old buildings connected by dark inner hallways or poorly roofed courtyards. It housed the all-female students and staff, plus many of the city's unwanted children in the east wing orphanage. Drearily Victorian, it was, however, one of the best establishments for learning, with practical hands-on experience, the intricacies of childcare. We slept in a large corridor divided into little cubicles, each with two narrow beds, and had to be in by 10pm curfew or the front door was locked. I soon fell in love with the babies and developed a knack of calming even the worst screamers. We studied every detail from pre-natal care of mothers to children up to five years, including basic psychology, wellbeing, diseases and ill health. Some of my peers found it hard to cope with the severely deformed infants in our care, but for me, those with mental disabilities were more distressing. On our first duty I was assigned Greg and told to take his legs off and bath him. Being used to my sister's artificial arm and all its straps and buckles, I managed the bath with no problem, just amazed at the dexterity of Greg's chubby little finger stubs helping me with his straps and buckles. His mother had taken thalidomide during her pregnancy, as had so many other women at that time, and we cared for several resulting tragedies. Physical tragedies yes, but every such child I met was blessed with a delightful attitude, rich personality and incredible determination. Part of our training included time spent at Chailey Heritage in Sussex, home to many more of these amazing children. My job was to assist the potter by measuring pelvic bones of those without legs, to enable him to make small 'flowerpots' on wheels, to fit each child's torso, to provide early mobility of a sort.

Around May 18th I went home to celebrate my parents' silver

wedding, and the photograph recording the day is priceless. We six squeezed on or around the couch, with only Alison and David smiling. I looked vacant no doubt wondering how soon my boyfriend would arrive to take me back to London. One of the other nursery nurses was dating John, and his friend Colin and I made a pretty groovy foursome. John and Colin each had a grey Mini in which we raced about all over London. They loved trying to outdo each other, and frequently played chicken by straddling the central white line, not swerving in till the last possible moment. Only my carsickness ever slowed them down, not our screams of mock or real fright. I'm sure now that there were guardian angels surrounding us. Colin lived in Balham, in a tiny house with his family. Colin was a dear, and often drove across London to pick me up from college, then all the way down to Sussex on a Friday evening, and reversed the trip on the Sunday evening. Unfortunately my mother could not get past his Cockney accent for far too long before realising he was a lovely person. He had a beard and a wonderful smile, and was exactly the same height as me. We had such fun together.

Back at college after the summer, we had a rota for lock-up duty each night, doing a head count for every student. On one of my nights going round with the torch I discovered an empty bed, but heard strange noises coming from the other bed. We knew they were good friends, but not that good. I knew nothing about lesbians until that moment.

Another part of our training was time at Queen Charlotte's Maternity Hospital and I loved working on the wards with the mothers and new babies, assisting as many births as possible. I have wished many times since that I'd gone on to do midwifery.

One of our class, Sarah, kindly lent me her car when I had to go home suddenly. I'd passed my test first time and was a reasonably competent driver, but a hopeless navigator and a worse mechanic. Armed with these directions: 'turn left out of college, head south through London and you will end up in Sussex,' off I went. All well as far as the Piccadilly Circus roundabout. Unable to see a single sign to anywhere vaguely south, I just kept going round and round sure that eventually I'd know which exit to take. The car solved the problem by chugging to a slow but distinct death. With traffic hooting and drivers swearing, I just sat there and wept. A policeman soon appeared, asked pleasantly, 'No petrol, love?' and pointed towards a distant hardware shop where I could buy a container. From there I was directed further on to the petrol station. Finally back at the car, and I hate to admit this, I had no idea where exactly to put the foul smelling stuff and no funnel to help. More tears, I'm afraid, and yes, a policeman soon appeared. Not the same one. He had long gone off duty. I cannot recall how I got home, having been in no fit state to drive, or indeed back up to North London.

A happier occasion to recount was the twenty-first birthday ball to which I was invited. I remember the dress, made from ruby red satin brought in some exotic land for me by my godfather. It had hand-embroidered beadwork of birds and flowers and was truly sumptuous. The lumpy body I squeezed into it was encased in so many whalebone-stiffened undergarments, it was a wonder any movement was possible. My date for the evening was a well-known politician's son, who is now well known in his own right. We were formally introduced, but the party did not start off well. The music was mostly the Beatles' songs and I danced a lot, but not with him.

We went to loads of London parties, and the Police Ball, and most of the activities put on by the Young Conservatives Club, an establishment far more social than political, which suited me fine. We walked on Hampstead Heath, drank Pimms or lagers and lime at Jack Straw's Pub. Some Sundays a few of us went to church and some Saturdays we got tickets for whatever was on at the Golders Green Theatre, up in the gods of course. Ice skating was also popular. One fateful time at the rink my tight pink trousers tore almost in half when I fell onto one end of a skate. Getting back while keeping the affected part covered was tricky. In letters home I mentioned happy evenings in the company of Peter, tall and bearded, who drove a gold MG sports car, and Steve who escorted me in a maroon Riley.

During the second year at college we were permitted to live off campus, and several of us did find tiny flats or bed-sits in the neighbourhood. I shared a room with Cassie in a big house on Rotherwick Road, and cycled to and from college. I knew Cass and her boyfriend were doing things I thought only married people did, and Colin and I were not. Not, I hasten to add, from morality or self-control, but more because we didn't know how to. We planned a week's holiday in Cornwall, arranged for the boys to join us down there but told people it was just Cassie and me going. We shared the driving in her parents' loaned Triumph Herald convertible. Colin and I didn't see much of the other two, but we had fun, especially on the beach, laughing and talking and a bit of canoodling too, but nothing more.

Exams came in the autumn of 1966 and in October I left with the Wellgarth Certificate, The National Nursery Examination Board and the Royal Society of Health Nursery Nurses Diploma. Tucked under my arm also was the wooden cradle and cloth doll I had made as part of the handwork project. The doll was downright ugly, but she earned me good marks. She had a jacket and shoes and a shoulder bag all made of soft well-worn brown leather which originally was my grandfather's motorcycling coat.

On the college notice board were pinned dozens of requests for qualified nannies and jobs all over the world. For months we had been applying to any we fancied, only semi-seriously to begin with. I wrote for details of one in Milan with good money; one in Nottingham caring for new baby plus helping in their riding school; a private house in New York; and also one in Canada. I didn't mention the job in Pennsylvania to my parents until it looked definite. It seemed the best of the bunch and my application was accepted, and a transatlantic correspondence begun. Finding out it would take several months to organise the necessary documents, I arranged a temporary position with a family in London to earn some funds and be accessible to the American Embassy in Grosvenor Square.

First I went home to the new house, since Brookfield had been sold. The parental move had taken place and the process of adjusting to retirement and settling into village life was, for them, well underway. We four had left, or were about to leave, the nest. The house was two ancient cottages joined, partly thatched, with roses round the door, hollyhocks and a well in the garden. Nestled almost next to the Sussex Downs, Amberley village is picturesque, calendar-perfect, a place Mother had always dreamed of living. My job in London was extremely difficult, having full charge of two hyperactive young girls. What free time there was needed to be tactfully divided between visits home and visits to the embassy, dealing with quantities of papers and forms. I was interviewed, photographed and interrogated. Not only were passport and visa necessary, but an affidavit also, which had to be sworn and signed by important people, posted to my future employers to swear and sign, then posted back. Everything about that job sounded wonderful; even Mother approved the credentials. So many phone calls, appointments, fees and frustrations, but at last I was summoned to collect everything. I had to place my right hand on the Bible and swear, but I cited my Quaker upbringing and was allowed to affirm that I was not going to America for reasons of anarchy or to work in a house of ill repute. Affirmation completed, I left, never telling them I was not sure what either phrase meant.

Christmas that year was not happy. My godfather gave me a beautiful pearl necklace, and asked Mum if she knew how dangerous America was and surely she realised if I went for a year I would never come back. She needed no help in feeling miserable. In the New Year we had a party; everyone tried to cheer up and it was a good evening, a joint celebration for David's belated twenty-first birthday, and early for mine. A cousin took me to Brighton for a late night meal and walk on the beach, maybe in an attempt to get me to change my mind. I was not longing to go, nor did I want to stay. I believe I was numb, or maybe just using Mother's trick of, 'if I don't think about it it's not there.' I'd always taken one day at a time, not from any great wisdom, more due to not considering long-term goals or planning ahead, certainly not anticipating consequences. I simply found out what had to be done, wherever I was, and did it. Choices and I were not yet acquainted.

The last few days were very tense. Great Aunt Ethel, who had been a mannequin, helped me pack by layering clothes with tissue paper to minimise creasing. My meagre wardrobe hardly compared with hers. Some life skills would have been more useful. Mother was not in a state to help with anything. January 18th 1967 came just as every day always does: too quickly for those who dread and too slowly for those who are eager. All the family came with me to Heathrow for the grand farewell. It was ghastly. A bon voyage telegram from relatives was addressed to me in care of Pan American flight 63, London Airport. Instead of cheering us, it just emphasised the finality of it all, and my terror covered with only the tiniest veneer of bravado. I wore a black and white wool suit and had a red silk scarf to wave, by prior arrangement, on arrival. Seated on that huge plane, strapped in and shot into the clouds was the start of a very bad eight hours. The veneer got left behind in the terminal, for I was facing alarming thoughts. Totally alone, never been on a plane before, never away from family or native shores for more than a few weeks, and never felt so bad. This was adventure minus excitement.

I wept most of that journey. The clinging smell of airplane fuel mixed with the turbulence sickened me, fear worsened it, and fear of the unknown worsened it still more.

I felt utterly adrift.

5

At Philadelphia Airport I struggled through customs and immigration in the now dishevelled suit, ready to wave the red scarf and look for the woman with three blonde children. Contact was made and we eventually reached her enormous car. Speeding through suburbs into beautifully rolling countryside, it seemed a hair-raising ride to me, on the 'wrong' side of the road, with small boisterous bodies clambering all over me, this long before seat belt laws of course.

Once settled into the huge old house, pleasantries soon wore off, replaced by disillusionment and unhappiness. Everything was so strange and new, and it became obvious that I had been hired as a servant rather than a nanny. The children, when not in school, were always out with their mother and I was expected to clean the whole house daily, taking special care when dusting the antiques. Constant laundry created mountains of ironing; every garment had to be perfect, including underwear. Never before had I handled any non-family intimate apparel. Often alone in the house, it took a while to get used to the cavernous basement's gurgling, roaring furnace, and seeing and hearing it through those holes in the floor above, covered with decorative wrought-iron grilles. Indoors was always too hot, but outside my British woollies were no match for the minus degree temperatures, and my boots too short to keep out deep snow. The riding horses I had been told about were a donkey and Shetland pony, both of evil temperament. The cars, also 'at my disposal' were only that when in need of a wash. How could employers write in such glowing terms of the welcome they offered, only to live a lie and be downright unwelcoming?

After working at least a fourteen-hour day, I was free to go out once the children were in bed, as long as the parents were home. They usually went out. When company came, I had to act as the imported status symbol, don a uniform and bring my charges down to say goodnight. Most evenings I sat up in my attic room and cried. Once, I did find my way into Philadelphia, the City of Brotherly Love. Discovering the Liberty Bell and Independence Park was fun. While enjoying my freedom, and not a little amazement that it was me, here, in the great USA, I had to watch the time for fear of missing the last train.

Getting mail from home helped. Dad wrote infrequently, but many lengthy screeds came from Alison. She who had ignored me when she could, or been unpleasant when she couldn't, began corresponding in a way I never imagined possible. Her letters became a regular source of comfort, amusement and hope. She opened my eyes to the legal aspects of my situation, writing warnings, suggestions and encouragement. Realising I could never stay the required twelve months, I somehow found strength to give in my notice after seven miserable weeks. What a torrent of rage that brought about, after which I was completely ostracised. A letter written by my employer was left open for me to see. Addressed to a friend, it said that they had to fire me because I was lazy and dishonest. Insecure maybe, but not idle or untruthful. Knowing little of exploitation or my rights, I obeyed when forbidden to leave until I had repaid every penny of the meagre salary given me. That didn't take long as there was little opportunity to spend. They never asked if I had somewhere go, and on my final day there were no goodbyes. They sat watching television as I carried my luggage down to a waiting taxi. Allowing for the fare into the city, I had less than three dollars left.

Probably it was pride which prevented me from admitting defeat, and phoning home for money to get the next available flight back. The plan was for me to stay one year in America, and I was determined to do so – somehow. I had to prove I could manage something. The only other option was the hurriedly- given, last-minute emergency idea, pressed into my hand as I left London: *'A friend of a friend knows a family. They'll help if you are ever in trouble.'* The scribbled address was still legible on the crumpled paper, so I found my way to Overbrook, near Philadelphia. Walking down Lancaster Avenue I decided to camp on the doorstep if nobody was home, knowing I had run out of strength as well as money.

Although unrecognised as such by me at the time, surely God was faithfully guiding me to safety. The Ashertons welcomed me with open arms, saying I could stay for a week. They pampered, cheered and encouraged me. I luxuriated in deep sleep and plenty of real human kindness, which had seemed unavailable in America. The children were sweet and polite and taught me many expressions, mannerisms and details of their lives; just everyday things to them, but which had been strange to me in the previous household. It was there my fondness for ice cream developed, sampling each of the many varieties in enormous cartons in the giant freezer. I soon rallied and together we searched through the New York City telephone books to find an agency job as soon as possible. An interview was arranged at Tempo Childcare for the next day. Following directions into Manhattan to the agency, I was delighted and relieved my qualifications were accepted at once. I could select any job from their files. I chose how many and what age children, but took advice on the better addresses. Finding an immediate placement, and after signing all the necessary papers, I returned to my friends in Overbrook for the last night.

There began a variety of homes lived in, experiences, and new friends made. All positions were temporary. I was to fill in while the existing caregiver was sick or on vacation, for as short as a weekend or up to several weeks. Each job had to start the same day the previous one finished because I had nowhere else to sleep. It required much planning, contact with the agency, and carrying my suitcases with me. Guardian angels hovered closely in those days. On countless occasions I should have met with trouble being so naive and gullible, venturing everywhere alone, truly unaware of dangers. The NNEB qualification, in my case stood for Naive Nanny Entirely Blinkered.

During explorations round the city I did get lost. I remembered 'when in doubt ask a policeman'… Though uniformed, he was slouching against a wall, revolting noises issuing from the open gum-chewing mouth. In reply he jerked his head towards the newsstand on the corner and, without missing a chew, drawled, 'There's a store, lady, go buy yerself a map.' Noticing a gun in his belt I sincerely hoped he was a policeman, though evidently not the kind I was used to. Sir Robert Peel's example did not extend far enough.

One afternoon around sunset I had to get across town; the map showed the shortest route was through Times Square. My walk was frequently interrupted by the small crowd of followers accumulating alongside me, amusing at first, but soon annoying. Twice my behind was pinched and several suggestions were either whispered or shouted, offering companionship for the night. I replied, 'That's very kind, but no thank you. I have a job to go to.' This elicited howls of laughter and more whistles. It was only much later that I was told that Times Square was known at that time for its unsavoury nightlife.

On March 22nd, being taxied to a new job and feeling sorry for myself, I blurted out to the driver:

'Today is my twenty-first birthday and nobody here knows or cares.'

A man of noble character, he handed me a box of tissues, then wished me the happiest birthday ever, adding shyly,

'If you'll talk to me some more in that beautiful accent, I will drive you wherever for free.'

I obliged and was almost sorry when we arrived at my destination. Across the street was a coffee shop and he asked if I'd let him buy me a coffee. I accepted gratefully. He was warmly greeted, indicating regular patronage there, and said to the waitress,

'Margie, it's her birthday, bring her the biggest piece of chocolate cake yer got.'

As Margie put in front of me a truly huge, luscious slice, she said it was on the house

and led everyone in a rousing version of the happy birthday song. I started the next job feeling on top of the world again.

The pay was good, averaging between $100 and $200 a week, always in cash, with agency fees and taxes paid, plus all meals and a private room in each home. Most families were wealthy, also employing cleaners, cooks and frequently a chauffeur too, so my work was purely with the children. Where possible I chose new-borns or pre-schoolers. Some were delightful, and each day with them was a pleasure; some were obnoxious and dreadfully spoiled. Some parents too were delightful, trusting me completely, giving me full authority; others were not pleasant to work for. I saw in action the results of loving care and discipline, and over-indulgence and lack of parental control. Such variety of practical child rearing should be a 'must' for all would-be parents. A video of the negatives might be a helpful contraceptive.

Substitute mothering can be very pleasant, especially when meal orders can be placed with the cook each morning, laundry professionally done, walks taken with silver-trimmed, high-wheeled 'English' prams, baby carriages or quality, spring-mounted strollers. For outings further afield the chauffeur is summoned. Many times I was asked to stay on and take the place of the person whose shoes I had been temporarily filling. Not possible, but a welcome compliment.

Accepting a new challenge, I ventured out of the city to Tenafly, New Jersey, to a family whose home help had just broken her leg, and the parents were going on vacation that afternoon. Only time for a quick briefing before the adults left for a week, calling as they went, in answer to my query: 'Oh, don't worry about the children; they're in the neighbourhood somewhere. They'll be back when they're hungry or before dark.'

Alone, I attempted to get acquainted with the home, even if I wasn't to know its occupants for a while. Putting my things in the only neat, obviously unused bedroom, I then tried to make sense of the hurriedly written notes and schedules magnetised to the refrigerator. Before too long, three rowdy kids exploded through the back door, pausing momentarily to look me over, then carry on as if I were part of the family. Eager to help fix supper, they explained who was who, and as many of the house rules they deemed necessary. Next morning we managed to get the right people onto the right school buses after a hasty breakfast. Less than three hours later, the kindergartener was back, bursting to tell me of her activities and present me with her vibrant water-colour – smudged and wrinkled, but my first American 'original'. She begged to have Susie over for lunch, and as I searched for a likely telephone number, Susie calmly walked in, greeting me like an old friend. The girls showed me how they liked peanut butter and jelly sandwiches to be made, inviting me to join their picnic on the back deck. That week with those wonderful children flew by. I thoroughly enjoyed it and I believe they did too. It was a great experience, for they taught me so much. The extra money given in addition to my earnings was gratifying, and encouraging.

Another New Jersey job booked for several weeks, for a toddler and new baby. It was great enjoying happy suburban family life. My opinions were sought on everything from baby care to plans for the vacation trip up to Maine. One hot, sultry afternoon the temperature rose over 100°F. Humidity and tensions rose with it. The storm crashed from a dark sky ripped open with lightning. Thankful not to be alone, I struggled to conceal my anxiety from the children, a useful habit used on countless occasions since. Then an amazing 25°F drop inside one hour; another strange American phenomenon for me to experience.

A future job required a return to Manhattan to interview. The prospective employer met me in Central Park during his lunch hour, soon asking me to visit his wife in their apartment on East 50th Street. The minute I saw her, my own discomfort disappeared in a rush of acute sympathy. On the couch, facing a large floor fan, she looked utterly miserable with an unbelievably enormous belly. Her long thin limbs lifelessly draped about, huge brown eyes sunk in a very thin face, the poor woman was immobile with still three or four weeks until delivery. We chatted while I fixed us both a tall glass of iced water. Agreeing to return when she and the babies came home from hospital, I left to find the bus back to Ridgewood.

Driving north on the toll way to Maine for the long Memorial Day weekend was an adventure in spite of the despised travel sickness. The beautiful scenery captivated me, as did stopping at intervals at booths to toss coins into baskets at car window level. Arriving at Kennebunkport I revelled in the fresh air, freedom, windblown beach walks, and fireside suppers in the evenings. We took the boys to the parade of flag-carrying brownies, scouts and war veterans in their – to me – unfamiliar uniforms. Another day we went along a rocky part of the coastline known for its blow holes, the most spectacular being Spouting Rock, which did just that at high tide. We drove into Vermont as well, for me to see all I could of the vast land I was growing to love, New England particularly. Those Pilgrims knew what they were doing when they named the area. Back in Ridgewood, it was sad when my time expired with these friends. My services had been paid for by the boys' grandmother, and not only was I paid well, but given a silver necklace.

As the excessively hot summer blazed on, I was offered far more jobs than I could possibly accept. One address was in still unfamiliar territory, the New York borough of Queens. I hoped the cabby had made a mistake when he dropped me in Rego Park, but he hadn't. Truly a concrete jungle, the tall, identical buildings were overwhelming from street level, worse from each succeeding floor up the fenced-in outside stairwells. Reaching the apartment number given on my papers, I rang the bell and waited. The door opened a crack. Showing identification, I requested Mrs Smith. From a now fully open door: 'I am Mary Smith. Please come in.'

We stood and stared at each other. Eventually I stammered weakly,

'Er… um… this is a bit awkward. Er… you can't want me as a nanny surely?'

Another silence then she shrugged, smiled and said, 'Well honey, I don't mind if you don't mind; my baby's poorly and I have to go to work, so what do you say?'

Warmed by her smile, I responded in kind, instinctively knowing a major milestone was occurring. Never before had I conversed with an adult black person, nor been invited inside, and both were happening at once. We were each surprised, and I felt angry with the agency for not telling me in advance, so I could have handled the introductions with more composure. Realising that one is learning a valuable life lesson is enlightening and humbling.

Mrs Smith ushered me into her elegantly furnished, refreshingly cool apartment and could not have been kinder or more charming. We looked into each other's face and shook hands, in unspoken agreement about the understanding and growth which had just taken place. When called, a young child dragging a well-loved teddy emerged from his room, unable to go to day-care due to a fever, but well enough to be padding around in pyjamas. We became immediate friends, so when mama left for the office there were no tears. Rather relieved not to have to go outside, I spent several relaxing days in that attractive home. The boy's health improved rapidly, but even while still unwell he was a pleasure to be with. Each evening when the parents returned, we shared hours of great conversation and classical music, without the customary props of cocktails and television shows. We did not merely eat dinner; we dined, discussing current affairs, and our different backgrounds which, in fact, were similar in many ways. On the Friday I should have left, they invited me to stay for one more evening: a most enjoyable finale.

The twin boys were born on time, bringing great relief to their exhausted mother. I went to escort them home, and settled in with my charges for the next eight weeks. At first I kept them side by side in one crib, moving them to opposite ends when they became too wriggly.

My job was to allow mama maximum rest, give each baby individual care and attention all the time, and remain alive myself. It was touch and go sometimes, but I did love it, even in the sweltering non-air-conditioned heat. Those boys became very special to me. Gradually routines were established, making it easier for all to distinguish night from day. The boys were christened at three weeks old, in St Patrick's Cathedral, on a very hot and humid day. The Roman Catholic service was beautiful, but so different and so long. As each baby was blessed with copious amounts of oil and salt, I couldn't help a tiny thought of potatoes ready for baking. When my time in that family was over, it was hard to leave.

6

Determined to see as many places as possible, I planned to visit cousins living in the Bahamas. Earning good money and spending very little of it established a feeling that I could go anywhere and do anything. Anticipating two fun-filled September vacation weeks, I didn't enjoy the flight, just the breath-taking, sun-dazzled views. The Bahamian Islands appeared out of the brilliant blue-green waters, carving through frothy wavelets to beckon and entice. My hosts' house seemed at first hardly substantial enough to qualify as a real home; more like a playhouse, open to the outdoors, sea breezes constantly flowing past wood louvers at the windows. Flowers were everywhere, sunlight and shadows chased each other across whitewashed walls and grass-fibre floor mats, with a concerto of birdcalls and the gentle hum of ceiling fans.

Unrealistically high expectations bring disappointments. If only I'd known then what I know now. As the Dutch folk of Pennsylvania say, 'Too soon old and too late smart.' Had I expected to meet someone tall, dark and handsome on the beach, and be constantly entertained? Something was certainly missing. I explored Nassau each day, either alone or with my infant cousin in tow. We all went out one evening to an open-air restaurant where local musicians played oil drums. That entrancing sound was lovely. I took a horse-and-buggy ride around the famous tourist attractions; and walked for hours along the beach enjoying market stalls set up close to the water's edge. A wonderful mix of vivid colours, strong smells, and a cacophony of laughing voices, a happy carefree place. Different accents loudly advertising the ripest fruits, best hand-woven straw baskets or hats, prettiest seashell trinkets. Lemons, bananas, limes and kiwis, tomatoes and melons all blending their perfumes in the sun's heat, set against the brilliant backdrop of sapphire-bright sea and sky. The water's clarity impressed me, lapping over the warm white sand. Being able to wade out chin deep and look down to visible toes was yet another new experience for me.

I'm glad I saw so much of Nassau during the first week, because it was almost obliterated the next by a hurricane. Storm warnings induced frantic activity everywhere. Shutters and storm doors were latched, outdoor furniture brought inside, boats tied down, shops emptied of batteries, bottled water, canned foods and cooking gas. Local residents, though busy, were calm and unflustered, emotions I was definitely not sharing. As predicted the storm swept in; but instead of moving on, it stayed, lashing the area for days, and, for me, sleepless nights. Finally it blew itself grudgingly away, leaving a trail of damage and debris, evidence of its strength and tenacity. No lives were lost, but many homes and possessions were. As others were clearing up and making repairs, I was packing my bags to leave. There was time for one last beach walk, but I hardly recognised it as the same place. Dirty sand was littered with branches, shattered planks, and seaweed by the ton. My beautiful, crystal clear ocean had turned into thick milky soup, choppy and unfriendly.

Returning to the Garden State of New Jersey, I marvelled at the fall colours. At Halloween I learned the art of costume concocting, and transforming a pumpkin into a jack-o'-lantern. The sadly overlooked original meaning of the day, All Hallows Evening, was the last day of the year on the Celtic calendar, the day before All Saints Day. A time for quiet reflection and remembrance of those saints who have died, rather than pretending to be monsters, ghosts and witches. How will future generations differentiate between over-done commercialism and overlooked reality?

Before seeking another agency job I had the weekend scheduled with the twins, plus an obligation. My father asked me to take out insurance as soon as I arrived in the USA in case of accident or major illness. An acquaintance of his worked at The Royal Globe Insurance Company, and I was to see him. That man was off sick, permanently. I was directed to his replacement. A Scottish gentleman rose from behind a huge desk to welcome me with a firm handshake. I liked him immediately. We talked a long time as I explained my reason for being there. He said his wife had recently had their first son and was desperately seeking professional help so she could return to work. Many questions later he, invited me go live with them as nanny for young Jamie, going home with him then to meet his family and stay for dinner. We cruised back uptown in a taxi, to his sumptuous Park Avenue apartment. I was given welcome, friendship, and a simple meal; I knew it marked the beginning of another wonderful job, and the end of my need of the agency. I thought I'd managed it all by myself.

Settling in with Jamie's family and re-adjusting to the swing of city life was not difficult. I took him to Central Park, to the doctor, whatever was necessary for the total well-being of the child. Entrusted to my care all day and all night, but surrounded by parental love and attention each evening and weekend, Jamie thrived. In the park we went to the statue of Hans Christian Anderson, or the Pond, or to the swings by the Zoo entrance, all good places to meet other children with their nannies, many of them English or European. Friendships began and my own social life developed. It was good to explore during my days off, particularly the museums. My favourite being the Metropolitan Museum of Art, although one visit to the Guggenheim was enough. We toured the United Nations buildings, sipped hot chocolate at the Russian Tea Rooms. We used busses and subways or walked all over the place. My surroundings became familiar by day or night. I soon learned which areas to avoid, especially when alone.

Late November showed me another way Americans celebrate together. Nearly everyone returned home for Thanksgiving, for mountains of food on best dishes, surrounding the mammoth, crisply browned turkey. Such a festive occasion but it seemed to me to rival Christmas just a month away. The homesickness for harvest festival intensified over Christmas when two record albums (one sadly shattered) of carols sung by choirs at King's College, Cambridge arrived from my family. I played it almost continuously. The entire season seemed so different from what I was used to: more glamorous, more entertaining, with more lucrative gift exchanging than I'd ever known.

January 18th 1968 came and went with mixed feelings but little else to mark the day. Yes, I'd made it, completed my year in the States but where was the pull to go back? Did I genuinely not want to leave a secure job with excellent pay and benefits, and some good friends? There were no serious thoughts about how long I would stay at the present job or even in the US, no major plans; just more shoulder shrugging, and 'let's wait and see what happens'. I had 'journeyed to a far country' like the Prodigal Son, with some 'riotous living', though there was a lot more to come. I lacked the Prodigal's sense, not allowing myself to literally go home, nor understanding the other meaning of that biblical parable.

Life with Jamie continued without great excitement but with much contentment. One English friend I'd met was Nigel, struggling to sell the *Encyclopaedia Britannica*. He had a tiny studio apartment and lots of friends. He took me to interesting places all over the city, sometimes accompanied by half a dozen canines entangling their leads in a frenzy to reach the park. He earned a few extra dollars dog walking, and we enjoyed watching them burn their energies racing around the fenced dog-runs, barking wildly. Nigel loved his guitar and unfolded the beauty of classical music for me, especially the works of Andres Segovia and Julian Bream, and took me to Carnegie Hall once to hear the latter. That was marvellous. I can see it now: the darkened stage, one lone man perched on a stool in a small circle of light, the fluid notes pouring out over a silently entranced audience. Nigel did not unfold any more intimate beauty for me, though we spent a great deal of time together. Our shy innocence was simply not believed by those in authority over us at the time, so when the venereal disease epidemic

45

arose (precisely three people known to us) we both had to undergo the extraordinarily painful duo of penicillin shots, every bit as bruising to the ego as to the posterior.

Winter finally gave into spring and I loved the magnolia blossoms in the park amongst the still skeletal branches. Saint Patrick's Day provided another parade to mesmerise all my senses, as Jamie and I watched from the warm security of the apartment window another example of New Yorkers doing things in a big way. On April 4th 1968 I was once again aware of history taking place as the whole country seemed to halt at the shocking news of Martin Luther King Junior's assassination on that balcony in Memphis, Tennessee.

One evening Nigel and I donned our best clothes and enjoyed a ballet at the Lincoln Centre, marvelling at the beautiful new building as much as at the performance. The euphoria affected my brain because, instead of having him escort me home, I agreed to go meet more of his friends at a coffee house. We walked across town, through rather seedy areas, then down dark basement steps. Horrors. Surely this was one of those dreadful places, a sleazy dive, where nice people don't go? In the midst of candle-lit, smoky noise I felt quite out of place in my red mini-dress beside Nigel in his three-piece suit. We were surrounded by bell-bottomed blue jeans, sandals, a great deal of long hair, and an unfamiliar smell. Friendly faces, handshakes and hugs, and a gift of strong coffee with a sandwich on thick chunks of black bread helped me relax and accept the welcome. The co-owners of that place were generosity personified, barely making enough profit to live on. From late afternoon until early the next morning, every day, they made gallons of coffee and tons of sandwiches, hot or cold (I'd never heard of a hot sandwich) and usually a huge pot of chilli or soup. One introduction among many stands out. He was a balding, bearded redhead wearing a green plaid flannel shirt and old corduroys, balancing a meerschaum pipe, a pencil, sketchbook, plus coffee mug in paint-stained, hairy hands. He had produced a caricature of me before I'd finished my meal. His name was Kurt.

Thanks to the natural ebullience of youth I was able to wake on time and take care of Jamie all day after only the briefest sleep, and found it easy to do the same several times a week. I continued to give my job 100%, while going out more and more during my time off. My long hair grew longer, and I hemmed my skirts shorter. We went to many parties and spent many evenings at 'our' coffee house, meeting theatrical, arty people, most of who were living alone in the vast city, cut off from families for various reasons, so my situation seemed entirely normal.

Kurt lived in a sixth floor walk-up apartment in a dilapidated building near 2nd Avenue at 78th Street. I recall no shock or revulsion when I first saw it, just acceptance. The dim, messy place was comfortable, and home to him. I did lose my thirst when finding the only receptacle was a chipped glass holding an inch of fine blue mould in the bottom. We enjoyed getting to know one another without any sexual pressures; again not believed by many. I knew I had a problem, but did not fancy the doctor's recommendation to get drunk and keep trying. Like Scarlet O'Hara I chose not to think about it until later. One weekend my employers left town to visit friends, so I stayed with Kurt. While preparing to go out for Saturday evening, I started feeling odd, noticing small red spots erupt on my hands, then arms, legs and face. Within an hour I was covered in a rash and really ill. Having crawled into bed, I stayed there two weeks, only taking sips of water now and then (out of a clean glass) forced by my very worried friend. Eventually he found a rare doctor who made house calls. Where she came from or how he paid her I never leaned. She pronounced the chickenpox bad enough to be smallpox, then disappeared to get a second opinion. She soon returned with one and they held a garbled consultation over my suppurating body. Once they heard there was no way we could pay for hospitalisation, the second opinion left. There was no pain medication. The revolting pustules were all over me, including sensitive areas. I scratched, resulting in several deep scars. Nobody else known to us had it, nor did anyone catch it from me.

Once completely out of quarantine, I returned to work, happy to be with Jamie again although it took a while to regain vitality.

Memorial Day weekend found us back in Southampton, Long Island, where most affluent New Yorkers went to relax. An elegant clubhouse was the favourite gathering place for the summer-home owners. Their offspring and nannies remained outside. We took turns looking after all the children at once, then enjoyed free time swimming or ice-cream hunting.

Memory seems fairly balanced, allowing one to re-live some of the good times along with those better forgotten. Is this process selective? Does one retain or block out things at will, or by instinct? Why are some happenings as sharply detailed as they were forty years ago, while some have to be dredged up and are foggy at best? One that isn't at all foggy is Robert Kennedy's assassination on June 6th 1968 and the terrible look on his dying face flashed across the country's television screens. It was the empty look, his eyes seeing his own eternity.

After Jamie was sound asleep one evening, the phone summoned me to a hospital way uptown in Harlem where Nigel was asking for me. Thinking it must be a joke, just him inebriated or on one joint too many, I responded in kind. Then I realised it was genuine when the voice identified himself as Officer Brown of the 125th Street Precinct. My boss called the hospital himself to verify, and there had been an accident and Nigel was calling for me. It was Harlem, and so late, and I wasn't allowed to go alone. Together we hailed a taxi and I was glad of his company although his irritation was clearly apparent. Doors locked, we sat in tight-lipped tension throughout the rattling drive uptown. In the hospital we traversed miles of corridors before finding Nigel lying on a gurney because the wards were full. His very British sports jacket was bunched up under his poor crushed head, the blood-soaked label below his ear whispering 'Harris Tweed'. His ashen face looked horrid, like the matted, unwashed hair. All they had done was stitch up the rips and gashes in the front and back of his head, and offer him one free call. He'd been driving with another salesman when the car had hit a concrete support for the elevated train tracks. He flew out the windshield then back again. All his so-called friends disappeared, so I was given extra time off to care for him as best I could once I got him back to his apartment. I had to throw out the sad remains of the tweed jacket but everything else, even his hair, finally gave up the last bloodstains and glass fragments. Countless hours crept by while I tried to spoon soup and eggnog into him, and he battled with recurring dizziness. Many months later he obtained a large sum of insurance money and was gracious enough to visit me, offering a bunch of roses. I felt sufficiently unrewarded to wish I'd not nursed him so well.

Kurt and I were walking arm in arm through Carl Schurtz Park one balmy evening. A few pathway lights had just come on. Earlier we had ignored a group of young boys messing about, but had not noticed they were following us. Within sight of Gracie Mansion, home of Mayor John Lindsey, I was suddenly shoved so hard that I fell to my hands and knees. Kurt yelled and I got up to see those boys running off with my handbag, and him in hot pursuit. The tallest turned, brandishing a knife which he obviously would have used if we'd reached him. Valuing our lives over possessions, we stood helplessly watching them melt into the shadows. I couldn't stop shaking as we ran to the police post at the Mansion Gate. Empty. Then out onto the street, certain of help there but no one, certainly no police in sight. How dare those kids steal my stuff? It was a beautiful navy-blue English leather bag, fully suede lined, and it held so much of me that I felt violated. The gold watch given by my parents before I left home was gone, along with my leather wallet containing cash and family photos, and my Alien Registration, or Green Card. Because I was supposed to carry that with me at all times, its loss created fear and fresh waves of anger, as did the realisation that I'd have to return at once to my employers, as their keys, with obvious identification, were also gone. They were sympathetic and understanding (amazingly so after all the problems and extra time off I'd had) and gave me my first ever drink of brandy. It burned its fiery trail down to my innards, successfully halting the shakiness.

The outward traumas were fairly easily fixed, belongings and locks replaced, sore back and knees soon healed, but anger and fear remained.

7

My family decided that I had become too involved with Kurt, so they arranged for an invitation from an unknown couple in North Carolina. My fare was even paid. The Potters were friends of my godparents. I duly arrived in Winston-Salem anticipating a good time. My hosts were kind, but I felt their scrutiny, as if they were sending reports home. Exactly that was happening. They passed on that I had given Kurt's address for mail forwarding, apparently proving beyond doubt that he and I were living in sin. Not true, but nobody bothered to ask. Since I stopped working and had no home of my own, Kurt agreed to house my belongings and collect my mail, as any good friend would do.

Carolina was horribly hot and humid. The Potters had no air-conditioning, nor any other creature comforts. They lived a severely simple life which seemed to me so dull. I was escorted on a few sightseeing tours, injecting a little spark of enjoyment now and then. That whole strange trip only improved when I left, and was woken on the return train ride, just outside Baltimore, by sunrise flinging gold at the grimy windows. Heading back to New York, deliciously free, to face whatever might happen next.

During the week of the twins' christening, their grandmother had invited me to visit her in California anytime, to thank me (she said) for lavishing such good care on her grandsons. The time was mutually convenient so, feeling very brave and adventurous, I set off once more. I was welcomed as an old friend and given a luxurious guest suite. The house was beautiful, high on one of the many hills, giving a view over rooftops to the Bay. From there we watched the aircraft carrier Enterprise come sliding in, bringing wounded soldiers home from Vietnam. My hostess saluted them, her emotion infectious.

We shopped, ate out at Blum's and Fisherman's Wharf, and rode up and down the switchback streets in the antiquated cable cars. We strolled through Golden Gate Park eating Ghirardelli chocolates, and walked in the hills of Marin County. One time we were half way across the Golden Gate Bridge as the famous fog rolled in, obliterating everything. We drove up along the curving cliff road with its perilously sheer drop down to the sea, to gasp at the views. What a land of contrasts. The confines of incarceration in Alcatraz so close just emphasised so much freedom, especially free love in the hippie sections of Haight Ashbury.

Hardly time to say hello to Manhattan before leaving it again, this time with Kurt, for a visit to his brother Bud in Washington DC. Details of that journey are sketchy, probably due to the creation of even better mind-blocking techniques. We did all the touristy things and I bought postcards of the White House, the Capitol, and Presidential Monuments. We ate ice cream while ogling the palatial homes of Georgetown, and wandered through Arlington Cemetery to see the eternal flame. I was impressed with Bud's artwork and that he was showing some of it, but it was all rather strange, like his whole way of life, similar to Kurt's. I never questioned this, but saw it as simply more of the American ways I was getting used to, determined not to dislike just because they were different. I was not at ease with the arty people we met, and sharing marijuana smokes was not the panacea it is thought to be. I was upset to discover, too late, I'd been given LSD, dropped invisibly onto sugar cubes. Mercifully it was not a bad trip but it wasn't good either.

Somewhere during the foregoing travels, Kurt and I decided to get married. It seemed a good idea at the time. We went out to call his parents – reverse charge of course – down in Florida. They sounded so happy, and his mother even cried a little. When mine replied to the letter in which I told them, their opposition was palpable. It was years before I understood the pain and grief I caused my parents, and myself, by which time it was far too late. Despite disapproval, and advice aplenty, I forged ahead, knowing I would cope somehow with whatever happened. I didn't know how to make real choices or effect changes or plan my direction, and what was worse still, was unaware I didn't know. A letter soon came from my uncle in New Zealand, offering cautious congratulations and a ticket to stay with them for a while. It annoyed me because I knew he was right. I should take up his offer but simply could not. It would mean going home defeated, still as hopeless as when I left.

In October my sister came to stay, sponsored I'm sure by the family, to see what Kurt was like, and just how mentally unstable I had become. I went to the airport with Kurt's friend Zac Goldberg and his mammoth Buick convertible. Awkwardness about sharing our abject poverty with Alison had to be buried. At home we were not raised in luxury, but the spacious, light-filled houses and acres of surrounding countryside were a far cry from the cramped railroad apartment with too few windows and too many cockroaches. If Alison was shocked or revolted she too did a good job of burying it, getting on with arranging the Canadian leg of our journey home to prepare for my wedding. Kurt had longstanding debts he could not pay. Having plenty of money myself, I saw nothing wrong with paying off all that before buying his ticket to the UK in December.

Back home again tough days got tougher. Alison and Mother had many private chats, the topic not hard to imagine. I was left pretty much to myself, preparing for the occasion nobody was enthusiastic about except me. I went to London and bought a dress and shoes from Pro Nuptia. In the evenings round the fireside, the atmosphere strained, I would be politely asked how my wedding plans were coming along, and I would politely reply that they were fine, thank you. Why on earth didn't we yell and scream at each other and clear the air instead? There are so many whys clouding that winter; it was not good. One problem was extremely personal and an American doctor said it would require surgery. I've not heard of anyone else having to endure the humiliation and pain of an abnormally thick, totally impenetrable hymen. Worse than the brief operation was the embarrassing discovery of the thick Pyrex glass tube inserted, to remain in place for six weeks, preventing scar tissue forming. Picture the bride walking down the aisle, terrified in case it dropped out and smashed at her feet.

Tensions were not eased by an absence of communication from Kurt. Snide comments and pleadings to call it off just made me more determined to go ahead. He did arrive on schedule. Dad welcomed him warmly enough, and Great Aunt Ethel wrote him a sweet letter of acceptance into the family. He and I went to buy our rings as Apollo 8 went circling the moon. Christmas passed in a blur, but I was very aware of Mother's decline the nearer it got to December 28th. On that day she looked lovely, but was frozen in her valium-enshrouded misery. Dad was magnanimous, but I knew he was sad too. Alison the bridesmaid was demure in dark green velvet, the same as the pageboy's trousers – that little chap I had looked after and so wanted in my wedding. The American groom looked fine for New York, where he belonged to a kilt-wearing civil war re-enactment group. He chose that attire having refused any kind of formal wear. It was Sussex, and my kilted Scottish relatives were unimpressed. I pretended not to notice the tight-lipped disapproval, and buried it all, beneath the mask I held firmly in place. There was one moment, kneeling in church, trembling, doubting, but I managed to squash those thoughts too.

Sunday lunch the following day, the farewell family meal, was heavy going. My siblings hardly contained their smirks, winks and nudges, though knowing nothing of the ever-present glass tube. Leave-taking, even if a relief, is never nice. We flew to New York where we had a five-hour stopover and a big fight. As we arrived in Florida I was close to tears and desperate for sleep. His large family totally overwhelmed me with endless hugs, constant talk and laughter, a huge meal and mountains of presents. The rest of the honeymoon (what a misnomer) was filled with humidity, mosquitoes, exquisite sunsets, pelicans lined up on wharf posts and visitors, the 'kissing cousins' type, lined up for me.

Optimism can be fickle. I had hoped that before leaving for England Kurt would have at least left the apartment presentable. Perhaps asked Zac to go in with groceries and maybe flowers for our return: dreamer, dream on. Climbing those six flights of dingy stairs, lugging suitcases, I was still hoping. Every hope came crashing down. No flowers or food, the bed unmade, stale. I wilted. Disappointment weighs heavy.

Yes, I'd made a dreadful mistake, but also I had made vows and would have to stick to them. No money left, no going back to England, so I had to make the best of it. That began with a trip to the laundromat for clean sheets, and an onslaught against the cockroaches. Zac appeared daily, hanging around interminably into the small hours. Soon it dawned on me he was not just lonely, but jealous, wanting Kurt's time for himself, as it used to be. There was no privacy in that little apartment, no door into the bedroom. When I'd give up on their military discussions and go to bed, sleep escaped me as I battled feelings of indecent exposure.

We lived on next to nothing, Kurt painted soldiers (military miniatures) when the rent was due: $75 a month. $12 a week was our average outlay for groceries. I used an electric fry pan for absolutely everything as that's all there was to cook on or in. We had no television, no phone and no car, of course. He taught me to paint the basecoats of the figures, and to drink strong black coffee. Zac was always with us. From him I learned about anti-Semitism, Jewish jokes and characteristics, things I had no idea of, even after two years in London's Golders Green. Jews, to me, were Bible people.

Much of my time was spent climbing up and down those six flights of stairs, usually with laundry or groceries. We stayed up late, often at the coffee shop or parties, and slept till noon. Sometimes Kurt would stay out much later than me, and one of those nights I woke hearing a stranger on those creaking stairs stop near our door, cussing. Our door was not sturdy. If he fell against it he'd be inside. In fear I fumbled for the Colt 45 always kept in the headboard. I'd been shown the safety mechanisms and how to fire it, but suddenly a deafening shot rang out. Certain of death, I froze, waiting for something to happen. Seeing the smoking revolver in my hand, following the trajectory angle (frighteningly close to my own foot) I saw the hole in the baseboard near the floor. Fully expecting downstairs neighbours and police any moment, I spoke my chilling thoughts: 'this is New York City, people get killed here all the time and no one pays much attention.' Thus I remained, unmoving, until Kurt's eventual return, hardly comforted by his scathing attitude to my carelessness and stupidity.

Some months into the marriage, Zac began talking about my size. I never thought to retaliate, though he was overweight himself. The obvious reason was that potatoes, pasta and chips were the cheapest foods. At that time it was the in thing to have a 'fat-doctor' to whom you would pay regular visits and too much cash in exchange for a supply of multi-coloured pills. Without questioning the wisdom of such a method, my dieting life began. It was not difficult to locate such a 'doctor', nor to pass his brief health check, and so to start on a course of his rainbow pills. Two purples for breakfast, a pink and two reds for lunch, and two greenies for dinner. Wonderful. No cooking, no clean up, more time to play. I think Kurt subsisted on onion rings and coffee for the duration. I lost weight, but was evil tempered, jumpy, and undoubtedly foul to live with. Severe headaches probably indicated an allergic reaction to something in those terrible tablets, but I stuck with them, and finished the last one, proud of my lighter self. One thought leads to another. The intimate side of our marriage was at last successful. An irritant remained, which could not be ignored. A small area of scar tissue had formed in spite of the specific precautions taken. I did not want any further medical help nor could we pay for any, so decided to see to it myself right away. Alone in the apartment, I showered, boiled water to sterilise the scissors, squatted over a mirror and with two snips removed the offending problem. There was less blood than anticipated, which helped, as I suddenly felt rather faint, but that soon passed and I got on with the day.

As many weekends as we could manage we'd join other military enthusiasts from all over the country attending what were known as Shoots, usually at or near battle sites in the east coast states from New England down to Virginia and the Carolinas. Primitive camping conditions matched Civil War re-enactment fervour, definitely not shared by all to the same degree, but fun nonetheless, most of the time. The men entered the competition shooting events, joined by a few hardy women, usually wearing uniforms or civvies of the period. Others set up tables for buying, trading or selling antiques and collectibles, mostly of military connections, probably where I first developed my taste for bargain hunting. Mingling with other regiments and old and new friends was pleasant, but I kept my distance from the noise and acrid smell of the black powder shooting ranges.

On July 28th 1969, we watched on a friend's television, in blurry black and white, the amazing moonwalk, hearing Neil Armstrong's now famous words: 'One small step for man, one giant stride for mankind.'

That summer Kurt's lease was up and, since he'd had some large orders for painted soldiers, we felt rich and decided to look for a better place to live. Also, I refused to be still climbing those stairs when pregnant, though I'm not sure either of us was seriously thinking of parenthood then. We found an apartment we liked and could afford at 312 East 90th Street, then summoned everyone to help us move. Zac drove the rented U-Haul truck, needed mostly for Kurt's books as we had very little furniture. One couple, who proved invaluable then, and on many other occasions, was Gordon and Annabel Stewart, who became good friends. They were engaged and prone to fierce fighting. That very evening she tore the ring off her finger and flung it to the ground, calling him terrible names, causing me to assume it was all over between them, only to find them twittering together like lovebirds the next time we met. Theirs has been a stormy, but lasting relationship.

Oh, the delight of settling into twice as much space. It felt like a palace. There was a real bathroom with a mirrored medicine cabinet on the wall, and a real bedroom complete with door. The large living/dining room with lovely big window we divided further, to create an art studio corner. A small alcove contained all a kitchen needed. There began my Salvation Army thrift shop decorating. I scrimped a few extra dollars now and then to buy cheap things and fix them up. I developed a keen eye for treasures, finding stuff, still quite usable, thrown out on the streets. We got to know several other tenants in our building through mutual use of the elevator, the incinerator, and basement laundry-room. Biddy was particularly kind and we became firm friends. Her apartment was full of vibrant colours mixed together riotously, and artwork created by her kindergarten students. Bid shared birthdays and most other occasions with us, always producing good things to eat. She had a sister who visited regularly, needing to 'see the doctor', wanting Bid and me with her. I never realised she was having abortions.

That autumn I returned to work caring for the twins. At nearly 18 months they were great fun to be with. I usually walked the twenty blocks in the mornings, taking the bus back at the end of my day. Thanksgiving offered yet another new way of doing things for me to experience. Kurt and I took the train to Connecticut to stay with his relatives in their Cape Cod-style house by the water. After a long journey and an evening of talk we slept late, rising to on-going preparations for the feast. While chopping ingredients for stuffing the turkey we stuffed ourselves with gefilte fish (pickled herring pieces in sour cream, tasting nicer than it sounds.) We walked off the over-abundant meal, along the river past a veritable fleet of small boats tied up for the winter. Returning from that festive weekend we had a shock. Our door was open, with utter chaos inside. We halted at the threshold, chillingly aware that whoever had forced his way in might still be there, more inclined to greet us with a bullet than a handshake. We shouted and yelled, raising rage, noise, and neighbours. A sick feeling pervaded, as if I personally had been attacked again. Cupboard and drawers hung open, contents thrown about, everything dirtied, torn or broken. Kurt's grandfather's fob watch was gone, also our radio and record player, but 'he' had the nerve to discard my string of pearls, my only good jewellery, and toss them on the floor. The gun was gone, so we feared the burglar would return and use it on us in retaliation for not finding more stuff worth stealing. I wished he had taken the tin of black powder from under the bed.

New door locks didn't erase the nastiness. The police were not helpful, telling us of many such robberies each week, where the loot is quickly fenced on the streets in exchange for drugs. Even after I had scrubbed and disinfected every inch of the place it took a long time for the invasion to fade. Kurt came home with a fancy new stereo set after the next pay-day which helped cheer us up; and together we went to The Pound to select a dog. Drowning in a sea of beseeching eyes, wagging tails, wailing whines and barks, it was nearly impossible to choose. We kept going back to a skinny, brown and white spotted creature whose long feathered tail thumped each time we looked or spoke to her. She stared at us, but did not bark or cower, just silently pleaded. It worked. For a $5 donation and a piece of string for a leash, she was ours. She marked her new home with an 'S' shaped puddle so we named her Samantha.

Christmas brought nominal feelings of goodwill to all men, nostalgia to me, but very little else that year. I had saved up to produce a UK-style dinner of roast goose served in candlelight on the card table. We found a tiny potted fir for our tree, barely a foot tall, for which I made a few equally small decorations, unknowingly starting a tradition. We were surprised by a gift of a small black and white television from a friend who had been more surprised that we didn't own one. We also acquired a Lavalite. A curious invention, giving little light, but fascinating to watch, as soft pieces of waxy lava rose and fell as they warmed in the coloured liquid. In a junk shop, for a very few dollars, I found a fur coat. It was curly Persian lamb, more holey and bare than woolly, with an odour that clung closer than the garment itself. So, happily smelling of long-dead skunk, I wore it everywhere.

We laughed at *Rowan and Martin's Laugh-In* television show, especially at Twiggy flaunting her pint-sized body. Using such expressions as 'you bet your sweet bippy' and 'sock it to me', we were in good company, as even President Nixon said such things on tv. We did silly things and giggled a lot, at least partly due to marijuana. Combining our earnings, we made enough for a summer trip to England, sub-letting the apartment to gain a dog-sitter and burglar-deterrent. We had a great time in wonderfully sunny weather. The countryside was lush and green, the roses in full bloom, almost smothering my parents' house. It felt different, though I couldn't have put it into words then. Cicero did, very aptly, when he said: 'Exile is terrible to those who have a circumscribed habitation, but not to those who look upon the whole globe as one city.' I didn't fit either category, but struggled to be both. Living so far away from home does create changes. You may feel the same, but that cannot be. I had done some growing up in a different world, a broader place, altering me enough so I no longer matched the family's idea of 'me'. I wasn't sure of the real me either.

Mother gave a garden party for us to see as many people as possible, and Dad tried to teach Kurt about gardening. They took us on woodland walks: up on the Downs and along the river, and in and out of sleepy villages basking in the welcome warmth of so much sun. Thirst was quenched at pubs specialising in honeybees and wild roses, and we wandered through ancient churchyards shaded by huge yew trees. We visited Hever Castle with its topiary and impeccably laid out Italian gardens, mostly designed by my great-grandfather. At Winchester Cathedral we watched an old stonemason at work, one of the last generations to use hand tools. We dined at a restored 15th century manor house, where my father had a small glass of wine in our honour – the first I had ever seen him drink. Kurt and I went on to Scotland as he wanted to see Edinburgh and hear the bagpipes. The long evening light provided plenty of time for more sight-seeing before our return to the USA.

8

Changing gears from one lifestyle to a totally different one, it soon seemed as if I had always lived in the City. All was well in our little abode, and at work the twins were pleased to see me again. They liked parading in the English policeman hats I gave them, and Sam loved their company for romps in the park. An increasingly bad smell in the lobby of our building got us wondering why the superintendant wasn't around to do something. Sadly, the smell was the super. The poor man had shot himself twice in the head, making a terrible mess before he died. He did it during a thunderstorm so nobody heard the noise. That was the same year Janis Joplin died of a heroin overdose.

During the summer I miscarried after two months, but hardly had time to be sad before realising I was pregnant again. This was neither planned nor prevented. Typically, I suppose, we never thought that far ahead. Once past the first risky months something happened to me. A baby! Me? A mother? After the scores of other peoples' children I had nannied, now it was my turn. Like at least 90% of all expectant women, I decided mine would be the healthiest, happiest, most well behaved, well-adjusted child on record. I stopped smoking and drinking coffee, made easy by my changing taste buds. Hunger and tiredness were my constant companions, but I blossomed and thrived, deciding that six children wouldn't be too many. A friend was disbanding his summer home, and offered us any furniture left. The only usable item was a dilapidated couch, but being couch-less we thought it luxurious. With the frayed, faded pink cover holding it together, it transformed our living room.

Christmas found us again in Florida, this time with Samantha who loved galloping on the packed sand of Clearwater Beach. She claimed as much attention as my belly. The entire family urged me to take lots of naps, never lift a finger to help, and eat many extra delicacies.

Back home in New York, while walking Sam, I discovered treasure out on the kerb for the garbage: an old three-drawer dresser plus arms to hold a mirror. Closer inspection unearthed the mirror, intact, held upright between piles of stained carpeting. What a find. I rushed as fast as I deemed safe for my swollen body, carrying the mirror carefully home to get help. Of course Zac was there, so I insisted they return with me at once and retrieve the dresser. I thoroughly disinfected, paying careful attention to the stains of what I was sure must be blood. The next day I saw, on the same street corner, a man dumping another dresser just like 'mine', only this one taller with no mirror, obviously a matching set. The man was not friendly, claiming it was for sale, so I argued, knowing this too was being thrown out. I bargained him down to $8. We were then the proud owners of the ugliest furniture imaginable, but I could see how lovely the wood could look minus dirt and paint. Never having refinished anything before, I went to the hardware store for advice and a can of Stripeze, a scraper and beeswax. Doing a little each day, I transformed those dressers, working by the open window, with no ill effects from the fumes.

I still took care of the twins, and Kurt's name was becoming better known and his work more sought after, so there was cash coming in, just not much of it.

While en route to the park on a lovely spring afternoon, one twin on either side of my obviously expectant self, a woman passing by whispered loudly to her companion, 'Some gals just don't know when to stop.' I couldn't help smiling while replying, 'Yes, and there are five more at home.' The look on her face was way beyond disapproval, almost worth my untruthful response.

The war in Vietnam progressed horribly and, though we were far removed from it, it still seemed to invade everyday life. The daily news bulletins and paper headlines saw to that. I steered away from anything political, ashamed of my lack of knowledge and lack of motivation to cure it. Having left England before I was old enough to vote, and being unable to vote in America, seemed like a good enough excuse to ignore it. That March not only recorded my birthday, but the death-day of those poor civilians in the Mai Lai massacre. One could not ignore that.

Another Americanism quite new to me was the baby shower. I was flattered by two of them, both great fun. The first was held at the home of Chris and Jim Melton, more military enthusiast friends, and was a total surprise for me, as planned. Their apartment was decorated with pink and blue streamers and filled to capacity with people, food and lavishly wrapped gifts. Somewhat overwhelmed, I recall being dreadfully teased for my lack of speed in opening all the presents. I simply could not bear to waste the beautiful paper and ribbons.

One person I met that day got woven into my life in a special way, like so many friends, with lasting threads. Doraine and I seemed to like each other instantly. She had two small daughters very close in age. The second surprise was 'showered' on me by Biddy, in her apartment. She and her then current roommate worked hard to produce another wonderful occasion. So many friends came, including the twins' mom, and Annabel Stewart who had recently given birth to Andrew. I wore my only decent outfit, borrowed from another friend: a silky pink blouse under a sleeveless tunic, also silky (probably polyester's predecessor) in pink and blue, and jeans of course, the one maternity pair in my possession. My hair was in two long braids and I rather liked the resulting photo. My dismay therefore was the greater when hearing later what my mother said. She thought it was a picture one would see in a clinic for unwed teenage girls, bearing the caption: 'This could be your daughter'.

Easter was unseasonably warm, so we gathered with many friends for a picnic in Central Park, referred to as a 'be-in'; a communal effort, with shared food and drink and much good will. Somebody provided a new garbage can, well cleaned, as a container for gallons of iced Kool-Aid. Samantha was panting hard so she had a long drink.

Almost at once she went peculiar with tongue lolling out, trying to walk on legs turned to rubber. I thought she was having a fit. I was not amused to discover a confirmed addict had generously spiked the drink. I was thankful I hadn't had any. Right after that Kurt left for Florida because his great-grandma was dying and he had always had a special bond with her. A bit of me thought it was rather inconsiderate of her to do it then, so close to my due date. I hope I didn't voice it. At the same time, my mother flew from London to New York to coincide, hopefully, with the arrival of the first grandchild.

On Monday April 19th the doctor pronounced me to be in good shape, but a full week or more away from giving birth. I rushed, lumberingly, through last minute preparations and cleaning, awaiting her arrival. I changed out of jeans into a light blue voluminous dress, trying to earn some maternal approval to start us off on the right track. Hearing the buzzer, not bothering to find shoes, I flew, lumberingly again, down to the lobby to greet her. We talked a great deal and she made instant friends with Sam. I was acutely aware of her every comment about the apartment, hoping she meant to be complimentary in her amazement at how small it was, yet how nicely I'd arranged everything. She did admire the beautiful antique brass bed, which I had only just finished polishing in time. It was a gift from friends who had obtained two the previous year. Nobody questioned the provenance.

I felt odd, but tried to ignore it. After supper I realised labour had started; the pains were strong right away, not a bit like the Lamaze instructor described. Kurt and I had attended the classes faithfully and I was quite determined to be 'awake and aware' throughout, concentrating on breathing exercises, loving every minute. After all, hadn't I studied this whole business at college, and helped deliver countless babies at Queen Charlotte's Maternity Hospital in London, and read all that had ever been written on the subject? As I discovered then, and many times since, book learning and other people's children mean absolutely nothing when it comes to one's own. I could not sit still, but paced about, feeling sort of claustrophobic in reverse: meaning, burdened with the sure knowledge that the distorting bulge wanted out and there were only two possible ways for that to happen, neither very attractive. The process had begun, and could not be stopped. It would continue to completion one way or another.

About 11pm we made a couple of calls to the doctor – yes, we finally had a phone – and Zac, who hastily arrived for taxi service.

Before leaving the apartment, Mum said, 'Now, don't be frightened dear.'

Until that moment it had not occurred to me to be frightened; now suddenly I was. She obviously knew what lay ahead. Driving uptown to Columbia Presbyterian Hospital on Broadway at 168th street, Zac must have run every red light and hit every pothole. Sweat was clearly visible on his balding head in the eerie neon glow of signs and lights flashing past. He kept mopping his brow and muttering, 'Not in my car, please. I couldn't handle it. Please, not yet.' If only we had known then how long it would take we could have crawled, by way of Staten Island. Thank you Zac, wherever you are, for getting us there, and for the many other times you chauffeured us.

The next thirty-six hours were ghastly. Contractions clamped their iron grip around me mercilessly, with barely a break between them for me to catch my breath, never mind the relaxing breaths I had learned about. On and on it went, with little dilation for all the work. Dimly aware of growing concern, I heard ominous whispers of 'dry-labour' interspersed with red-hot wrenching. Somebody wielding a scalpel broke the bag of waters after agonising slashes that I couldn't scoot away from, as someone else pinned my shoulders down. Then they tried to give me a 'spinal' during a contraction, with me sitting on the edge of the bed, leaning over my own belly, held firmly still. All I could see was a pair of once white shoes splattered with blood – was it mine or that of the prior user of the bed? In the early hours of Wednesday I was given pitocin to hurry things along, but that then worked too well and the monitor showed foetal distress. No monitor necessary to show maternal distress. I do remember a mad stretcher dash along miles of corridors, seeing ceiling lights hurrying by, presumably to the operating theatre. Someone attempted, during each contraction, to push my baby back where he was coming from, to get him out by caesarean section. Then they gave me morphine. I was past being any use for anything.

Finally, at three minutes past three on Wednesday afternoon April 21st, Garth was born naturally, wonderfully alive and intact, if rather sleepy from medication. I stared in wonderment at my infant, unblemished and perfect, when the outcome could have been so different. My son was utterly beautiful, like a ripe peach with pink-crowned golden fuzz. Big blue eyes, slowly blinking, stared back at me in recognition: 'So it's you who's been talking and singing to me for so long.' He had a blister on his thumb plus a corresponding one on his top lip, indicating weeks of contented sucking *in utero*, a habit he continued for a long time. My transformation from a lonely island of terrifying pain to a live person, a mother, happened the instant they handed me the clean, warm package tied with heartstrings, wrapped in a white wool shawl.

Unknown to me, there was a gathering of friends in the waiting room, eager for news. They brought champagne and paper cups, and were undeterred by Mother who wanted no one to disturb me. In they came and we sipped the bubbly, although I could not have been very entertaining. A couple of days later a cable arrived from my sister saying: 'The flags are flying all over England to welcome Garth.' In reality they were to celebrate the Queen's birthday, but it was fun to imagine it. In the apartment Mum and Kurt had been coexisting. They never were the best of friends. Mum was fearful of city life, unwilling to walk Sam, and bothered by all the locks on our front door, but managed well, all things considered. It felt good to be back but impossible to settle down due to the constant stream of visitors bringing more lovely gifts. Kurt's parents drove up from Florida, staying with an old family friend. Mum delighted in seeing her grandson wear the little gowns she had so carefully made for him. Before she left, we went out to West Caldwell, New Jersey, to visit friends in their enviable, pre-revolutionary war house. There was no crib so Garth slept happily in a padded dresser drawer. Suddenly, late one evening, acute pains in my chest made breathing difficult. A doctor called it angina from delayed post-birth trauma but it was the pancreatitis again.

We had lots of impromptu parties, all friends, and friends of friends welcome. Each person brought something to eat, drink, and in many cases, smoke. Candles were the only lighting used; folk songs or jazz the only music. Nobody got roaring drunk, or totally spaced out, but we did have good times. One evening there had been a good crowd in our home and someone brought in several joints to share. Because I was still nursing I did not smoke. Nor did I realise the widespread effects even on non-smokers, until the next morning when Garth did not wake for his early feed. I panicked then, opening every window and the door, for what fresh city air there was, fervently praying to the God I had been far too busy to acknowledge that my son would be alright. I vowed never to smoke any more dope, nor allow it in my home, and never to get even slightly tipsy from alcohol ever again. Mercifully Garth was fine, waking later, as hungry as ever.

Every summer Kurt's wider family held a reunion in Michigan and we decided to go. It was new parent pride more than familial duty. We joined with Bud and his wife Dee, the dark-eyed Spanish beauty, renting a Volkswagen van so we could take turns driving straight through to Long Lake. I had only recently obtained my licence – and that was a story in itself. A month before giving birth I took and passed the written and vision tests, then on to the driving school in lower Manhattan. Barely able to fit behind the wheel, I squeezed in, grateful that the young German instructor was patient. The traffic was fierce. I started off in the direction he pointed, driving superbly, cornering excellently, to a smooth halt when told, all on the left side of the road. Assuming failure, I smiled and prepared to turn back to base and hand over the keys. He returned the smile saying, 'Don't vorry, I unnerstand dat mistake. Ve'll start again and you vill pass. You are reelly a goot triver.'

Back to Michigan in the August heat, to an abundance of white-haired relatives, screaming children and watermelon fights. Ignoring advice, Kurt took the small sailboat out, got marooned and terribly sunburned, which postponed our departure for a couple of days. The sleeping arrangements had to be seen to be believed; perhaps the others were used to that sort of thing, but I certainly wasn't. Upstairs was a huge room packed with wall-to-wall beds of every description: camp cots, air mattresses and regular ones, fold-ups, roll-aways, and a few cribs. Upon arrival one was expected to dump luggage on any free bed, as quietly as possible, because several might contain optimistic nap-takers. The worst part for me was waking during the first night to see Uncle So-and-So's face six inches from mine as I stared into his denture-less, snoring mouth. And Americans think the British are strange.

Garth's first Christmas was marred by croup and tonsillitis. The only interest he took in his gifts was to eat the wrapping paper. His first birthday was more fun. Kurt must have painted a great many soldiers, so we got back to England. At that time travel inoculations were required. Ours were still good from the previous trip, but Garth had a sore arm from his. The day before departure we went to the Stewarts to leave Sam there for our five-week trip. She was always happy with them and got on well with their dog, Tank.

Expectations of trips home were always high, but not always realised. That one was good. Having produced the first grandchild, I felt truly welcomed, and everyone loved my son. There is a treasured picture of my paternal grandmother, my father, myself and my son. Garth was christened during the morning service in the village church on May 14th. He wore a vyella romper suit, white knee socks and red button-up shoes. Part way through, the vicar realised there was no water in the font, but nobody minded. Mother had borrowed a pram and other baby needs from neighbours, and she loved pushing him round the village. Everyone stopped to admire Mrs Cheal's American grandson. We took Kurt to castles, an Elizabethan manor house, and more quaint villages with, to him, odd names. There was a day in London to see St Paul's Cathedral and the changing of the guard at Buckingham Palace. Leaving Garth with his grandparents, we went to Paris for a few days. Missing my baby, it was not fun for me, nor was it the marvellous time imagined in that famous City for Lovers.

9

The Stewarts were at Kennedy airport to meet us, which was nice, but their faces showed disaster of some kind. The kind that causes stomach and heart to change places immediately. They no longer had Sam. Our faithful dog had disappeared. As we collected luggage and headed for the car, the grim details came with tears. On the first evening, the two dogs were let out to run in the woods for a few minutes. It was thundering, and Tank returned alone. They waited, whistled and called, donned rain gear and went searching. They contacted everyone, including the police and animal wardens, even putting messages on local radio stations, all to no avail. Of course we agonised over each possibility, wondering what had happened, hating to accept that we would probably never know or see her again. Bad dreams followed : of her appearing outside our door, having found her way home from upstate New York, bedraggled and exhausted, but we'd moved on and she could never find us. Reality was just a gaping hole in our lives.

We took care of a pet bird while its owners left town briefly; Garth loved chatting to it through the cage bars in a language known only to both of them. He ended his stationary existence one day by getting up and walking, suddenly, just like that, no struggles with crawling. Once upright there was no stopping him. He also developed larger and more irritating blotches of eczema. Kurt brought home a free puppy, from the man at the corner newsstand. A mistake to accept an unknown animal, but a kind-hearted attempt to fill the gap left by Sam. This new, adorable ball of brown fluff caused nothing but trouble. Not nearly so easy to train as Sam, Jemima had frequent accidents and showed no remorse. Looking like a blue-eyed husky, she was, I am sure, part wolf. She would nip or scratch until she drew blood, follow that with much licking before curling up for a nap. Unsuitably near-wild behaviour, I hoped she'd outgrow.

Grandma and Grandpa drove up again to stay for two weeks. Our apartment seemed very overcrowded. When it all got too much I retreated to the shower to weep in the only available privacy. Grandpa liked beer, and spending time walking around the city, seeing the sights. Grandma wanted to spend every moment with her grandson who, she confided, was a lot easier to handle than her husband. In their youth they had eloped because her mother had not approved of the engagement. One could see why.

I answered a newspaper advertisement for volunteers to test new products and see if the promotional efforts were successful. The extra cash was handy, and I met a new friend who lived just across the Hudson River in Jersey City. Our sons were the same age and we all got on well. Visiting them meant venturing on the PATH subway under the river. Each time it got easier.

So too, mastering their Polish surname and the source of their income: they lived in a funeral parlour, responsible for the embalming. I was uncomfortable with their apparent indifference toward Good Friday, and Easter in general. Not that I could claim many sincere observances but it did seem wrong to go grocery shopping on a day traditionally set aside for quiet reflection. Kurt told me that my thinking was Victorian, and that what little religion I did have was force-fed from childhood, and not real at all. Being unable to counteract with anything solid, I couldn't help thinking perhaps he was right.

With those friends we learned the joys and pitfalls of buying cheap houses to fix up and sell, mail order shopping from the huge Sears catalogue, and the bargains to be found at K-Mart. In what was a crazy dream to me, they persuaded us to leave the city and find a house near them. No worries, provided we could produce the enormous down payment. Enormous being relative. Nowadays it would be considered next to nothing, but to us then it was out of the question. Unless I brought over my inheritance money, sitting untouched in my English bank account since my grandfather's death. It seemed fine to me, so I ignored the unasked for advice, given in urgent torrents from family, and started on the complicated transfer. Funny how the Prodigal Son comes to mind again, saying, 'Give me my share' – which he then squandered in a far country. It didn't seem like squandering, though I did have to work hard drowning out a nagging inner voice of warning. Eventually we exchanged title and keys. The front porch of our new house hung lower at one corner, looking as dangerous as I am sure it was. It never got fixed. Known as a two-flat, the house had a kitchen and bathroom upstairs as well, and plenty of room, so it was decided that Biddy should leave Manhattan too and come and live upstairs. It was great to have her company, and some rent money. There were two front doors, side by side, hers leading immediately upstairs, ours into the tiny hall, then the living room. We respected each other's privacy, but there was still a lot of visiting back and forth. The long thin house stood on a long thin plot, giving us a small fenced yard, with neighbours on three sides.

One of the first things I bought was a green stretch slipcover to camouflage our old couch, whose faded pink looked worse than ever against the gold tone carpet. More space naturally required a much bigger Christmas tree, on which our few ornaments looked lonesome. Gathering what materials I could, I made more, mostly by sketching figures of Father Christmas, or Santa as I was learning to call him, on clean Styrofoam meat trays from the grocery store. Painting them was easy, then I cut them out and pushed a tiny metal hanger through the top and hung them up. Copying a magazine picture, I spread glue on waxed paper, inside circles of string, setting flattish seashells into the glue before it hardened. When dry the paper peeled off leaving semi-transparent disks to hang on the Tree or in a window.

Although we had nothing luxurious to offer, the house was usually full of friends and neighbours. I went out to say hello to a girl I had seen walking past a few times with a child about Garth's size. Her name was Mary Delpeto and she was as eager for conversation as I was. Her son Jerry was just two months older than Garth, her husband quite a bit younger than Kurt, but we all became firm friends. For some time Kurt and I had been learning Scottish country dancing at a Monday evening class in the city. It was tremendous fun and we were pretty good. Those who had kilts wore them, and we all wore the soft, black leather ghillies, similar to ballet slippers. We never had extra cash for baby-sitters and even after I weaned Garth, we still took him everywhere with us. He was no trouble and would sleep anywhere I settled him.

Spring of 1973 was my first taste of gardening, and I was thrilled when a few bulbs burst from the barren ground: some wizened daffodils and three scarlet tulips – what riches. They remained upright because we had said farewell to Jemima, who continued to insist upon her nasty attacks. The vet agreed she must be unbalanced, and put her gently to sleep. We were invited to the Delpeto house for a magnificent Italian Easter dinner, and many new foods I'd never heard of. The antipasto trays of manicotti and lasagne, meals in themselves, but only to be sampled because the main course was next. A vast ham, potatoes and vegetables, all washed down with generous gallons of dark red wine. Everyone sat around the table for hours, giving time to produce appetite for the wonderful desserts.

The next international experience was not so nice. The elderly Polish couple next door were quite private. We only saw them occasionally, or said hello over the fence. Suddenly we found out the old man had died. They invited us to the wake and it seemed rude to refuse, though I didn't know what a wake was. The only person I had known to die was my grandfather, and his had been a quiet, graveside service amongst the ancient moss-covered tombstones at the Quaker meetinghouse. I imagined something like that for the dear old neighbour. At the funeral home I thought I had mistakenly walked into a florist. Never before had I seen such massed blooms nor been overpowered by their mixed scents, except at London's Chelsea Flower

Show. I found myself in line, slowly progressing past weeping people to where I could see the most elaborately decorated coffin imaginable, but nobody had closed the lid. Surely it must be empty, they wouldn't all be leaning over, touching and kissing the deceased? He was lying there looking no different from when I had seen him pottering about his back yard, but now reposing on crisply frilled satin. Afraid I would giggle, and mortified by my inappropriate thoughts, I slunk away. I did manage to mutter condolences of a sort to the bereaved before going shakily home.

Nels moved in upstairs with Biddy. They had been dating for a while and wanted to be together. There was little if any discussion or agreement. He simply brought his stuff and was there. Bid paid us more rent, which was good, but my relationship with Nels was not. He was noisy, and so heavy that our kitchen light swayed and shook when he walked about above. He wanted use of the yard without helping with its upkeep, and he took over most of the basement for a workshop. Down in that dank, cavernous pit lived the antiquated washing machine – ours only because the previous owners could not get it up the curving, narrow staircase. We inherited other interesting things that were never moved away from that basement, including a box of very old Christmas ornaments.

How did we manage trips to England? We had no bank account, indeed no credit to open one, so even cashing a cheque was tricky. It was living hand to mouth. Kurt did excellent work on the miniatures he painted, collecting anything from $25 to $200 or more per figure, depending on detailing, and individuals or group dioramas. When we needed more money, he painted more figures, but there were many lazy days, too many. I was upset when the mortgage was late, then overdue. Occasionally I would see men on ladders climbing the side of the house to cut the telephone wires. After the first time it doesn't frighten anymore, just shames. The same with the utility bills, including the heating oil company. I knew nothing about collection agencies until a big black car slithered to a halt outside, disgorging four similarly rain-coated men. Two went round the back through the alley, one came to the front door, one stayed in the driver's seat. Certain it must be the mafia – we did have Italian friends – I tried to smile as I answered the door. They told me how much money they wanted. Not sure whether to laugh or cry, I went up to Kurt (his studio was the one room up there that we used). He found a $10 bill for them, which had to do, with several promises. Then he told me of his anti-government leanings. He felt it his duty to cheat 'them' whenever possible because taxation was so high, and he planned to continue his evasive tactics. Continue, apparently without concern for his wife and child. That day a chilly tentacle grew round my thinking.

In spite of altering and rearranging most of my priorities to fit the circumstances, I still held onto inbred awareness of good quality, correct behaviour and speech. This included a strong sense of the goodness of God, and my duties towards Him as well as the world. Because I exhibited few of the preceding characteristics during those bohemian years does not mean I discarded them. Rather, that they were on hold, to return to, possibly, after I had tried out other ways of living. Now I can look back and see the desperate need to break away from cloistered, labelled, presumptions, of thinking that anyone unlike us could not be right or even acceptable. My temporary condemnation of all religious personae began with thoughts like these, unchanging until I learned a little wisdom and understanding. First came the attitude of each to his own, which heralded the mantra of the late 60s into the 70s: If it feels good, do it. Christianity was surely the way to go, on one condition: that I could pay lip service to Christ when convenient, or when particularly worried about something. I taught my son about Jesus, and we said prayers at bedtime. I took him to church and taught him to sit still and behave suitably. Kurt would not come with me, suggesting I would outgrow my need for such hypocritical stuff. In a way he was right, because my heart wasn't in it. I went because I thought I ought to.

A lot of responsibility did come with motherhood, and I was

determined to do my best. Maybe that was reassuring because marriage was not a bit like I thought it would be or should be. I just kept plodding on. A neighbour started coming round more often, frequently when Kurt was out. He was always very nice to me. One time in the front hall, his farewell hug turned harsh and before I fully realised what was happening or how to stop it, it was too late. His strength and determination turned a mild flirtation into a battle. It was horrible and I suppose could be called rape. I never told a soul because I felt what he jeered at me must be right: I'd brought it on myself. So nothing was done about it and he never showed up again. It became more of an effort to keep the mask in place.

A small pair of Clark's sandals arrived in the post for Garth. I did so want him to have nice shoes. I'd drawn an outline of his feet and sent it to Mother, with a five pound note left from our last UK trip, to help pay for them. Thanks to the generosity of many of my past employers, with whom I remained in touch, my son had lovely clothes and fine toys. Grandma and Grandpa came back for their annual visit, she alone exhausted from the long drive; he was relishing the remains of a six-pack and his foul Limburger cheese. We went rubbernecking, as Grandma called seeing places and people, in their car. Kurt stayed at home, as usual, mostly to paint.

Grandpa went alone into New York. Later I found out that he frequented 8mm film peep shows. One evening he was very late for supper and Grandma was angry. When at last he arrived I opened the door. Dishevelled and drunk, he exposed himself to me, right there on the threshold, but out of anyone else's sight. My own father-in-law doing that, so soon after my recent 'neighbourly' experience, nearly exploded me. Again, my coping method was to bury and not speak of it.

On a hot morning I was woken early by faint cries outside the front door: a tiny puppy, mewling and blindly seeking comfort, obviously not old enough to have been separated from its mother and callously dumped. After two days of warmed milk from a dropper and lots of loving, fading life returned. I did not want yet another dog. This one had nowhere else to go, and I sympathized. So began the task of raising, mothering and training, all over again. A new perfume, Charlie, was being widely advertised, in a yellow bottle portraying a windswept blonde. Our pup was pale golden yellow, Labrador type, so she became Charlie. She was great and stuck to Garth faithfully, in spite of his over-enthusiastic hugs. He called her 'mine bubby'.

I felt ragged, always cleaning up messes made either by the dog in the house, or by Nels in the basement, and must have been mad to attempt to pack everybody up and go to the Shoots as well. A change is meant to be as good as a rest. Those weekends were usually fun, though anything but restful. The smell of black powder is bad enough around guns, but gets indescribably worse on a sweaty body in a small tent with you, without benefit of a shower. One of the campsites was on a hill in the Shenandoah Valley overlooking miles and miles of rolling hills and woodland. I remember a blustery night at one such Shoot. Kurt was still lingering by the fire with his buddies, on guard for blowing sparks (which meant prolonging the alcohol-embellished tall stories). Garth, warmly bundled, was asleep in the tent, me beside him having been out to secure the ropes for the umpteenth time in the mounting gale. Both of us were suddenly lifted completely off the ground, billowing skywards. One lone guy-rope held firm in the ground, forming our link with safety during that frightening ride.

The Meltons were at most of the Shoots we went to. Their grade-school age boys still played happily with Garth. That family loved food. At their house we were always warmly welcomed. They were such sweet people, but we ate the entire time. Dinner began with cheese and cracker snacks, then the very large and filling meal, and various pies for dessert. As soon as the dishes were cleared, there was a bowl overflowing with buttery popcorn, plus potato chips to munch on through the evening. After one such binge, while the popcorn was popping, our host cleared some wall space on which to project a 16mm movie he had rented. Never in my life had I seen anything like it. I never knew people would do those things while being filmed. Thankful the lights were out so my scarlet face didn't show. I was shocked, then fascinated, then revolted by what I saw. The 'hero' in a hurry to perform his 'duty', had torn off all his clothing, as well as that of his friends, but he forgot his socks, somehow making the whole scene ludicrous.

10

Trick or Treating for the first time with my own child did not prepare me for how much imaginative creativity was to be expected in the following years. That October we went with Mary and Jerry around a few streets. Garth soon caught on to the idea of filling his bag with goodies. I dressed him in a brown paper grocery bag, with cut out armholes, and a smaller brown bag for a hat, on which I printed 'Trick or Treat' in bold letters; a cheap but effective costume.

Eventually we obtained a car, doubtless through a shady deal of sorts. It must have been practically a throwaway, with over a hundred thousand miles on the clock. I drove everywhere, thrilled with the freedom of wheels. It was a dark blue Mustang convertible, as breezy with the top up or down. The road was visible through several holes in the floor, including the boot/trunk floor, and the driver's seat allowed interesting freedom of movement on its runners. I wedged it with the old raincoat I kept in there for some protection when it poured. Parking wasn't a problem on Liberty Avenue. I could nearly always squeeze in beside the hydrant, or at the corner where the telephone pole was very close to the kerb. I hit that pole a few times when reversing, but the dents never really showed.

It felt so good to drive to the airport myself to pick up my sister. Alison made me laugh by asking how I could drive such a big car. Recovering from jetlag, she loved her three weeks of walks with Charlie and Garth, trips into Manhattan, and a whole day wandering round the restful Cloisters, way up-town. She also spent quite a bit of time with a friend who joined us for Thanksgiving dinner. He had rather inviting dark brown eyes, and used them to his advantage. After her departure I got to work planning the playgroup my friends and I had talked about for some time, and through it we met new people. One of these became and has remained a dear friend. Ev and I liked each other immediately, even with my calling her *Eeevelyn*, the English way, and my unconcealed amazement that she could be three months pregnant and still so skinny. Her husband Tony was pastor at the Methodist church on the far side of town, the distance no barrier to our frequent visits.

Christmas was as nice as I could make it, and being blessed with many generous friends, we received wonderful gifts. Underneath was always the pang of homesickness. Like a weighty wild animal, it would sometimes threaten to crush. It was hard work keeping it at bay.

January brought a great perk-up: David and Jan came for ten days. He was to be transferred to New York City, so they came to find a place to live. They chose an elegant apartment high up on the 27th floor of Waterside Towers, overlooking the river with spectacular views out over New Jersey. I could hardly believe I would soon have family living so close. Gus came over fairly often to talk soldiers with Kurt, and liked staying for my definitely non-gourmet meals. Being a bachelor, he was pleased to be away from home when he could. His friend Kerry had recently finished a tour of duty in Vietnam, and returned to find his teaching job gone. Not a fitting reward for fighting for one's country. Poor Kerry wandered about aimlessly continuing with his main love, playing the bagpipes. He and Gus were in a pipe band, always busy on parade days and at many of the Shoots also. Kerry tried teaching Garth to squeeze music from the pipes, and he often helped me with the children when playgroup was at our house.

When the weather got warmer I attended to a project long in need of completion. From street level up to our front doors were six cracked concrete and brick steps, with loose or missing grouting. They had to be fixed before somebody tripped. At the hardware store I picked up a sack of cement mix plus a few tips on how to do yet another thing I'd never tried before. Following basic instructions, I mixed, stirred, slapped on and scraped off quite happily, transforming those steps into a work of art. Twice, while trowelling the muck off my hands, I noticed some whitish strands but paid little attention until the job was done. Only then did I realise that it was my own skin sloughing off, eaten away by lye in the cement. Staring at my hands numbly, then suddenly not numb, but hot and searing and very, very painful. Tears flowed with the tap water as I attempted to wash any remaining acid off, knowing I would be useless for days while it healed. Kurt was angry to find his putty knife beside the trowel, encrusted with hardened cement. Thank God, my hands did heal completely and promptly, and yes, I did thank God because I knew I could not care for my son without hands, so I had prayed. How great and loving He is, to keep in His care even those who do not pay Him any attention until they are in trouble: 'I am the Lord, and there is no other; apart from Me there is no God. I will strengthen you though you have not acknowledged Me' (Isaiah 45: 5). How well He knows what we need before we even know of the need, how steadfast is His love for us.

Restored once more, I planted lots of seeds, crowing over my small horticultural successes of the previous year, determined to produce some edible zucchini instead of only the umbrella-like leaves and to try again with zinnias. Daily tending and careful watering was paying off. The seedlings were sturdily growing and I was Earth Mother. One morning I noticed immediately a new shininess in the chain-link fence between us and the two elderly sisters next door; they must have spray-painted it the previous evening while we were out. They were pleasant enough, I am sure, though our conversation was limited to the minimal English they knew, and that was heavily accented. How could those women have been so blind, or so unthinking, or both? The entire flowerbed along the fence, so painstakingly dug, de-rocked and constantly weeded by me, contained nothing but row after row of grotesquely bent, shrivelled, silver seedlings, very dead. When my shrieking brought the offenders outdoors, they pretended to have lost what few words they did know, just smiling and running their murderous fingers over their nice shiny fence before disappearing indoors again.

81

David and Jan settled into their lofty new abode, and how elegantly and beautifully they furnished it, with artefacts and treasures gathered from around the world on their travels. It was an odd sensation to stand at their window, the glass of which came down to the floor, and see nothing but water, many hundreds of feet below. They came over to celebrate Garth's third birthday, which was warm and sunny, but had an unpleasant ending; more than just Charlie stealing a chunk out of the birthday cake. Jan kept piling the kids into Garth's little red wagon and taking them for rides around the back yard. Repeated tumbles were par for the course and no one minded, until the last time. She pulled the wagon in decreasing circles, eventually flipping the squealing contents onto the grass again, all on top of each other in a giggly heap. One by one they disentangled and got up, except for mine, who stayed sitting and crying. Assuming over-excitement, I herded him and his friends in to wash before the cake and juice break, but he would not be comforted. Knowing that the birthday person often shows the worst manners, I tried to ignore him, glad it was nearly going-home time. He sobbed all through the farewells, not wanting to be cuddled, so I put him right to bed. That night he woke crying several times, fussing even more when I tried to make him comfortable. Awake again early, he was still fretful and I was staggered to see a large bruise on his throat and shoulder with a golf-ball sized swelling on his collarbone. Feeling like the worst kind of mother, I took him for X-rays which confirmed the break, and the doctor wrapped a thick ace bandage round in a figure-of-eight, to brace his shoulders and help healing.

Soon after that we went to David and Jan's apartment for a party. Gus and Kurt were standing in front of the étagère, several glass shelves on a fine chrome frame, containing African treasures. Someone's elbow rested on the top shelf a little too forcefully and the whole lot came crashing to the hardwood floor. The mess, the breakages and the awkwardness can perhaps be imagined. Even more alcohol was consumed then, particularly by Kurt who became loudly obnoxious. I had to take him home in a taxi. Not a good journey. Getting home, I paid the driver as Kurt crawled up the steps, fumbling to get the key in the lock. Giving up, he silently vomited into the keyhole instead, all down the door onto the mat. Coming up in the dark behind him, I got the door open while trying not to slip. We trod it well into the carpet. That took me so long to clear up, but worse was to come. By the time I got to bed I could still smell it. Pulling back the covers I found he had rolled onto my side, vomited again over my pillows, rolled back onto his side and passed out. I very nearly put a pillow on his head and held it there.

As if to compensate for the silver seed disaster, the rest of my flowers were beautiful, especially the *Lavatera* shrub by the front door. When the violets faded the roses opened and were lovely all season, enticing many people walking past to stop and chat over the wrought iron railing. I never left Garth out in the front yard alone because of his tendency to call out to everyone equally, 'Hi, mans', whether it was to a hurrying housewife, the mail-lady, or delirious wino.

A couple of years previously Kurt had given me a book about open marriage, wanting me to read it and tell him what I thought. Harmless enough surely, and our marriage did seem pretty free and relaxed, though I knew Kurt was bored, resenting my time spent on parenting. Yet another eye-opener; a kind of freedom and openness I knew nothing of. Well, why not? Being married to one does not mean you never fancy another. Sneaky affairs were condemned more strongly than conventionally monogamous marriages, the idea being to share intimacies with good friends openly and freely, with no secrets between spouses. The whole subject knocked me sideways, and it took a while to sort out what I did think. We talked back and forth about it. Needless to say he was keen, but I was frightened, and, yes, a little excited too. He reminded me again about my Victorian ideas being so outmoded, and it was high time I got with it. The awful part is, I was quite unable to come up with any serious reasons against this. The fact that it is diametrically opposed to everything the Bible says on the subject didn't occur to me, or if it did, I must have squashed it as being too 'holier than thou.' Gradually the idea grew into our lives, adding to conversations with friends until it seemed acceptable. I must have reckoned that the rest of my life was so wacky anyway, so utterly different from my expectations, or anyone else's, that what harm could a little more craziness do?

This does not mean that we began having hot, passionate sex with each friend who arrived at the door. We did not. There were however, many occasions when friends stayed for dinner – we'd been sharing potluck meals for years – and in the late, candlelit evenings we'd all get pretty comfortable together, sometimes going to different rooms, but not always. There were other duets, private, but not secret. David and Jan were with us one time and David was horrified, even though nothing major happened in their presence. He gave me an unwelcome lecture. I tried to think of him as just a party-pooper, but I knew his anger held deep, brotherly concern which underneath I appreciated and could not ignore.

Like any abuse of something meant for our good, the thrill, the ego boost, the sense of 'living free' was sadly empty, and only very briefly exciting. It's that emptiness which seeks more, urges on to wilder things, causing addiction. It created in me an awareness of my sexuality, a sense of power, and new worth, especially when willing to share it. However, it showed me starkly what had happened to my marriage. Forcing me to look at what I'd been avoiding: what would soon happen if we didn't make changes. A pastor in a different town did counselling so I went to see him, only to find out that marriage counselling for one is, of course, only 50% effective. He was very attractive. He kept his distance, encouraging me to work at the marriage, while agreeing with me that the extra-curricular activities must stop. Kurt grudgingly agreed to accompany me once, even though he despised the man, sight unseen. Any self-esteem I had struggled to accumulate disintegrated in that pastor's office when my husband shrugged and said, 'Nah, it doesn't have to stop. I don't care who she does it with as long as she saves a bit for me.'

In that instant it was all over. My play-marriage, exposed to the light, held nothing of substance. Being rather short of alternatives, I had to bury what had died, down deep, and plaster over the mess with forced hope and determination. No more men. I busied myself with the playgroup which was hard work but great fun. I took in other children also, whose mothers had to go out work. For quite a while I was the only mum at home during the day on our block. I wanted another baby of my own, in fact for ages I dreamed of having six eventually. Maternal instincts worked well in me and, in spite of being in essence a single parent, I did my best. I loved being pregnant, being a mother, and I adored Garth and I longed to produce a daughter next. Although certain Kurt was continuing to spend time with others, I did not refuse him.

One night I deliberately forgot precautions, and knew I'd conceived. And I knew it would be a girl. Whether it's medically or scientifically possible to know didn't bother me at all, I just knew. The next morning, unwisely, I did not conceal my forgetfulness. Kurt was furious first, then scathing, saying it would all be over in a month. When it wasn't, he got angry again, this time very angry, and insisted on an abortion. A most unpleasant time followed and I was quite frightened. He threatened to beat it out of me if I did not get an abortion. I counted on his basic laid-back laziness preventing him ever expending that much energy. It did, but our relationship deteriorated even further. Part of me felt sorry for him. His Peter Pan lifestyle, into which I had slotted so easily, did not include responsibility for anyone else. My role was to continue taking care of him like his mother and grandmother had done before.

Despite the angry atmosphere between us, life just carried on. Because I grew so large so quickly there was some doubt about my dates. Looking the doctor in the eye I said, 'I know exactly when this baby was conceived. I was there.' He then said it must be twins. That's the only time Kurt was interested. He made me take out insurance with Lloyds against twins, so we'd get lots of money. In October my parents came and there were some happy times. Together with David and Jan we rented a Ford LTD station wagon and all drove down to Florida. It turned into an epic journey. Dad asked how much further while we were still in New Jersey. For those only familiar with the British Isles, such vast American distances are impossible to comprehend. We stopped in Williamsburg, and stayed in a motel on the South Carolina border. Hot and tired, we separated into three small ground floor rooms, omitting to mention air-conditioning to Mum and Dad. We immediately turned ours on, as did David and Jan, and slept in the welcome cool. At breakfast we heard how the poor parents had been so hot, stuffy, and sleepless that they'd opened the door directly onto the parking lot and the great Interstate 95 Highway, and propped it open all night. Mercifully, nothing worse than humid air went in. We finally arrived in Gulfport on Monday evening. My father's notebook simply reads: 'Very warm – temperature and welcome.' It was a picture, him complete in shirt and tie being met by his Floridian counterpart in nothing but shorts and a tan. Both sets of grandparents got along pretty well considering their many differences. United in their love for Garth and longing for the next grandchild, many potential trouble spots were avoided. Grandma and Grandpa were always superb hosts, showing us their Florida favourites. I was excused from many of the outings in order to rest my expanding girth on the beach – lovely.

In December Garth had a flu bug and earache, best described in his own words:

'Mom, I gotta coupla rocks in my stomach an' a hot germ in my ear.'

For Christmas I continued the tradition of making dozens of cookies and frosting them all, and he and I had great fun doing that together. Another baby shower, and everything was pink, even the wrapping paper. My certainty that this child was my longed-for daughter was no secret. I'd had to sell the Mustang for $50 and use the cash for a maternity outfit which I wore almost daily. Much later I found out the car was a real keeper, a sought after classic worth a lot.

On February 21st Kurt left for a long weekend Shoot. As sure as I was that the baby was my longed-for daughter, I was also quite sure she would arrive on her due date of February 25th, whether she was twins or not. During Saturday supper with Ev and Tony, I became unable to sit still as labour had begun. In the night Tony drove me to Belleville Hospital and stayed until I was fairly well settled. Knowing Garth was fine with them, I tried to concentrate on the Lamaze technique. Ev spent hours with me as my coach but most of those three nights and two days are mercifully blurred. I felt very alone and very afraid. Desperately wanting to get up, I was forced to remain on my back, locked into pain, sure it could only end badly. The masked faces around me showed only worried frowns. As before there was a stretcher ride through long corridors with glaring ceiling lights to cower from. There were more attempts to assist nature by repositioning my stuck baby, going against each contraction, to prepare for a Caesarean section. As before it was unsuccessful and eventually, at 11.33am Tuesday February 25th, Kate emerged naturally, furiously screaming. Although both labours and deliveries were similar, the actual pregnancies and results differed greatly. Garth had been as calm and placid *in utero* as he was on arrival and for his first few years of life. Kate had kicked, rolled and stretched from the moment she was able to, and from birth on had a hard time lying still. Usually scrunched up, her little fists flailed about, far too twitchy to suck her thumb as it would not stay in her mouth.

The next few months were difficult. Caring for two dearly loved and cherished children alone with their father alive and well under the same roof, creates a certain amount of tension. That tension, however well disguised, is felt by all concerned with different reactions. Kurt slept more than usual, worked when he had to, and went out a lot. He showed little interest in his offspring, and less in me. Garth's eczema worsened, requiring oatmeal baths and frequent creaming and bandaging. Bad headaches worsened for me, and poor Kate just screamed. For five months she screamed, most of each night and the greater part of each day. Thinking she was hungry I nursed her almost non-stop, feeling permanently unbuttoned. I had plenty of milk and soon realised her problem couldn't be hunger alone. I tried everything I knew, including carrying her in a 'front-pack' pouch all day sometimes in case it was just comfort she needed. She gained a little weight very gradually. She showed no other symptoms. The doctor thought it was colic, but no amount of gripe-water helped. Someone lent a Silver Cross pram and when out pushing that I felt almost like a normal mother. One time my brother walked with me to the park and I pretended we were a normal family.

That spring Grandma and Grandpa came up again, bringing Bud with his new family. He and Delores had divorced, so we met his new lady and her two children. They were with us when I went for surgery on my toes, hoping the extra people would help care for my children. Kate utterly refused a bottle, with my expressed milk, or formula or water; so she was brought in to me for each feed. One doctor in that hospital was far too free with his attentions and I had no strength, of any kind, to stop him. Frightening, yes, but was he right saying it was my fault? He successfully guessed that would guarantee my silence.

In June, at four months old, Kate got sick. I had to take her to the Medical Centre Emergency at midnight; it was otitis media, a painful ear infection. Two weeks later, same again, this time with tonsillitis also. With a fever of 104°F she was admitted and put on an IV drip. Nurses held her down, and removed me forcibly from the room because I was fighting to get to my baby. They were inserting more fluids through a stent in her temple. No permission was asked or explanation given. It seemed outlandish, but, thankfully, she recovered quickly.

In August Garth, Kate and I returned to England for two months. We must have looked pretty haggard on arrival as Mother took us straight to her doctor. He was thorough, then truly shocked me, pronouncing Kate's problem to be malnutrition. If he had accused me of murder I couldn't have felt deeper blame and guilt. How did I not see it? My milk, gallons in quantity, was more like water because of my wrecked emotional state. No wonder my beloved daughter had been so unhappy. From then on she drank cow's milk from a cup, plus a nightly teaspoon of sedative. I was allowed the sedative too. Improvements began at once, we both slept well, Kate gained weight, smiled all day, and so we all enjoyed the English summer.

We went to Bath where Alison lived, and met her fiancé, and there's a lovely photo of my son sitting by the Roman baths, which he called 'that hundred-week old swimming pool.' Seeing the black slab in the Abbey floor commemorating one thousand years of British monarchy was very special. In the back pew I used the brief rest to change Kate, but had left it a bit late. There is probably still a stain on the ancient flagstones, though of course I cleaned it up as best I could.

Cousins and aunts, old friends, flower-filled garden tea parties, plus great fun on the tyre swing Granny roped to a convenient tree branch. Downland walks, harvest fields, and cricket matches on the village green, all bathed in lots of sunshine. A favourite photo shows Kate wearing nothing but a big grin, sitting in Gramps' arms, contentedly leaning up against his chest. Thirty seconds later he had to wash his hands and change his clothes. Garth and Granny ran races together and, regardless of who won, he puffed, 'We nearly beat our chothers, didn't we?' That one found its way into wider family usage, along with his other classic comments.

September 12th was Alison and Chris's wedding. Kurt returned from his militaria convention in time to join us for the ceremony, without much pleasure in reunion. I hoped Alison's marriage expectations would not be as crushed as mine, as we all gathered in the same church for the same service. The bride looked stunning and everyone loved her unusual colour choice of sage green and cream. She'd also chosen to revive an old custom and walk through the village, both to and from the church. Our parents must have pulled out all the stops as there was a huge marquee covering the back lawn, with flowers twined up and around the poles.

As before when facing the end of a visit I was full of conflicting emotions, this time worse than ever. Not just the goodbyes then eight hours flying, but what lay ahead. Certainly no real marriage to return to, and part of me very much wanted to stay. Perhaps it was the obvious relationship breakdown between Kurt and me that loosened Mother's tongue. She spoke of things never mentioned before, or only alluded to occasionally, such as her own early life and broken first engagement. So much sadness unleashed onto shoulders unable to carry it. If she wanted sympathy, I let her down – again. I felt angry. Why didn't she tell me things like that far earlier, before I left home; surely I'd have been better equipped to face life? Maybe she simply could not.

11

Coping, as usual, meant keeping busy. There was absolutely no money. Desperation was close. We got another car, for $10 no questions asked. I accepted the challenge of two foster children because the payment was $100 a week. 'Busy' then took on new meaning. Sam and Irma were 8- and 7-years old, but each exhibited behaviour more suited to 3- and 30-year olds by turns. They came with pitifully few possessions, quite happy to adopt several of our resident teddies; naturally they picked my children's favourites. Sam took a can opener the first evening and carved his initials on to the top of his cupboard. I was angry but told him I'd done a similar thing many years ago, protesting unfair treatment, guessing he felt the same. It forged a bond between us that survived even when I produced sandpaper and polish and explained their use. Thinking a few swipes would do, he found out just how much effort has to go into refinishing wood.

Those kids craved my attention, soaked it up and demanded more. Both scratched a lot, their heads overrun with lice. That did make me heave. I'd never faced the problem before but knew what it entailed. When shampooing and combing through each head bent over the basin, every louse got crunched between my fingernails as I shuddered. Then bedding and clothes were changed and boiled. My un-boilable wool blankets I washed, and hung outdoors on the line for days. Nits and eggs perish just as completely in freezing conditions as in boiling, and we'd had several hard frosts. Next came Garth and Kate's hair and bedding. Every stuffed toy and teddy had a turn on the washing line, pegged by their ears till thoroughly frozen. When it got to my own treatment and bedding, insisting Kurt use the special shampoo, he ceased being amused at my 'fussing'. Being hirsute, his de-lousing became a lengthy operation.

Kate's first birthday meant real celebrating. Her earlier miseries had given way to a sunshiny disposition. Everyone delighted in her company, and she slept all night plus two naps each day. Like Garth, she was equally happy with her own company or with lots of others. Playgroup still took a lot of time, but was such fun. Most of the children at five, including Garth, would be ready for school in the fall. Before that we had to say goodbye to Ev and family as they moved away to Iowa. That was a big wrench. Ev was such a support and comfort. We had shared a lot. We got out and about a bit in the 'new' car, a huge blue station wagon with a mind of its own. I talked to it a lot, and learned to flick the butterfly under the hood whenever it wouldn't start.

Ev and Tony knew before they left about the sad state of my non-marriage, and once settled in their new home, sweetly sent me three tickets to fly out for the summer in Iowa with them. Perfect timing too, since Sam and Irma had just moved on to an aunt. Arrival in Low Moor was a better tonic than pot-smoking or other pastimes I'd tried. The wide-open spaces and vast expanse of sky brought such light-heartedness. There were flat acres of corn ripening under hot sun, and miles of country roadways lined with orange day lilies. Sometimes Tony joined us and we took picnics and explored, once driving parallel to a tornado. It was far enough away not to be dangerous, but the black, twisting funnel cloud was close enough to be clearly seen. Happy hours were spent in their garden, Garth and Charissa used to swoop together on the big swing. After a sudden sharp thunderstorm, we heard their delighted shrieks having discovered a downpipe overflowing from the roof. They were bent over, soaking themselves gleefully. Saying goodbye at the end of that visit was awful.

Jersey City hadn't changed in my absence, nor had my spouse: both just looked shabbier. The fresh air vitality found in the mid-west evaporated as I sank back into the mundane. All the late night talks of encouragement and determination seemed wasted back where there was no conversation at all. One question kept repeating in my mind:

'Does Kurt love you and do you love him?' The long silence for an answer said it all. That's as far as my thinking could go, so I quickly returned to busyness.

Garth was not excited about going to school. He wanted to go back to Iowa for long carefree days with his special friend. His other friends were either going to the Catholic school or private kindergarten, both fee-paying, so out of the question for us. He and I visited our local school in Journal Square, trying to be positive, but I didn't want to send him there any more than he wanted to go. Ninety-five percent of pupils were Hispanic or black and my poor son stood out like an albino. Morning lessons were taught in Spanish; English after lunch. Garth had been reading since he was three years old, and writing also, knew his numbers, and drew amazing pictures. I believe he gave more of his calm, above-average maturity to that school than he ever got out of it. October brought a cheering visit from my younger brother Jonathan. He was on his way to a new life in Hong Kong and apparently he wrote home saying his fortnight in my home had been much better than expected. He and I had some deep talks and I was surprised I didn't resent his questioning, but instead felt strongly moved by his concern. At one point he asked outright about my sex life. A one-word reply was sufficient – dead. How ironic, considering the amount of activity, marital and other, earlier on. Jonny said, 'Well, old girl, if you haven't got sex, you haven't got a marriage.'

Nowadays, I am sure both he and I would agree that in a good marriage there is so much more than just sex. It is the icing on the cake. When there is no cake to ice is when things are bleak and need to be attended to. Dropping him at Newark Airport, it was time to face up to the problem.

Bracing myself for sparks, I tried raising the subject with Kurt several times. He would not talk. Eventually I went up to his studio where he was painting, with a cigarette stuck on his lip and a pipe on the go also. He shrugged and agreed that we didn't have much going for us anymore, but then he leaned back on the rear legs of his chair, paint brush tucked behind his ear and looked at me for the first time in ages, saying, 'Do you remember what Nels told Biddy after they moved out of here and she wanted to leave him? He said there was no point in her running off because he would find her and kill her for it. I will do that to you too.'

At that instant something very weird happened. Kurt's painting table was in the corner at right angles to the window, above which was a wide pelmet used as a shelf. Up there was a large Toby-jug tankard with an ugly gremlin face. It suddenly tipped forward and fell, not straight down as gravity would decree, but out in an arc, directly towards my husband. We watched it curve as if in slow motion, neither of us moving. It passed so close to his head that it knocked the ash off his cigarette, crashing on the edge of his overfull ashtray, spraying the contents everywhere. The momentary silence was soon shattered by foul language and accusations, although it was obvious even to him, that I had nothing to do with it, as he had not. We were both quite shaken.

Once when Garth was still tiny, Kurt started groaning, saying he felt ill. I paid little attention, assuming it was due to over-indulgence of some kind while he was out late the previous night. Onto the floor, doubled up and rolling about in pain, I saw beads of sweat on his forehead. When I could decipher his mutterings and heard there was an elephant sitting on his chest, I'm afraid I gave up and left him alone. The elephant must have followed my example, because soon Kurt was in the kitchen making coffee. Now I know that was the first of his many subsequent heart attacks, but neither of us thought of such a possibility then. He chewed a handful of antacids with his coffee and kept off onions for a while. I never wished that on him again, but knew the children and I could survive if something did happen to him. I could not even peek at the dreaded word 'divorce'. That word is obese: it carries within itself so many other nasty ones like pain, hurt, ugliness, failure, fear, rejection, anger and grief. I was so desperately hanging on to making the best of a bad job, not admitting defeat, that I could not permit anything else into my mind for fear of losing the lot.

I rang David, whose New York boss had just transferred him to Fort Wayne, Indiana. The timing of that move was an amazing coincidence and I remember thanking God. Now I know it was a God-incidence. I told David I needed help and was very uneasy. Only that morning the bank had approved his mortgage, so he could shortly offer us refuge in his new home. The tiny apartment he and Jan were temporarily renting prohibited children. That felt safe enough, rather like a holiday, with no need to mention any nasty words, even separation. Some days later I tried talking to Kurt again while Garth was in school and Kate slept. He had to know, though I didn't yet know how or when I could go. He was cleaning his guns and checking bullets in preparation for the upcoming Shoot. I sat on the stool watching his meticulous care of the pistols and rifles, specially his favourite Charleville. Each hand-made bullet was checked, excess lead carefully trimmed. Same routine for the Colt, the replacement for the stolen one. I watched him oil the chamber and fill the eight places with brassy shells. Then he cocked the hammer. Suddenly, like a rabbit caught in headlights' glare, I froze. Very slowly my husband – sober and unstoned – leaned back; very slowly turning to face me, he lifted that primed and loaded gun till it was pointing directly at me. That room contained more than just us two: angels must have been on protection duty, and now I freely and openly thank God for it. Staring at me for a long time he finally spoke. 'I think I will just do this now, and that'll put an end to your stupid talk of leaving.'

His finger was on the trigger, but he still didn't pull it. Instinctively I knew any sudden reaction from me would bring disaster and I wasn't physically capable anyway. Still mostly frozen, I asked what plans he had for caring for the children, as I would like to know that first. After what seemed ages, but probably only a couple more minutes, he put down the gun, turned from me snarling,

'Oh just get the hell out and go, I don't care, and take the two of them with you.'

As quickly and quietly as possible I got Kate up from her nap and went out, walking the streets till it was time to collect Garth from school, then we three walked around a lot more. When we ventured home Kurt had gone, and stayed out all night. When the children were asleep I rang David again, only then my shakiness dissolved into tears. Jan left then and there to come get us, escorting us back to Fort Wayne. She made it in two days, having slept just a few hours in a motel en route. Kurt had gone to his Shoot, but we didn't know when he'd return and no one wanted to be there when he did. Jan helped select a few major items for each child and myself, hurriedly packing all we could into both cars. If I'd known then that I would never go back, would I have chosen different things?

I owe an enormous debt of gratitude to my sister-in-law. I couldn't have managed those days without her. It was very cold that November morning as we prepared for the journey. Mary Delpeto came round to hug us goodbye, promising to keep an eye on my house and garden, as if we were just going on vacation. Kate got strapped into her seat with a giant box of Cheerios, of which she was very fond, and Garth climbed into the space made for him on the back seat, and we left Liberty Avenue. By then I was a zombie and certainly not fit to drive. Divine intervention and protection was the only way my car stayed on the road. I glued my eyes on the rear of Jan's car and simply followed; where she overtook I overtook. All through Pennsylvania and Ohio, through rain, sleet and snow. When she stopped for gas I did too and we must have eaten and slept somewhere. I do remember walking stiffly into a motel restaurant near the end of the trip, realising Kate was very cold, and still in the same pyjamas and blue zippered sleeper that she left home in. She was so good hour after hour stuck in that car seat, playing with Cheerios, eating them and chucking them around. Garth took turns riding with me or with his aunt. Once during heavy snow, she pulled over onto the shoulder so I did, and sat there watching her get Garth outside in the light from my headlamps. Poor child couldn't relieve himself into the coffee can provided, so had to get out. It was like watching someone else's family movie, with the wet snow cutting diagonally across the screen in the arc of light and the music was the constant swoosh of traffic thundering past. It was real, not a movie; and mine not someone else's.

Eventually we reached Fort Wayne, continuing to feel like someone else's family movie. For the first couple of weeks we had to pretend we weren't there as they were still living in the no-kids apartment complex. Fear of being discovered and reported was ever present. I was anxious about everything. At last we all moved in to the new house. What a mansion! In the whirl of adjusting, we had to get Garth into school. It was called Indian Meadows and there was no walking downtown to it. Big yellow school busses stopped at certain spots so all children from that immediate area congregated for collection, getting dropped off there also each afternoon. Garth had his lunch-box and knew what to do. His teacher, Mrs Connington, was lovely and so good to him. Unfortunately, she had no jurisdiction over the bus journeys and it was during those that my poor son was so unhappy – and I could do nothing about it. Nearly every day he would come back miserable with new taunts about divorce, and being a bastard kid. Excerpts from my journal dated Tuesday November 23rd 1976, read:

Am dead inside. Tremendously strong 'it's not fair' feelings after all the effort. I tried to be better, make it work, and so on. Anyway, much encouragement and support from lots of people, but what to do now? Big bro saved my sanity. He and J have opened their home to us. The children have settled amazingly well, tho' Garth speaks and weeps about his daddy a lot. My mind is blank most of the time. Bad headaches.

That winter broke records on the weather charts, sub-zero cold for weeks on end, many feet of snow and dangerous drifting in howling winds. Arctic gear was essential for any exploration outside, and still all moisture in mouth, nose and eyes quickly froze, and was sore when thawing. Many days schools were closed – the children would get frostbite waiting for the bus. I learned driving skills never before

97

necessary, and always kept a shovel in the car, old sacks and a bag of kitty litter to improve grip. David took us to a tree farm where we chose and cut our own tree. Jan did everything so elegantly and produced a perfect English Christmas lunch, valiantly trying to keep us cheerful. She invited friends and we all played in the snow, sledding down onto the frozen lake. More friends joined us for New Year's Eve but my leaden heart was uncomfortably aware of being single amongst happy couples.

Later on Jan and I did have fun attempting cross-country skiing. A pocket flask of whisky glowingly kept hypothermia at bay but did nothing to improve balance and coordination. When some of the snow melted there were ice storms, turning leafless, groaning trees into exquisite frozen sculptures, from which branches split and broke, while zinging fence wires hummed. We hardly met any neighbours as only the most adventurous went outdoors, but one guy did come knocking. A new pastor was openly drumming up business in the subdivision, a vast area in the middle of flat farmland with many new homes being built. Josh Kelly said we'd all be welcome in the church and there'd be loads of other young children. I went and he was right. Garth, Kate and I were warmly welcomed and met lots of new friends. On one of our earliest Sundays there Kate wriggled off my lap and started wandering, which she'd not done before. Silent and unpredictable, she sauntered up the main aisle towards Josh in his black cassock, busy preaching on the dais. Still silent, Kate reached the steps and laboriously climbed up them, showing her diapered bottom to all. By this time Josh had lost his congregation's full attention. At the third and final step Kate reached over, tugging on the hem of his cassock. Possibly he thought he'd try ignoring her first, but she tugged again, so without losing a word from his sermon he bent down, picked her up and settled her comfortably in his arms as he continued. There she stayed with an enormous grin of satisfaction, perfectly quiet till the end of the service. She was adopted into every heart in that place.

Josh told me about an eligible man I should meet and finally did set up a date for me on March 17th, Saint Patrick's Day. Matt arrived precisely on time, his huge stature filling the doorframe. We had a good evening out and many more to follow. Spring eventually came to Indiana, marking my thirty-first, Kate's second, and Garth's sixth birthdays. David and Jan both had high-powered jobs so I kept house for them, repaying just a fraction of all I owed them. It was necessary to be resident in the state for six months before starting divorce proceedings. Someone said that doing the divorcing is better than being divorced by your spouse. It's still a no-win situation. However viewed, right or wrong, it shouts failure, defeat, exhaustion, finality. The hard part is existing through the eons while that decision is forming. That was the real me, but impossible to dwell on if there was to be any attempt at normal living and certainly, continuing parenthood. That was my priority. I was absolutely determined to be the best I could be for my children. If I was to be all they had of parental love and security then they would have it in double portions from me.

There had been minimal contact with Kurt. He sent his children birthday cards, but on the wrong dates. He sent some child support, but the cheques bounced and I had to pay bank charges. He intended to come see us, but as he didn't drive I never thought he would. He did, and what a visit it was. I agreed only to meet in a very public place. We chose the zoo, and I had back-up protection and support waiting in strategic spots, just in case. I was deeply afraid he'd shoot one or all of us, then possibly himself. I dreaded seeing him yet also wanted to, realising the kids must never be prevented from seeing their father. We were curious. At least Garth and I were. Kate was confused. It was weird and unreal. Who waits around by the monkey house to meet up with the one who had been your life, who fathered your children, who was supposed to have loved you? We should have been behind bars, not those chimps. He arrived by coach at the time he said he would. We three were rather weepy, and Garth's eczema flared up. Not a pleasant day, but he didn't shoot us, or argue over the children. He did not object to divorce and was happy for me to have sole custody, and take the kids to England whenever. He even agreed to put that in writing and did so and signed it.

I accepted a housekeeping job back in England at the school my brothers had attended. Garth would be educated there. I thanked God, and meant it, even if I wasn't sure I wanted to leave America. The term didn't start till September, and I couldn't go at all if the divorce judge wouldn't agree to it. The legacy of Kurt's visit was indeed no physical damage, but something more lastingly painful, especially for Garth, than a quick bullet would have been. Kurt took his son on his knee in farewell, saying he loved him, and added: 'Now you watch your mailbox every day because I'm going to write to you lots. Yeah, I'll send you something every day so you won't forget your old dad. So no sleeping late. You get up early and wait for the mailman, OK?'

Hearing those words I wanted to kill the speaker on the spot because I knew they weren't true, and I knew what anguish would come. From the next morning on Garth was up, washed and dressed, waiting expectantly for the mail, for days and days that stretched into weeks. Each trip down the driveway to the mailbox was a little slower and each empty-handed return a little more dejected. It broke my heart as I could see it breaking his.

The journal entry for July 21st 1977 reads:

This has been a day unlike any other and, I trust, will never have to be repeated. I went to court and became divorced. Eight years of marriage wiped out in eight minutes. Matt took me to dinner and said, 'Welcome to the world of the un-married.' Throughout the day there were tremendous storms, but in the evening it cleared for a lovely sunset and a million stars came out in a velvet sky. The world keeps turning. The beat goes on. So must I.

The farewells from the USA and the return to UK were so difficult. Not only in leaving everyone in Indiana, but we stayed three days in

New York with Doraine and saw the Delpetos too. The final evening with Matt had been a real wrencher. Not one to scrimp on life's niceties, he organized flowers, champagne and a hotel room. He'd spoiled me during the preceding five months, literally wined and dined and danced me through many a late night. He knew so many people and good places to go, was recognised and welcomed at the best nightspots Being on his arm, as it were, these red-carpet treatments extended to me also. Only a couple of times was I hailed as Carla, his ex-wife. I just had to ignore that. We talked of marriage in a roundabout sort of way, agreeing we'd both been through too much to try again. He'd kicked Carla out after discovering her second affair. As a pilot he was away on trips a great deal so was the last to find out about it. I thought she must be mad to throw away such a wonderful man. He appeared to be everything Kurt was not, and I wanted him and he said he wanted me. He was nearly fifteen years older than me and his three teenagers towered over my 'babies'. The end of our last night together felt like the end of everything. He pressed an envelope into my hand, not to be read till on the plane, so I knew it must contain a goodbye brush-off. It was beautifully written for an un-love letter, leaving me with the merest glimmer of hope.

12

At Heathrow an official took all our papers, yelling at me for being in the wrong passport line. On reaching the desk everything was double-checked. They said I could stay but the kids must leave in fourteen days. Trying to stay calm I explained we were all three coming home and my children were staying with me. The man glared, repeating himself while stamping visas. I never expected a trumpet fanfare welcome back to my native land, but never expected to be turned away either. I sat down on a suitcase, held my children and together we wept. Immediately the men came out of their kiosks. One redirected people behind me to a different queue and the other took us plus our luggage into a side room. Cups of tea and tissues were produced with lots of stammering apologies. Finally they brought forms for me to fill in and sign for my children, to allow them unlimited entry.

Occasional culture shocks can be difficult, frequent ones even more so. We seemed always in a state of adjustment and adaptation and that's hard work. Within one week of starting the new school job, we all got a vicious bug and were sent back to Granny and Gramps. Our allocated flat was cold and draughty. By cold, I mean cracking and removing ice from the kettle before the morning cuppa, and scraping more ice from inside windows in order to see out. I rebuilt the ancient fireplace in the upstairs living room, knowing what effort it would take to carry logs and coal up there, and take ashes down. It created warmth in one corner of the large room while the rest remained windswept in the draughts. Thick newspapers under the rugs did stop some cold, and I stuffed more under the mattresses. Poor Garth caught pneumonia that autumn. He'd fussed all day, woken about 10pm wailing that his ribs were breaking. He had to be in the school sick bay for ages, off games for six weeks.

Kate trotted up the long school drive each morning with me and 'helped' with my work. Sweeping and mopping was what she liked, specially in the dormitories, seeing if the boys' beds were made. She liked their teddies. Nobody minded which bed she'd nap on each day. Her favourite job was lunchtime sweetshop, when I took the cash as the boys replenished their tuck boxes. If a boy dithered too long, Kate pushed his hands away saying, 'Dat's 'nuff, boy.' At the end of term she ran about, scrunching up her face, gleefully announcing, 'It's ormosh Kissems-time', but when ready for the Nativity play she suddenly backed out whispering, 'I don't want to be anybody else. I just want to be Kate.'

We three had fireside supper on the floor quite often and the first time she sang out, 'We're having a widdow pinkit' (little picnic). Meals for her were easy: peanut butter, raisins, carrots and cheese. Garth wasn't much better but he did manage school lunches most days. I fell into the habit of eating just peanut butter also, but washed mine down with whisky. That did take the edge off the cold, and my loneliness. I longed for Matt. I had felt accepted in Indiana, even as one of the church's dreaded 'single parent problems', but not so here in school. Being neither domestic nor staff I didn't fit anywhere. When I did venture into the staffroom, conversations ceased and newspapers came up in front of faces. I invited some to my flat for coffee or tea but they didn't come. Disapproval reigned.

That winter was generally bad. Garth was angry, hurting, confused and needing his dad. The only person he could vent it on was me and although I understood it and ached with him, that didn't make it any easier to cope with. His nightmares meant none of us slept much. In schoolwork he did excellently, even in French and Latin, and playing a quarter-size violin. He read a great deal and even read to Kate when he wasn't cross. I felt so protective of them both. One comfort was Peg. She must have been the mainstay of that school kitchen since 1801 at least. When my brothers were there she could spot a lad who needed a special touch, saving extra cake for him at tea, or seconds of a favourite pudding at lunch. Then my son joined the ranks and Peg took to him, and Kate too. She often pitied 'the littl' un wot's got no Yankee dad no more', and made sure he had many extra cake slices. It was particularly difficult therefore, for me to caution her about smoking while peeling the potatoes, or dropping ash into the stew.

January 11th 1978 was my grandmother's one hundredth birthday, and a great party was held for her. Resplendent, she sat next to her telegram from the Queen and innumerable other tributes and cards, quietly muttering, 'Blessings on you, my wee lamby pets,' in her usual manner. Everyone enjoyed the celebration, including me, although I was so sad about a letter received only that morning. My dear friend Ev poured out her heart on paper over the death of her premature twins. Being torn and divided between two such different worlds was my reality.

Dad helped me buy an old Cortina which served me well and did provide a bit of freedom. I didn't visit my parents much because I couldn't manage Mother's emotional demands. The steamy letters from Matt added more pressure. We'd agreed not to write. That lasted a week. He wrote first, to make sure I was alright, so I had to reply. Then the phone calls started and they were lovely, yet made everything worse. Suddenly he was coming, flying himself to Gatwick on business, coming to see me. I'd draw curtains of privacy round those few happy winter days if they'd been as blissful as anticipated. I was recovering from another bug then got a shocking migraine requiring a doctor with a needle. We did have fun, though, and he managed to say, 'I love you.'

Gradually Garth lost some miseries, almost regaining his old sweet self. Every boarding-school bug found its way to our flat, bringing colds and croup. Garth broke his collarbone again but in spite of it did not revert to the black moods. It was more often me dealing with moods and miseries. Frazzled by daily survival, I was pulled in too many directions. Knowing Mother was desperate for my company plus an assurance we'd remain in England forever, I could not give her either. It was too hard to be 'daughter' while unsure if I was going to change from 'ex-wife' to 'second-wife' while retaining 'divorcee' and on-going mum. No wonder the headaches escalated.

Matt's letters were still a regular source of pleasure, but they contained no commitment. Yet on Valentine's Day he sent a huge bouquet of yellow roses. Did yellow have a strange meaning such as: 'I don't love you enough for red ones'? From someone who never bothered much about the future, I became someone who needed to know now. An old friend reappeared, also newly single, came over a few times and was good company – suddenly far too much good company. A dental appointment also went wrong. The dentist injected into a vein. Instead of numbing one side of my mouth, it made me feel very drunk, then as if I had run up-hill fast, then terminal. I sat in that chair twitching, trembling and sweating, barely able to breathe or see. I heard someone phoning to London for advice. I remember thinking it was all over. If they thought I was dying, I surely must be. Sometime later I was returned to school by taxi, assured I would be fine, with just a few days of amnesia and drowsiness. Too true; the next morning I even forgot how to keep standing up. They gave me the day off. The dentist rang to apologise and see if I was alright. I did not book a return visit.

Prior to that fiasco Matt called at 5am saying he had another European trip and could visit for twenty-four hours, which he then did, and proposed. After supper by candlelight he got down on one knee asking me to do him the honour of becoming his wife. Jumbled stuff charged through my head, namely a line from *Oklahoma*: 'I'm just a gal who cain't say no'. Now he has finally asked, should I tell him I might be brain-damaged by the dentist? Damaged goods as well as a 'second hand rose'? By then I'd said yes and shed a tear or two. Soon felt like shedding more, when, in referring to my precious children, he used an odd phrase. I'd heard him say it a few times, but it never hurt as it did at that moment: 'the calves come with the heifer.' Warning lights flashed. Remembering about Christian marriages needing God, and all the prayers I'd been flinging towards the ceiling recently, I asked, without looking at him, if he was a Christian. 'Of course,' he mumbled, just a tiny bit terse. Slightly braver, I mumbled something pious about putting God first in our marriage. In the silence that followed I reckoned, 'You've done it now. He'll un-ask you next.' Instead he said clearly, 'Naturally we'll put Garth first if you like, but it'll be equal first with my three. 'No,' I said. 'God, not Garth.' 'Ah, right. Of course, that's fine too.' End of discussion. Further warning lights had bricks thrown at them hastily by me.

We had to finish the school year, so planned to return to the States at the end of July. Although still passively letting things happen I had to be even more busily active to keep at bay oppressive thoughts, and heightened awareness of straddling two worlds. Was I leaving home again, or was I going back home again? Both were true.

In the meantime my school job had to continue, while contacting shipping companies and booking tickets. It was exciting to share my children's enthusiasm for their new dad, but not my fearful anxiety. Was it out of the frying pan into the fire? Was it a golden opportunity not to be missed? As a distraction we three went to the South of England Show, where I bumped into a man who worked occasionally on the school gardens, an itinerant jack-of-all-trades. That day he was selling country antiques. I spotted a set of brass scales on a marble base, bearing the seal of King George. As we bargained over the price he suddenly grabbed my hand in his huge, grimy one and told me I could have it for nothing if I married him. Two proposals in as many weeks! I retrieved my hand, declined politely, and backed away. He followed. He became a pest. He began entertaining my children, and got them up onto huge farm machinery like their Tonka trucks, which they loved. Then my children disappeared, just like that. One minute with me, the next gone. I retraced frantic steps, revisited each stall and exhibit we'd been to, trying not to think of what that man might have done. A message went over the loudspeaker system describing my children, calling me to the St John's Ambulance HQ, the furthest point from me. My feet seemed cast in lead, as in a nightmare, but I was wide-awake and running.

'Why don't you come this way dearie, and sit down, and we'll get you a nice cup of tea.' Inner panic had become externally obvious. My children were totally fine, enjoying biscuits, squash, and a great array of toys. Garth welcomed me with, 'Where have you been Mum? We've been waiting here ages, and thought you were lost.' Kate was keen to point out the giant horses nearby, decked out in lots of brasses, with braided manes and tails. 'Look over there, Mum. He's got a necklace on his bottom.'

On July 10th the shipping firm collected our trunks and boxes. We were moving into a well equipped home, so would only need our personal belongings. The remaining weeks we lived out of a suitcase each. End of term excitement was helpful. 'Oooh, off to America to marry a rich pilot.' It did sound glamorous, and the congratulations were nice, but I kept quiet about the niggling doubts. After school we went to Wales for a family holiday. Much effort went into having fun, which sadly backfired. It was so tense with a build-up of emotion, particularly Mother's barely concealed bitter sadness. I was only 50% there, the other 50% already way ahead getting Americanised again, keen to be free, yet sad to be leaving once more. That journey we started on the final Welsh day, just me and my little ones, carrying heavy luggage and heavier hearts, did get better, but was exhausting. By a variety of vehicles we went from Fishguard to Paddington, overnight in Bromley with friends who took us to Heathrow. On to Chicago where we changed from the 747 jumbo jet to a very small Lear jet with Matt at the controls. Safe landing followed by a short car ride, then home – again.

Matt's house was only a few blocks from where we'd lived before. The whole area was familiar and we knew lots of people so this homecoming was wonderfully different. With his family's help he had spruced up the house to perfection, and everything gleamed and shone. The spare room had two beds, each with a new quilt made by

107

his mom for Garth and Kate. Flowers everywhere and champagne in the fridge; if we hadn't been semi-conscious from tiredness it would have been better.

While I was bathing my kids Matt knocked, entered the bathroom and proposed again, presenting a ring box. Much earlier he'd asked and I'd found an old curtain ring that fit my finger exactly and sent it to him. He also asked me to draw my choice of engagement ring – the sky's the limit, he added, and that from a pilot. I wanted a diamond deep-set into the ring, not out on prongs. So, having dried my trembling hands, I opened the box. A large diamond sparkled atop tall prongs. If I had spoken truthfully at that moment, telling him it was the opposite of what I asked for, how different things might have been. I couldn't bear to appear rude or ungrateful so I silenced the pushy little voice whispering: 'You aren't that important or he would have remembered,' not knowing just how many times I'd need the silencer on.

The informal wedding ceremony was to be in the unfinished church building, taken by Josh Kelly who had introduced us. Matt had arranged a baby-sitter but I felt Garth and Kate should be present. He strongly disagreed. His children rang, one by one, saying they wouldn't go through with the boycott and would come after all. At the last minute both boys came home, needing to borrow Dad's ties, and Sara appeared in her jeans. So I insisted on my two being present also, which seemed obviously right and proper. Another huge mistake loomed, but if I couldn't tell my very-soon-to-be-husband that I didn't like the ring, hated being in his first wife's bed and putting my clothes in her dresser drawers, how could I tell him we should not marry? We were married. Jon asked me to promise to take good care of his dad, Roy said nothing, Sara wept, apologising for wanting her mother there in my place, and my two just looked bemused.

We had a four-day honeymoon between the ceremony and the reception party. He wanted to fly me up north to the Michigan woods, and wasn't pleased with my request to stay on the ground. It was a long drive requiring an overnight stop which he had not planned for. Once at the real destination, only two things spoiled the idyllic hideaway for me: concern for my children, though they knew and liked the friends who had them to stay. I soon learned to keep such things to myself. The second was discovering the origin of the necklace I'd not taken off since receiving it as I left for England the previous year. Suspended from a gold chain was a gold rectangular box filled with Lucite, in which stood the number 1 made of tiny diamonds. I thought I was his number one. He had bought it for his first wife, who'd given it back when she left him.

For weeks Matt had been planning our party. He did an excellent job and it was lovely. Friends came from far and near to the Bakers' superb rural home. Don and Jen had scrubbed out their huge garage and decorated it as beautifully as the house, and lined the driveway with candles in sand-filled brown bags. There was plenty of food, drink, dancing, and gifts galore, each boxed, wrapped, ribboned and bowed in fine American style. Afterwards Ev stayed a few days, which was such a help. She made several meals and snacks, as I seemed to have forgotten how to cook.

We were less than a week at home before Matt left on a flight. They varied from one night away to a couple of weeks, and we all acclimatised quickly. That first absent night showed me a different side of his younger son who, at fourteen, had been charm itself up till then. Roy burst into my room, where I was already in bed, and bounced beside me, asking, 'So how do you like Mom's bed, huh? She'll be back soon. Let's talk about the wedding, huh?'

Producing an opened album, he thrust it in front of me, saying, 'Now that was the real wedding. You do know that, don't you? See how happy Dad and Mom are.' There followed a torrent of talk and persistent demands that I look at each and every photo and hear every little detail about Mom and Dad. Then suddenly, like a deflating balloon he bid me good night and good sleep, and left. A murderer trained in psychological warfare could not have done more damage.

Then, and on countless other occasions, I tried to understand and feel compassion for that boy, obviously so hurt by his mother leaving his father and so desperate for them to reunite, but it was never easy and seldom successful. Sara had moved out 'to make room for me', going to live with her mother; and Jon was away in the marines. My journal states: *I am again a married woman. In spite of whatever traumas and problems I have inherited, I am happy – well, I have to be. The alternative is unbearable. So I will be happy.*

Our belongings arrived from England but the fun of that was spoiled by embarrassment. My husband couldn't believe how little there was and how few clothes I had. He insisted, ordered me, to go shopping.

The night that Matt was due to return from a trip, Roy volunteered to babysit. Keen to improve my relationship with this stormy stepson, I decided to trust him, going out with friends in their car. My children were both asleep and mercifully stayed that way. Roy's friend came over and they took my car for a joy ride, throwing firecrackers into neighbours' driveways. Coming home I was thinking of the champagne I had put ready in the fridge to welcome hubby home at midnight. Instead I welcomed him with the local sheriff who had been waiting in our driveway for me. Nobody bothered that Garth and Kate had been left entirely alone, nor the joy riding, but a major fuss was made about the firecrackers and neighbours' complaints.

Everyone was deeply shocked and revolted by the Jim Jones cult leading to mass suicide in Guyana. How could any person become so obsessed with another that they would follow his every command – even poisoning babies and children, then themselves, because they were told to? I was profoundly disturbed by that. Only much later did I recognise the link with my need for subservient obedience to keep my husband as sweet-tempered as possible, and show our gratitude to him for having taken us on. That is sadly pathetic, verging on something worse.

Matt bought a bulldog while we were still in England. Often alone in the house, he was used to life in the basement, but also well trained for good manners upstairs. All humans he knew were tall until we arrived, whereupon he fell in love with Kate, convinced she must be the lady bulldog of his dreams. He constantly knocked her over, becoming possessively amorous. My daily struggle was keeping the peace between the two families, always trying for the desired goal of blended family. For me to insist on the dog's departure would have disastrous repercussions. It did, for a long time.

Matt changed jobs so we needed to move, and managed to sell the house and buy another on the same day. I was hoping to enjoy Christmas in 'our' new home rather than remain in 'her' house, but it didn't happen. Most of us tried to enjoy the festivities, but I was not permitted to touch, re-arrange or decorate any piece of furniture or part of the house unless it matched what Carla, his ex, had done before. Roy insisted on that, poor lad. I had to feel sorry for him, but also for me. The move to Zurich, Illinois, happened in a blizzard over New Year's Eve and Day. Frustration, foul-ups and fury flew between us and the moving men, but I didn't mind because I loved that house. In the first two weeks, while hubby was off somewhere hot and sunny, another blizzard trapped us indoors as twenty-eight additional inches of snow piled up, dropping the temperature to minus 50°F.

Once the snow finally melted it was good to see new friendships and flowers blossom. In March I went on the first of many aviation convention trips, that one to Los Angeles. I almost enjoyed flying in the little Falcon Jet. The photographs I took then from far above the Grand Canyon and Colorado River looked amazingly similar to the first televised pictures of Mars. Early on my birthday morning in the California hotel room, Tony called to say Ev had just produced their second daughter.

Playing outdoors in the summer Kate and Garth made many friends, so I met more parents. Our houses were set back on an acre or so each, and the roads were quiet through the Woods subdivision, allowing the kids safe freedom to ride bikes and visit each other. Quite often mine needed to talk about their father, and stepfather, and similarly deep matters. Most days the mums gathered at the lakes so the children could run, play, and learn to swim and jump off the floating dock. Always checking for two blond heads above the surface, I did not find it restful. We were even more vigilant after one little girl had to be pulled out, upended, and thumped hard. She brought up quantities of lake water and promptly revived.

Lengthy enquiries produced an elderly woman called Veronica, highly recommended as a reliable and trustworthy babysitter. Willing to cope with children of all ages, animals, and houseplants even, she became a regular visitor, whenever I needed to go with Matt to some exotic place or function. At summer's end we flew down to Miami for three days to meet up with Jan, David and their baby Alex, en route from Brazil to their new life in Puerto Rico. In October Carla came to visit, but it wasn't an enjoyable time. I wanted to be welcoming but I also wanted her to go, particularly when she and Roy wept together. He would not live with her because of her new husband and hated living with his dad because of me. He was in trouble at school, constantly bullying Garth at home and diabolically rude to me. He desperately wanted me to leave.

When winter came round again we discovered the nearby lakes were great fun for ice-skating, ice hockey, and sharing gallons of hot chocolate or hot cider afterwards. I made more friends at church and the kids enjoyed the Sunday School. We had lots of visitors through the years, something I always enjoyed, and I never minded all the extra cooking and cleaning up. On Scouting Sunday in February Garth won his God and Family Award. He had worked hard on all the requirements for that and I was so proud of him. He liked Scouting, except the bullying. Another surprise in such a fine tradition was after one of the camps he came home telling me the Scoutmaster, Mr T, camped with them but the woman in his tent with him wasn't Mrs T.

In a sad letter from England I learned my grandmother had died on February 13th 1980: 'Annie Grace, aged 102, beloved wife of the late Earnest Cheal, devoted mother, grandmother and great-grandmother, loved by many in four generations.' Her funeral was at the Quaker meetinghouse where it was said, 'Her long journey is over, she has gone Home; absent from the body but present with the Lord.'

Later there was an American letter, written by my stepdaughter, shown to me:

She and Dad have a lovely comfy home. You'll never know how much I appreciate the way she has brought happiness and joy to my dad's life. They're both lucky people. I only hope Roy can be more pleasant to her. I think time will help; she's a super, super lady.

Although essentially too late, those words were comforting.

In May 1980 my parents celebrated their Ruby Wedding. They came to stay with us en route to David's family in Puerto Rico and we had some good times, but they were not sorry to leave. I tried to provide meals they'd recognise at fairly normal times, but they struggled with doughnuts for breakfast, a sandwich lunch and dinner at differing hours. I struggled with keeping my mask firmly in place, trying to have everything appear normal and just fine, preventing them, or anyone, seeing the double life I'd so quickly learned to live. One as Wife and the other as Mum, and never the twain could meet. When it was just him and me, or with any adults, he was fine and we had fun. He expected my children to be perfect, literally no noise, no mess, certainly no fussing or tears, absolutely no thumb sucking. At night no hallway light left on or even a small nightlight, no contact after scary dreams. I married him because he was so terrific with his children, and I was sure he'd make a super father for mine too.

It was difficult to know where to draw the line between interfering in brotherly tussles that naturally occur in all families, and forcibly halting Roy's bullying and teasing. Being so much bigger and stronger, he liked to pick Garth up, toss him in the air, hold him upside down, generally making life miserable. He was often too rough with Kate

113

too. He would go on and on until tears resulted, then, of course, taunting with every sort of degrading name. My son's tears were a mixture of fear, hate of such treatment, and also frustration at his inability to retaliate. I knew because I felt exactly the same. Once when I could take no more, I tried to protect us with a broom handle. Roy certainly let go of Garth, but in half a second I was flat on the floor with the broomstick pressing on my neck. Though I loathed greeting Matt with such tales, truly appearing the wicked stepmother, I was more scared of not doing so. My husband chose not to believe his son capable of such behaviour, which naturally put more strain on our relationship. He then felt a need to even the score and remind me of my children's wrongdoings. This tit-for-tat attitude worsened until I gave up and stopped telling him or anyone of Roy's atrocious activities. They were hard to believe, I knew, because he never exhibited anything unpleasant when his father was home, nor when anyone else was around. When that continues unchecked it makes you wonder about your own mental health; thoughts all too familiar to me. Garth joined a judo class to toughen up and learn self-defence. In only the second session he fell badly and broke his collarbone again, grating his pride as much as his shoulder.

That autumn I braved a test flight of a new Sikorsky helicopter during a Kansas City convention. Not something to repeat. Each convention I attended (full of anti-motion-sick pills of course) was similar, always in very nice places. While the pilots conferred over business charts, and deals, the wives were organised with military precision. Every leisure hour arranged throughout the day, complete with printed schedule, to meet up again with spouses for cocktails and evening entertainments. At the first few I did everything I was supposed to with all the other women. I took the coach tours – one memorably tedious one around the Hollywood homes of the stars – not into the homes, just past them. There were variations of fashion shows, lunch speakers, aerobic workouts, flower-arranging classes, and so on. Gradually I just didn't go, being far happier reading by the pool.

Matt vented his displeasure, telling me how much extra he always paid for me to have these treats. There was no discussing it. What should have been great times away became great times of stress, most difficult to avoid. Slowly I saw through the glitz that it wasn't me as me he wanted, but just me as the correct public picture. My headaches and migraines increased, often with sickness and dizziness. When I could not accompany him, or worse, got ill while away with him, his anger escalated and our relationship crumbled further.

13

Early in 1981 we accompanied Matt on a Paris trip, taking all three children out of school. From the air the views over Greenland were spectacular, not green at all, just thousands of square miles of frozen empty space broken up by floating ice-islands and bergs. At Reykjavik in Iceland we stayed in the Loftleider Hotel where their dubious English was 100% better than our Icelandic. Supper was described as 'sticked potatoes and encrusted fish'. A different appearance and taste, but still fish and chips. For sleep, each bed was a mini sofa with just a duvet. Next morning we had more spectacular views and were amazed at so much Icelandic green visible, mostly fir forests. At last we descended through thick cloud to see the wonderful patchwork of southern England. Soon back to Amberley, looking as sleepily picturesque as always, and hugs all round, and 'How was the flight?' and 'My, how they've grown!' Mother produced a superb roast lunch, at which Roy said, polite in intention, that she had forgotten the ketchup. He jumped up to fetch it, not hearing her slightly frosty, 'We do not serve ketchup with roast lamb.'

After the meal, Matt and Roy agreed, not willingly, to go for a walk. They failed to see the purpose of simply walking for walking's sake. Walk where to? What for? Why not take the car, or even a bus? It's about to rain: why go? To give credit where due, they went, realising it's part of what happens in the country in England. They did not enjoy it. Even the stretch along an ancient Roman road did not impress them, and anyway it was raining by then, the kind of solid, very wet rain that relentlessly soaks through every garment. Two teenage daughters of a friend happily escorted Roy to London for a day's sightseeing which he loved. He then went with his dad on to

Paris for a few days, before coming back to collect us for the return flight.

Medical problems and many appointments resulted in a date set in April for my hysterectomy. More dates had also been pre-arranged for me to take Garth and Kate to Puerto Rico, and it was wonderful. David, Jan and Alex lived in a 17th floor apartment on the beach at Isla Verde, and the views from their balcony along the crescent shaped shoreline were incredible. We toured old San Juan and El Morro, the fort, shopped and ate out, drank fresh coconut milk on Goat Island, played, lazed, and collected beach shells. The flight back was bad. I was in pain and didn't handle it well. It was a relief to get to hospital and have the surgery and a bigger relief to wake up and hear it was successful, and that scanned shadow was not cancer. I'd been warned I might feel less of a woman, and need at least six months to recover, but within six weeks I was absolutely fine.

During July, Ev came with her three children to stay. I loved those visits but they made me tense because Matt could hardly stand my little ones, never mind three more. Fortunately he was not home on the 29th as we were up ridiculously early to watch live coverage of the Royal Wedding. I was glued to the screen and unwilling to deal with any interruptions, including the breakfast needs of my children and guests. Ev was more charitable, making toast and refilling juice glasses while I fed on pomp and ceremony, drinking in tradition, nostalgia, homesickness, and the beauty of Princess Diana's special day. I saw glimpses of a riotously happy England, with fireworks and flags, street parties, and a chain of beacons lit on hilltops across the land. When it was over of course I had to ring home and re-celebrate and mop up a tear or two. The physical ache of being so divided was not diminishing. So totally Americanised yet still so totally British, happy in one country but always pining for the other. Whichever side of the Atlantic geographically I was on, part of me was on the other. That began in 1967 and looks set to continue.

In September Matt took me to Palm Springs, California, the heat was fierce, 110 degrees, but manageable because there was no humidity. We drove through desert and up into mountains. While he worked I soaked in a Jacuzzi pool with unforgettable results. Unaware of the customary ten-minute limit or the reasons for it, I spent most of one afternoon bubbling away out in the open under a blazing sun. Sauntering slowly back to the hotel to change for dinner, I felt most peculiar. I could not hurry. Apparently I was a rather bland dinner companion. Matt needed to introduce me to some frightfully influential people, but my eyes kept closing and my face hovered over the soup. That truly was not my intention. Blood pressure must have been so low it's a wonder I didn't pass out completely. I felt ill, and worse after the ensuing row and long, silent drive back. I knew he was fuming by the way he slammed the car door and the gas pedal, so I retreated inside myself trying to escape the third party on the front seat between us. It was a large, ugly lump of black ice, stretching more freezing tentacles around my heart and gradually filling the entire car.

In October Jan came to take my place, bringing Alex, so I could leave for England to help Alison with newborn Nick, brother for recently adopted, eighteen-month old Claire. Watching Alison work out ways to manage infant-care was great. Holding nappy pins in her teeth, and leaning over her tiny son willing him to reach up to her so she could lift him from the Moses basket. My time there raced by, requiring the usual mental gear-changing prior to returning stateside. As always the dreaded plane journey kept the two well separated. Certainly in the early years, I think my family assumed: 'She's landed on her feet. She has married money this time. She's fine.' As long as I kept burying the bad stuff I could keep writing positive letters home, without mentioning the almost daily hurts of slowly growing apart – again. Little put-downs, mini rejections, small snide comments, all add up to big pain. Matt went faithfully to his children's school events, sports, and parent evenings, but always managed to be away or too busy to go to anything of my children's. Asking him would always get the same cold response: 'I've served my time.'

The winter of 1981/82 again broke records when temperatures sank even lower and the wind-chill one January day registered minus 81°F. Such cold increased the severity of pain and stiffness in many of Matt's joints, particularly his hands. It made him bad tempered, as it would anyone, and we all felt sorry for him. He compensated by taking most of the flights to sundrenched places. Doctors suggested we should move to Arizona's dry heat, not to cure his rheumatoid arthritis, but for pain relief. He applied for a job in Hawaii but nothing came of it. His pain medication gradually became stronger.

Jonathan came to us on his way back from Hong Kong. He'd grown a beard and considerably more self-assured, the latter perhaps due to living the high life with plenty of people to do his bidding. I was not quite so willing and found him rather difficult. When Matt criticized, I flew to Jonny's defence; we humans are contrary beings are we not? I can say what I like about my brother, but when someone else does, well then: 'Hey, how dare you, that's my brother you're complaining about.' The kids thought Garth's crazy uncle was wonderful because he drove much too fast taking them to soccer. He and I drove to Earlham, Iowa, a small, rural place, home to some of our distant cousins. Back in 1830 my paternal great, great grandfather's sister gave birth to George Standing. George married Deborah Fox, from the English Quaker dynasty, and with their five sons emigrated in 1870, joining the wagonloads of pioneer families travelling west from New York. They settled in Earlham because it reminded George of England. He built a tiny cabin for his family and cultivated the eighty acres he'd bought for $5 each. The family became, and still is, an important part of the Quaker community there. They welcomed us warmly. We stayed with Minnie, one of the great granddaughters, and saw the original cabin right next door. It was a delight to realise I was neither the first nor the only family member to leave my native land to live elsewhere. Like George and Deborah I learned to love so much of the New Land without ever giving up my loyalty and love for England.

For months I had been secretly planning a fiftieth birthday party for Matt. Roy, who'd left to join the marines, returned for the weekend, as did Jon, each with their girlfriends, plus Sara. Garth, Kate and I presented our gift – Grace, the best bulldog ever. At eight weeks old she fit into two hands, a solid yet rubbery body packed in a silky skin several sizes too big. Everyone fell helplessly in love the moment they saw her. In the afternoon, as we lazed in the garden, Wonder Woman arrived as a singing telegram. Wearing a scarlet cape and little else, she spent a long time on Matt's lap crooning to him. More guests arrived, then the Big Surprise – the belly dancer. She was big too, but amazingly lithe, making the most of her 'dance of the seven veils.' She was well worth her fee. It was a good occasion. Matt was always radiant when any of his kids were around. He was a good father, concentrating on them and enjoying their company. Excellent, as it should be; except for two small, fatherless hearts, being brushed off as one brushes away a nuisance. That is what broke my heart, time and time again and crushed the pieces underfoot.

My parents had often said they would love to have their grandchildren to stay. Something was needed to ease the mounting tensions between my son and husband. A solution, if only temporary, was to let Garth travel alone to England for the school summer vacation. He would have a wonderful time and be well looked after and my parents were delighted. I still felt uncomfortable about letting him go as he was only eleven. British Airways ticketed him as an 'unaccompanied minor' guaranteeing an official would stay with him from when I handed him over until my parents collected him. After the initial call announcing safe arrival, I had to resist the urge to ring every day, knowing it was time to let go a bit. I've always liked the axiom: 'The two most important things you can give your children are roots and wings.' I had tried my best to do so, not realising how hard it would be to see those wings flexed and spread so far away so soon.

Taking his boss to California, Matt called me from the cockpit. That could only mean trouble. He'd just had a call from my mother.

120

Garth was 'sort-of all right'. I should call her and go at once to England. You do what has to be done, reactions follow later. From Mother's tearful explanation I pieced together a ghastly picture. The previous evening Garth had not returned for supper. Neighbours had been contacted, then the police, by which time my parents' nightmare was very real. About 9pm a woman returning home saw a child in the verge, put him in her car and drove to the nearest house. He was recognised as Mrs Cheal's American grandson, so they rang my parents, the police and the doctor. Although bruised and dazed, my son was coherent. The very thing that all parents warn all children about happened. A car passed slowly, turned, came back and stopped very close, almost pinning Garth to the hedge. The man chatted, offered a lift but became angry when Garth declined. Leaning out he grabbed my little boy into the car and sped off, threatening to hurt him if he yelled or struggled. Knowing it was bad, and he could not escape, Garth figured he'd better obey in case the guy had a gun. They drove through the village, up to a lonely part of the Downs where Garth was forced to participate in deviant sexual activities. The man drove him part way back, then dumped him out of the car, where he was found later by the 'good Samaritan' woman.

Through our tears, all I could do was tell Mum I'd get there as fast as possible. Kate decided her brother must be dead and raced as fast as her seven-year old legs could go down the road to my friend and neighbour. Dear Jeannie did come and was the ideal person for such a time. She offered to keep Kate but I knew she must come with me, to see her brother was still alive and that we three could be together. Somehow we got a flight, arrived the next day and shared mutual consoling. Mother could not believe that I did not hold her responsible and think her negligent. For days we stayed in the house, seeing countless police authorities, photographers, legal people and many kind friends, family, and neighbours who had heard and read it in the papers. At one point a very young officer was going over Garth's statement with me when he broke down, unable to continue reading out the gruesome facts. David and Jan arrived with a large bottle of scotch. Never before had I sat drinking whisky in the morning with a policeman on duty. All officials were amazed at Garth's mature behaviour, and we were much comforted by their sensitive handling of him, and us. I had always been frank and open with my children, answering their questions about their bodies and how they worked, and Garth's class had done a sex education course, so he knew what his kidnapper wanted, and he understood it was sick and evil but the man probably couldn't help it. Even in terror, Garth's cooperation, I'm certain, prevented further anger and possible death. That same summer two other children were similarly abducted and attacked, then murdered. How I thanked God, truly thanked Him, for preserving my child's life. Yes, I was pretty angry with Him too.

My desire was never to let either of my children out of my sight ever again, but Garth begged to be allowed to stay on for his last two weeks in England, so Kate and I returned to the States without him. Matt and I decided to tell no one but the immediate family. Garth didn't need all that publicity again, and have it discussed in school and around our neighbourhood. My stepsons were surprisingly supportive, wanting to assemble their marine friends and get to England to find the attacker and rip him apart. Somewhat impractical, but the very idea warmed my heart; maybe we could be a blended family after all. Hope springs eternal. The doctor had to know, and school recommended a specialist in child trauma, but Garth was unwilling to be alone in a room with a male. When Garth returned we did have a reasonably positive family meeting. My husband insisted that we would not let the incident ruin Garth's life, nor could he use it to gain extra benefits or reprieves. It did make him wiser and more aware of life at an earlier age. Kate too, because I had to explain what happened, thereby telling her things I would never normally have talked about with one so young.

That autumn was a time of turbulent emotions, from anger – utter blazing fury in me needing to go find and slowly dismember my son's attacker – to great heaving compassion for my son. Naturally his asthma and eczema worsened and few nights were unbroken by dreadful dreams. The dark hours were the worst. No adequate words describe that awfulness. In November I tried to cheer us by going all-American and making a super Thanksgiving dinner. Even the pumpkin pie worked. We enjoyed that four day holiday weekend. Then Matt's arthritis flared again. Being a master of control, having a disease impossible to control did not suit him. His alcohol consumption steadily increased, and he paced about at night when hurting too much to sleep. Between him and Garth I didn't sleep much either, but when I did, I too was plagued by bad dreams. Always the same three, so I guess they were recurring nightmares. One went back to childhood pets, and the tortoise whose demise was particularly nasty. He was eaten by rats, as far up as they could get into his shell. The rats gave me the same treatment. The second dream was inside a Salvador Dali painting of an uphill beach at low tide. I was free to walk on the sands yet trapped and confined within the frame. Stinging sea anemones in rock pools caressed my bare feet, crowds of human faces were superimposed onto others so you could not tell who was who, and nothing was right. The third dream was losing, permanently, one of my children, either falling off the gangplank of a huge ship, or left behind at the subway station as the train pulled away. Sudden waking agony of mind was the inevitable result.

One escape I created for myself was by answering an advertisement for half shares on a horse. I joined with a couple who needed help with caring for their five-year old quarter horse, Stormy by name and nature. The 16 hands creature was hugely handsome, but still green and skittish. It was a challenge to get him tacked up as he tossed his head, way above my reach, even when close tied. Always hard work, he was difficult to manage, but I loved riding and went as often as I could. Another positive was that Roy's bullying finally lessened after I appealed to his reason, and spelled out how it made Garth feel after the incident in England.

Matt was away in Florida most of that fall and winter, preparing to take delivery of a new plane. His boys had marine duties, Sara would stay with her mother, so we agreed it would be smart for me and mine to spend Christmas in England. I certainly wanted to contact Sussex police to see if any progress had been made, as all I had were their letters assuring me of their utmost diligence in the matter. Garth and I chatted about going back to where it happened, knowing that sensitive feelings needed careful handling, but it'd be worse the longer it was avoided.

Changing trains at Gatwick we clickety-clacked past sodden fields and farms, over level crossings through villages, with familiar names whizzing by: Faygate, Roffey, Billingshurst. Surely I'd never lived anywhere else? Tumbling out at Pulborough station, we found a phone-box then waited for the car. Raindrops chased themselves down the windows as the Victorian clock above the door counted time in the same deliberate manner as it had for a hundred years. Into the teeth of the gale whipping across the forecourt, we made a rather un-British spectacle of hugs and kisses with Granny. Reunions should always happen in the rain so tears can mingle in nicely. We pushed those nine bags, four people plus dog, all dripping wet, into one small car, and tried asking and telling everything at once. The over-laden vehicle groaned and swayed through town, over Wiggonholt Common, under the leafless beeches of Rackham into Amberley, where Gramps was waiting.

Was I a sad, homeless waif with ever-divided loyalties, or someone fortunate enough to have two wonderful countries and families? Another cup of the steaming British cure-all, tea, soon brought reality back. That night, in my old pre-nuptial bedroom, previously shared with my sister, now with my daughter softly slumbering in the other bed, my mind was busy. Sleep eluded me. With wind howling through chinks in the leaded windowpanes, I wasn't cold under a mound of woollen blankets, with, of course, a hot water bottle, thankful for the accomplishment of the long journey, and that there was a whole month before it had to be repeated. Bright eyed children surfaced very late, refreshed and hungry. The wild weather had calmed slightly and we needed exercise, so trundled off to Rackham Woods for a couple of hours. We clambered up the ancient sandy rocks (some doing more clambering than others) along well-worn paths through winter-crisp bracken, almost noiseless on the deep carpet of leaves shed annually there since before time was even recorded. The way opened up a little, providing us with a view best described as one of John Constable's greatest paintings. Pale, yet vibrant, watery sunset poured itself over the flooded wild brooks, illuminating bovine backs against the darkening fields. It required no gilded frame. We spent long minutes just being, absorbing the beauty of it and thinking of WH Davies' words: 'What is this life if, full of care, we have no time to stand and stare?' Dusky twilight encouraged us back to the cottage hearth.

Sunday morning's low temperatures had coated everything in a rimy opalescence. Rich, mellifluous notes rang out from the church belfry, inviting everyone to worship God and give thanks for another beautiful day. We walked along the High Street, a delightful misnomer for the narrow lane, past thatch-roofed cottages, and the shops, closed and shuttered for the day. Friends and neighbours came from their front gates to join us with happy greetings and dragon-puffs of white breath hanging in the cold air. The black cassocked vicar stood outside, directing his flock apologetically into the hall for the service because the church boiler had burst a vital part and frozen. Sunday lunch was still considered the most important meal of the week, and the traditional fare created havoc with the waistline, inducing post-prandial soporific thoughts. Perhaps that's why all but the infirm go for a walk, dog owners or not. However, the young American palate, more used to peanut butter and jelly sandwiches, or burgers, fries and ketchup, is not so appreciative of roast meat, parsnips, and brussels sprouts. Gramps tackled the mountains of washing-up; Granny took the children and dog out while I pulled up the old wing-backed chair for a fireside snooze. All too soon six rosy cheeks and one wet nose appeared, and Gramps came unsteadily in with the tea tray.

Dad/Gramps had arranged a car for my use for the month. Although I passed my UK driving test at seventeen anyone watching my first efforts in that rented Renault would question my right to be on the road. We hadn't planned to go down to the castle where the road tapers to a track but, since I could not get into reverse, we had to. Our mirth helped drown noises getting into then out of, reverse, to proceed forwards into Storrington. The highlight for the kids was in the bank exchanging carefully saved, crumpled dollar bills for crisp pound notes, and even the newly minted pound coins, then deciding how to spend them.

Later Garth and Kate dragged in the tree from its bucket outside, and we all helped decorate. It made me feel old to see my own children discovering the battered blue tin with the clip-on candleholders that my mother used on the trees of her childhood, as we did. It was a small tree, perched on a big log, so that the candles, once lit, could shine out through the ancient square-paned window.

The vicarage children came to tea. We cut elegantly small sandwiches and buttered wafer thin slices of bread, with plates of cheese or sweet scones. An abundance of good things, washed down with many cups of tea, or orange squash. Granny wanted to pass on the enjoyment and awareness of truly old-fashioned games, played by all ages in the days before radio and television. Rather apprehensively I agreed to help, thinking that today's children – and adults – might find it tedious, missing the point altogether. Oh, ye of little faith. We played Old Soldier of Botany Bay, the Memory game, and the Flour Cake game. Dad, a known anagrammatist, had his own contribution. Long ago he made a set of numbered cards, each with one anagram, all words to do with Christmas. He placed these around the room, semi-hidden, for each player to discover, solve, and list them in correct order, in fifteen minutes. Nobody was ever able to decipher all twenty, not even Dad, who mislaid his original list and couldn't remember it.

A successful evening happily ended as we lit the tree candles and joined together round Gramps playing the piano, singing carols.

We needed new wellies, a vital part of country life. Suitably booted, we went to Ringmer, near Lewes, to stay with Alison and Chris and their two for a few days. Strolling around the green, Garth sat with us while his sister and cousins played, the wind whipping their laughter away as they swung higher and higher. Our pub lunch of fish and chips – no longer wrapped in newspaper – tasted great. Exploring, we meandered along between fields of sheep ready for motherhood, under ancient oaks arching overhead, listening to raucous, iridescent rooks wheeling against clear sky, to Barcombe and Spithurst, Bentley and Horsted, twisting, narrow lanes through Chiddingly, Muddles Green and the Dickers, returning through Ripe. Sunday brought us to Southover parish church, as tranquil inside as it surely has been since its corner stone was laid in 1346. Alison and I returned there for the evening Carols by Candlelight. The choir processed up the main aisle carrying their lanterns, sending heavenly music floating upwards through the ancient rafters.

Back in Amberley the rain worsened with fierce gales at night. Kate woke anxiously calling for me, wondering if we were quite safe. I assured her that Granny's house, solidly standing for the last five hundred years or more, wasn't going to blow over.

A long day in London presented opportunities for much more than just the required medical appointments. In Knightsbridge we met up with Jonathan for lunch in Harvey's. Jonny hailed a taxi for us and asked the driver, while winking at me, 'Please take these American tourists through Green Park to Buckingham Palace.' Our cabby obliged, earning every penny of his exorbitant fare. After the doctor, one more taxi back to Victoria, listening to the radio announcement of a bomb scare at the station. That driver showed commendable concern for his own safety by dropping us and disappearing without waiting for money.

Hardly out of the station, the train's overhead lights flickered ominously and dimmed as we inched along the tracks. Travelling thus for some time, suddenly plunged into total darkness, the train ground to a halt. There we stayed for nearly sixty minutes. Dim light returned while the heat continued blasting its breathy comfort from under the seats, but the silence was the worst part. All those people confined together all that time and not a word was spoken, except by us three, very quietly. Nobody else laughed, no one swore, only occasionally was there heard a discreet cough from a well-covered mouth, and the rustle of newspaper pages. Here were live examples of British stiff upper lips in action. Chatting, sharing the humour of the situation, getting to know someone, making a new friend, was clearly not fitting. On an American train I think it might have been rather different.

A promise of holly for Alison sent us out to Rackham Woods. Squelching along muddy paths and up slippery banks searching for the one tree we'd previously noticed still held berries. Nearly all the scarlet gems had gone to those wise enough to pick in good time. By the time we found some we were very wet, cold, and short-tempered. I recall wondering what I'd found so alluring about those woods. Then I thought of the previous Christmas when I'd been so eager for a little bit of England in my decorating that I'd gone to a florist near Chicago and paid $10 for one small bunch of holly with precisely three berries.

14

We three drove back to my parents' home, wreathed in wood smoke and the pure Christmas smell of evergreen boughs and pinecones. Chores accomplished by three o'clock, we gathered in the drawing room for an auditory delight, the Service of Nine Lessons and Carols. Solemn words read with perfect enunciation, alternated with exquisite singing. Even Kate sat through the hour with very few disturbances. Later we sang round the piano, lit only by flickering tree candles, with the top half of the stable-type front door open to the unseasonably mild evening. Yes, there was a bright star shining, hanging above the dark silhouetted line of the Downs: 'As with gladness men of old did the guiding star behold, as with joy they hailed its light, leading onward, beaming bright; so most gracious Lord may we evermore be led to Thee.'

At six-thirty I took the kids along the quiet street to church to join a carol-singing group. We stopped at many houses, warmly complimented by all who heard. Nobody minded when the rain began. The Black Horse publican invited us to sing amidst clinking glasses and the gurgle of drawn pints. We only had to cross the road home, cheery 'Happy Christmas' calls floating out with us on the night air. Mother's elegantly late dinner was too much for Kate who fell asleep at the table. Raiding Gramps' sock drawer, we dug out the longest pair, thick brown wool, and laid one on the end of each grandchild's bed. With the usual beeswax candle safely placed at each bedside – the only night of the year candle-lit bedtimes were allowed – the two youngsters fell promptly asleep.

Just before midnight I heard bells pealing out, now and then silenced by the wind tossing chimes away. Leaning far out of my bedroom's tiny window, looking over at the closed pub's now darkened panes, I was thinking deep thoughts. There was no room at the inn for those long-ago, wearily expectant travellers; was there room for me anywhere? Where did I really fit? As if windborne, words rang in my mind:

'It came upon a midnight clear, that glorious song of old, from angels bending near the earth to touch their harps of gold: "Peace on the earth, goodwill to men from heaven's all-gracious King," the world in solemn stillness lay to hear the angels sing.'

Where and what is that peace? I had not yet discovered it.

As I dressed hurriedly to combat the freezing cold, joyful notes rose from downstairs as Dad played: 'Christians awake, salute the happy morn', a Christmas Day tradition fondly remembered. My children were delighting in yet another, having found the stockings stuffed full of treasures. Chocolate, tangerines, new crayons, a diary with a pencil, a tiny doll or car; and they loved those treats as much as we always did. Assembled at table once more, dressed in our best, we enjoyed succulent slices of cold gammon with toast, coffee and juice. Certain appetites seemed smaller than usual, possibly due to confections discovered earlier. We opened only gifts from each other, and I particularly enjoyed seeing faces and hearing comments, instead of imagining same, as in most years when the Atlantic separates us.

Just in time we trooped into church, taking up two full pews, bathed in refulgent light shafting from the stained glass windows, whose deep sills were decorated with holly and trailing ivy. That small Norman church still looks out on the same view as it has for a thousand years, still hears the same lowing and bleating of sheep and cattle, and still calms all who enter. Steeped in history we became part of it, joining in the oft-repeated words of the prayer book and the hymns. Back home, greeted by the almost tastable smell of turkey, slowly roasting since early morning. The table gleamed with silver and crystal. Willing hands carried in platters of food, Gramps said a beautiful grace, thanking God for the joy of being together, and asking a blessing on absent loved ones. We drank a toast to Her Majesty, then to each missing family member. Quite a bit later Granny turned out her magnificent pudding from its steaming basin, lit the brandy over it and brought in the masterpiece softly haloed in blue flames. Cheeses and nuts, port or coffee, all finished just before three o'clock so we could watch the Queen make her televised speech. Finally the children's patience was rewarded by the mess of ten people opening lots of presents. Calm of age mixed with haste of youth, showered with happy gratitude made a wonderful afternoon.

15

The first few weeks back in Illinois were very difficult, the adjustment harder than usual. Jet lag was only part of the problem; it was finding Matt even more closed up than when I'd left. Knowing your spouse is in more or less constant pain, and being unable to ease it, is dreadful. Knowing also that he is shutting you out causes pain about equal in both of you. There was still plenty of conversation between us about his planes and our dog and our children, but that was all. He would not discuss 'us' and certainly not anything personal. He'd been made Aviation Director, a well deserved promotion, but it looked like the future death knell for his flying, akin to cutting off a bird's wings. Certainly it meant more money, but I would rather have had more smiles and real communication, and no need for his insistence that we move to a bigger house. He took me to meet his 'other woman', the Gulfstream III jet, stunningly upholstered in leather and gold-plated fixtures, with every luxurious convenience and comfort. He was away flying it, and 'directing', so much that house hunting was left to my half-hearted efforts. The children did not want to leave the Woods and I was quite certain we should stay. It was a lovely neighbourhood with good schools and great friends.

Kate only wanted to recreate the English party games for her birthday. Matt was away for weeks in London, Paris and Zurich, but was back for my birthday and presented me with aquamarine and diamond earrings and a matching pendant. Garth claimed his birthday was the best ever. He and his friends danced in the downstairs rec room (usually referred to as the family room, or even the wreck room) which Matt had refurbished to resemble an English pub, complete with large slate pool table and dart board on the wall. Garth's friends fixed their own pizzas and drank gallons of coke before going outside to play flashlight tag.

His interest in Scouting diminished, as mine did, after one survival training meeting. A leader brought in a lively rabbit which they all petted, then killed it in front of them, skinning and cutting it up while still warm and twitching. Garth said its eyes were brown and soft like Gracie's until they bulged out while it screamed. It seemed an unnecessarily heartless lesson, causing much distress and more bad dreams.

In May Matt returned to France, this time as a Concorde passenger. He came home full of his visit to the Normandy beaches and the serried ranks of gravestones. Then it was back to England for me, taking Kate but leaving Matt, Roy and Garth to fend for themselves. I went to be nanny for another nephew, David and Jan's second son, Richard. The amazing thing about that trip was Jan's ability to fall asleep and remain asleep with her infant son crying. Even when I picked him up, changed him and attached him to his mother for a feed, she could still stay sleeping. I've never known any other new mother with such talent.

Matt's arthritis steadily worsened. I tried so hard, unsuccessfully, not to let his moods affect me and the kids, but he was so cross and difficult. Constant pain does that, I know, but knowing didn't make it any easier to deal with. Because he still loved Gracie, if not the rest of us, I started looking around for a second bulldog, realising of course all the extra work of training a new puppy would again fall on me. It was worth anything to try to cheer him. House hunting seemed only to create further tension and aggravation. He never liked any place I thought vaguely possible, he wouldn't even get out of the car to look if he didn't fancy the exterior. He wanted new, low maintenance and rural for peace and quiet. Garth was desperate for a town house, 'where it's all happening, man'. Kate set her heart on five acres with a horse. I craved an old house anywhere out of the Midwest ragweed allergy area but not isolated as Matt was away so much. He thought a four-bedroom was adequate; his kids insisted they had a room each when they came to visit. I defy any real-estate agent to make something of all that. The obvious answer was to stay put, which was what everyone wanted except Matt, who insisted on being close to his new airport without a commute.

On September 14th Matt and I flew to Connecticut for his good friend's fiftieth birthday. Don and Jenny had hosted our wedding reception, and Don's own party was similar to Matt's fiftieth. They even brought in a belly dancer. I spent a lot of the evening chatting with Scott, the son of another pilot, an encounter which left a deep impression on me. The previous year Scott had been run off the road by a speeding drunk and left for dead. Virtually all his bones were broken. Before the accident he'd been training for the 1988 Olympics, and his eventual aim was to fly a spacecraft. After it he was a quadriplegic. Surviving many months in intensive care, and numerous corrective surgeries, his determination brought results. When I met him he was walking unaided and attending college part-time to help regain some memory and brain function. Although unable to drive, he was striving to run by Christmas. He told me how important Jesus Christ was to him, and that he'd learned to trust Him in spite of, and because of, the accident. Scott said he knew the Lord had something special for him to do, so he had begun by speaking at meetings and schools about drinking and driving, making wise choices, and choosing to follow Jesus. I must admit he made me uncomfortable. Great that he had such faith, and had made such an amazing recovery, but all that openly shining talk of Jesus was a bit much.

At last Matt agreed to return to the doctor. He'd lost strength and flexibility in both wrists and some days could hardly write. Fairly often he would drop a full cup of coffee, or send a fork skidding across the dinner table, neither of which improved his mood. Whenever possible I prepared meals which needed no cutting, but that made him cross too. The doctor prescribed Feldene, which did help the arthritis somewhat. A late night call brought more trouble. My husband, on a

California trip, had been taken to hospital with what turned out to be a kidney stone. Further agony for the poor man. The smallest of my kitchen strainers got sacrificed to stone-catching duty and once caught, the minute pellet was sent off for analysis. The stone proved to be calcium, but he who despised any sort of ill health, or any malfunctioning anywhere, refused to omit his nightly tub of ice cream.

The second bulldog was not a success. Grace had been so responsive and easy to train but Elly – short for Elegance – was the reverse. Hopelessly slow to understand what was expected, she still wasn't reliable indoors. Twice she made a mess right at Matt's feet and once peed against his briefcase, which may sound amusing, but was not. Matt had absolutely no patience with her or the rest of us. At a very low point he did admit to being vile to me, coming as close to apologising as is possible without actually doing so.

One day in winter Garth did not come home. Not on the late bus, nor did he call for a ride. No answer at school, even the janitor had left. It was almost dark. None of his friends knew where he was. By 5pm it was quite dark, and he came up the driveway. He was frozen, very tight chested, and elated, having achieved what Roy sometimes did when he missed the school bus: walked home, taking a short cut along the railroad tracks. It took Garth an hour and a half and I don't believe it entered his head that I'd be imagining his kidnap again. He was scared of my expected fury, nor was he disappointed. The very next day he made a big fuss about not wanting to go his school Christmas concert. I had to find out why. For months he'd hardly attended any orchestra rehearsals, obviously just enough to keep the teacher from calling me. Instead he'd joined the chess club and been playing in high-ranking tournament games. I'd been paying instrument rental for other kids to play his cello while he played chess.

When Roy asked what Garth and Kate would like for Christmas I happily provided some ideas and began to feel a little hopeful. As usual I'd arranged two dinners and two present opening sessions to accommodate my stepchildren being with their mother and with us.

Then Roy said he'd been too busy and too broke to get anything, except for his dad. He wasn't joking. Garth and Kate had taken money from their minuscule savings accounts and thoughtfully chosen and wrapped their gifts for their stepbrother just as for everyone else. I never had to tell them to, even after the earlier years when they made their gifts with much enthusiastic gluing, cutting, painting and secret excitement, only to see Roy sneer as he opened them and groan, 'What do I want that for?' My husband's ability to overlook his son's inexcusable rudeness made it so much worse.

Months rolled into years and we celebrated our seventh anniversary. Certainly we had some happy days, but underneath there was a black pit hungrily awaiting those who bent too low beneath the heavy clouds. There were yet more fights between children and stepchild, and trying to deal with Matt's explanatory excuse of any of Roy's failings: 'my children come from a broken home,' while still choosing not to see that the same applied to mine. Garth felt so wretched he attempted to cut his wrists. Usually that is 'only' a cry for help but should never be ignored. Any parent whose child has been suicidal will instantly recognise the wordless, guilt-ridden agony of such a time. How can I have failed so badly that my precious child sees life as no longer worth living? How can I repair the damage? Instead of keeping Garth's injuries from Matt, I showed him, fully expecting more of his predictable anger. He amazed me by being as parental as after Garth's incident in England. Why was it only possible to feel cared for in times of serious trouble? He spent the worst of the winter in Florida and Texas, while the kids and I stayed indoors a lot. Once when the cold was down to minus 29°F and Gracie needed to go out, her muzzle brushed the metal storm door and instantly froze and stuck to it. I had to pour warm water to release her. Both dogs liked to drink immediately before asking to go outside and would often return with icicles hanging from their jowls.

Matt and his boss invited me to join them on the new Gulfstream III for a five-day European flight. Business naturally, but I'd have two days with my family. In whirlwind preparations I managed to get a prescription for the new drug: one little transparent patch stuck behind the ear released enough anti-motion medication for three days, and they worked. Great to see everyone again, however briefly, but the return journey was rather eventful. Due to thick fog at Gatwick, our early flight was cancelled so we rushed to Heathrow, catching the first available flight to Paris. We were only at Charles de Gaulle Airport long enough for a call through to Le Bourget Airfield where his plane, crew and boss were waiting, engines fired, as it was way past the scheduled departure time. I prayed they'd wait. I begged God to listen because I dreaded being anywhere near Matt if they left us behind. Did I think, yet again, God just existed to answer my pleas when things got bad enough to warrant it? We rushed again, to grab a taxi. Our luggage was secured in the boot when the driver saw the address we wanted; he burst into torrents of angry French. Yelling and gesticulating were not hard to translate. He pushed past us and began wrestling our bags back onto the sidewalk. Precious minutes were ticking by. A fistful of francs changed his mind, but then he drove off almost before we'd been able to jump in and slam the doors. It was a death-defying journey at the hands of another bad tempered man. At Le Bourget he raced right up to the edge of the runway, depositing us under the wings of the still waiting G III. Then he disappeared with more shouting and squealing tyres, as we climbed the steps and sank into leathered luxury. None of the others had minded waiting, and within two minutes we were aloft, for a smooth seven-hour run to Bangor, Maine. There we fuelled, passed customs and immigration, then flew home.

The following few days I was incapacitated with vertigo and migraine. Matt also was bad, his pain, twitching and jerking more intense for having kept it hidden from his boss. My children were quite open about wishing we'd stayed away longer as they were very happy with the sitters, and neither of us was any fun at all. Veronica had proved unreliable. She had gone to bed soon after 8pm leaving the children to take care of the dogs and lock up. Her charges didn't object in the least, but their mother certainly did. I substituted two lovely college girls who brought loads of fun things to make and do.

Singing was a great outlet for me. I'd been going regularly to church and had made some good friends, mainly due to the choir. I loved the practices just as much as the Sunday services and seasonal cantatas. It amazed me that I should be thought good enough. The leader, Howard, was quite a character. With perfect pitch and ear, he could detect who, in which section, had missed a note. If he wasn't such a nice person he'd have been too daunting to sing under. Spring was slow to arrive, and delayed further by our bedevilled Elly. As soon as the bulbs sprouted she chewed them, lying innocently sunbathing upon the remains. I put everything into training that dog, with precious little to show for it. Even the vet eventually agreed no normal dog wets its own bed ever, certainly not past puppyhood. So there was no great sadness when I met a woman who fell instantly in love with Elly, and it was obviously mutual. I did miss the wretched animal as she'd brought laughter as well as frustration. Later the woman called to say how thrilled she was that Elly was so well trained and such a wonderful dog. Hurrumph!

Matt was on new pills. Called Ridora, they contained gold and were known to cause unpleasant side effects, including vision damage. He had to be checked every two weeks, and we all awaited his pain relief.

We were capable of happiness together when everyone was well and Matt's pain was controlled, but that wasn't too often. Take the mountains of laundry I always had to do, for example. Were we dirtier than most people, or far, far cleaner? Did we have more troubles than most families or were we just more aware of them? I longed for peace but it felt permanently just out of reach. Matt expected to be soon off flying altogether since the arthritis had spread to his hips, knees and feet. His oldest, Jon, requested my honest opinions on marriage, remarriage, and taking on someone else's child. Not easy topics anytime, especially when your stepson is asking. We all thought Kim was lovely, but also felt concerned that they'd only met so recently and had a super-quick romance, arranging the wedding rather too fast. I told him honestly things were not as idyllic with his father and me as I'd expected. Jon said he loved Bridget, Kim's little daughter, but I warned him that when his own baby arrived he would naturally love it more; he didn't want to hear that. It was a mutually unsettling conversation. Wedding plans raced ahead. I agreed to go because Matt said it was my duty as his wife to do so.

I had never felt like his wife, just his second wife. Never that he and I were a partnership; just that he and his kids had allowed me and mine to live with them so that I could cook and clean because Carla was gone. Of course they shared regular communications over their children's education, finances and insurance, I accepted that; I even agreed to invite her for lunch again as Matt wanted. That visit shattered any remaining illusions: from the moment she arrived they became again the happy family reunited at last, if only briefly. To see clearly that one is surplus to requirements in one's own home – again – is emotional death. In case, dear reader, you think I'm exaggerating, here's one more vignette from that year. After a minor fender-bender I went directly to the insurance office on the way home to report the damage, thankful that the other car was fine. Consternation on the face of the man processing my claim alerted me to trouble. He asked me to repeat all details and show him proof of identity. Looking uncomfortable he cleared his throat, several times, before telling me I was not insured, and my car was registered to Carla and Matt.

When too much alcohol has been consumed, careful and precise movements are necessary to prevent falling about and slurred speech. I was like that then with no drink whatsoever. Extricating myself from the man's compassionate handshake, I drove home to call my husband. I was rather concerned by the strength of my own anger, never mind his. As always, he excelled in talking around the situation, explaining it away, leaving me feeling silly for having mentioned it. He did mutter something close to an apology, promising to set the policy aright.

After all, we'd only been married seven years. A chap shouldn't be expected to change his papers right away.

The journey south to the wedding was not good. Sitting next to a frustrated pilot on a commercial flight can never be good. Lots of marines in full dress blues all oozing *esprit de corps*. My mother-in-law was sweet; she clutched my hand several times and whispered how glad she was I was there and what a strain it must be and how nice I looked. At precisely the correct moment we all entered the chapel, each marine removing cover (hat) and sword first. Kim was radiant in a creamy, pearl-encrusted gown, enhancing her dark-haired Irish beauty. After the service they emerged through an archway of drawn swords in fine military style with a great deal of saluting, and heel kicking.

Matt was overly particular about most things, insisting that his planes, hangars and offices be kept neat, orderly and pristine. He expected me to be equally fastidious in the house and garden. He wanted the leaves raked almost before they'd left the trees, and snow shovelled before it settled. He was away while most of the leaves fell, and kindly winds blew a lot into our neighbours' yards and back into the woods. Two days before he was due home I thought I'd sweeten his arrival by raking every single leaf into a bonfire. For two days I raked and swept, and raked some more. I did the entire (acre and a quarter) yard, plus the patio and the driveway. Making the bonfire at the edge of the lawn beside the road, where we'd burned leaves each year, I kept it small, under control, and not in the way of any traffic. Exhausted but proud of my achievement, I raked the last pile to the blaze as he came home. Ready with a smoky hug of welcome, I was not prepared for his growl from the car window about dangerous fires in the road. I knew it meant his pain was intolerable, but he was making things intolerable for me as well.

There was a company merger pending, and none of the pilots' jobs were secure. He and I were living proof that stress worsens both arthritis and migraines. He got the job, and insisted we had to move upmarket. It would be particularly bad to uproot the children, well settled in their schools, and it was clear the family would fragment even more in a much bigger house.

Along with the Feldene and the gold pills, Matt had a cortisone shot directly into each wrist, meant to relieve pain for up to six weeks. I wished he could have had two more into his hips. Jon brought Kim and Bridget for a mercifully short visit. He was tense, she was newly pregnant and very weepy, and Bridie was dreadful. No wonder, poor child. So many adjustments to make, and suddenly having to share her mother. She whined and screamed continuously. Her mother clearly felt the same; it was her first Christmas away from her own folks. She told me she already saw the same controlling chauvinism in Jon as was evident in Matt and Roy, and she was determined to force it out of her new husband. I liked her but could see stormy weather ahead for them.

16

In spite of a full house and much socialising, Matt and I had no communication at all, and I'd about reached the end of my fraying rope. All was made worse during the month Roy was home. One afternoon, in his father's absence of course, he went outside my bedroom window, knowing I was in there trying to sleep away a headache, and repeatedly let off firecrackers. Even as I leaned out asking him please to stop, he just laughingly carried on. More than once in the past, again, only if his dad was away, he had come home in the early hours with too much beer in him, creeping to my door with veiled suggestions and much mirth, but only once did he try to force my bathroom door open while I was showering. The physical strength to keep him out was, I thought initially, adrenaline-pumped fury. Later I believed there was a guardian angel on my side of that door with me. The day I managed to tell Matt about that, he became so incensed by what he described as an impossible lie, he went straight to the airport and flew south to ask his son face to face. Naturally Roy did a superbly smooth denial to placate his father.

I knew an elderly woman whose frail husband depended on her for everything. They'd been married sixty-four years and she bought a bulldog pup to cheer him, but could not possibly cope with it and him. So she put the pup, Maggie, into the bathtub to relieve itself, but then couldn't lift the squirming bulk out again, so there it stayed. Once I'd got the dog home and washed her thoroughly I found she was white with one ear brindle brown, adorable and eager to please. Basically untrained, she took just two days to figure out that the back door was where to head for, not the bathtub, when nature called.

Millions of people around the world were plunged into grim sadness at the death of seven individuals, strangers to most, when the space shuttle Challenger exploded in the air one minute after takeoff. A great adventure turned into the worst video nasty; a jarring reminder of our own mortality. Sombre days followed, with memorial services on radio and TV, a five minute silence taken out of school recess; and flags everywhere at half mast. The *Chicago Tribune* had a full page spread featuring the well-known words, '*They shall not grow old as we who are left grow old, age shall not weary them nor the years condemn. At the going down of the sun and in the morning, we will remember them.*'

Sara was forging ahead with her May wedding plans. She'd heard I wasn't going and wrote such a sweet letter saying she understood why her brother's wedding was so difficult, but hers would be different and she wanted me there as I meant so much to her.

Matt had lost twenty pounds since the previous summer, and developed a hernia. Poor man hardly needed more pain, but was always too busy to get it fixed, though if a problem was found in cars or planes he'd see to it at once. Garth argued with a girl at school who stomped on his feet with her high-heeled boots. The resulting broken toe and severe bruising put him back on crutches. Maggie insisted on attacking his good leg and the crutches every time he clomped past near her, so they usually ended up in a heap on the floor. Her behaviour changed. She began using her teeth too vigorously when playing, especially with the crutches. On March 4th she had a seizure. On March 5th Kate was on my lap when Maggie suddenly raced across to us, biting Kate's thigh. A fifty-pound pet that cannot be trusted cannot be kept. On March 6th Maggie was put to sleep. At least we still had Gracie.

After that I started seeing a psychiatrist. A year earlier a friend had commented on the distress she saw and felt in our home, and gave me the number of a therapist, said to be a Christian. Being a keeper of good quotes, I'd tucked that number in with a description of a woman trapped in an unhappy marriage: '...*she struggled to build a picture of the happy family, even though the harmony was artificial and the pain and heartache of the effort threatened to send her over the edge into hysteria.*'

My fortieth birthday might have had something to do with it, and realising I'd spent half my life in the States. That life of mine was going downhill whether I admitted it or not. So I called the man and began regular weekly sessions. I felt safe with Dexter: he was a good listener. There were unexpected discoveries about me and mine, and nicely sorted things came tumbling apart upon introspection. Different hats and masks came off so I could look at the real me. From the start I asked Matt to go with me, for our mutual benefit, but eventually gave up, squashed by his total lack of interest. Going home after one evening session I was upset, not only by his non-participation, but by a scathing comment asking if I'd 'had fun learning to be a woman's libber'. I blew up at him. It shocked both of us, but it did open some doors long closed. The next morning a large bouquet of flowers arrived from him at work, with a sweet message.

On April 26th 1986 a nuclear disaster sent waves of fear around the world. We'd hardly heard of the Ukraine, never mind Chernobyl, but it instantly became a household name, a place of dread where nobody wanted to be. How strange that in a little over ten years' time I was going to spend a month just south of there, near Kiev.

Matt found a house and sent me to see it because he was buying it. In a quietly rural area, in the worst school district that we'd agreed to avoid, sat a huge house looking like Noah's Ark on Mount Ararat. The generous acre of land was very green, with plenty of trees but no flowers whatsoever. With heavy heart I washed and polished every inch of our dear little house in preparation for the arrival of dozens of estate agents. Showing them through, in the dining end of our spacious kitchen, they gathered round the table as I stood in the bay window. Leaning to open a cupboard, my shoe slid on my highly waxed wood floor, onto which I fell, legs akimbo and skirt billowing. Silence, at first, then they all leapt as one to my rescue, all talking at once, pretending it hadn't happened, and the house tour continued. A day later an offer was made and accepted. I was very bruised.

We did all make the four-hour drive south to Indiana for Sara's wedding. The hot, humid weather did not help. As Matt rained unpleasantries on me outside the motel, we met up with Carla and others, to whom he was charming. It was nice that Sara had included Garth as a groomsman. He looked so smart in his grey suit and buttonhole. The photographic session was, if anything, more humiliating than at Jon's wedding. I was told to 'run along and check on the children' so the pictures could be of the 'real' family.

Returning to the Woods, Matt insisted our house be left spotless for the new people, just like the previous move, with no trace of our existence remaining. Friends and neighbours kept arriving to help and bring complete meals as my kitchen disappeared into cartons. On the last day, June 16th, I could not stop crying, without hope of an optimistic future. In the new house we rattled around getting used to so much more space. My legs nearly dropped off at the end of each day, after climbing two full flights of stairs plus step-ladder into the attic, dozens of times, carrying cartons that always needed to be somewhere else. The carpets were thick with cat hair, as were the kitchen cupboards and pantry shelves. I had to scrub everything, thinking all the while of the sparkling clean home I'd left. I did find a lady decorator to paint the living room's cathedral ceiling; our old house was small, warm and comfortable, as was the neighbourhood; the new was none of the above, the decor was atrocious throughout and the whole mess was overwhelming. My husband went to the airport each day, happy with his short commute.

Matt and I had hardly spoken since the move, but Roy arrived, plus Jon and his family, for July 4th weekend and Matt was, of course, the perfect host, loving father, and life and soul of the party. Gone were the twitches and groans of pain, except in the most unguarded moment, and the hard, cold expression which was all that I'd seen for ages. Jon and Kim introduced five-week old Seth, with Bridie needing even more attention. They lounged about on the deck, enjoying the sunny holiday weekend. Roy stayed on in the new house while Matt,

Garth, Kate and I flew to England for my brother's wedding in London's Temple Church. My father, although walking with a stick, looked every bit as dashing as all the other groomsmen in their long tailed morning coats and scarlet boutonnieres. Unaware that it was frowned upon, I took a couple of photos inside the church and heard tut-tutting from someone behind who whispered too loudly, 'That must be his American sister, so no wonder'.

Matt returned to the States leaving us three to enjoy a few more weeks. On the last evening Mum took her grandchildren for a long Downland walk and Dad and I had a wonderful time singing together. Dad played old hymns and choruses from memory, on his recently acquired keyboard. That was the last time I saw him alive.

Driving up to London was successful, with Garth navigating and Kate reading out signs once we got into city traffic. Finding Rosedale Road in Dulwich, Jonny and Miriam's tall thin townhouse, they fed us excellently. Next morning we drove Jonny to work in Belgravia, and to the M4 to Heathrow. Car back to Hertz, we bussed to Terminal 3 for a marvellously smooth return to Chicago.

The new routines necessary for my children to get to the new schools were ridiculously complicated. Garth had to leave the house at 6am and make two bus connections for the first class at 7.30am. Kate's bus picked her up at 7.30am and dropped her at the bottom of our driveway just after 3pm. The autumn pollen count was depressingly high, increasing my allergies accordingly. The lady painter increased her hours, and a plumber and carpenter also had plenty of work. All I could do, through many frustrating hours, was stay in my small sitting room with an air-purifier helping me breathe and reducing the dreadful itching and sneezing. As for Matt, he was frequently unable to write or even lift a pencil. Odd that he had no trouble with a wineglass. Driving wasn't difficult either, all our cars being fully automatic. He'd anchor the steering wheel between his knees, a trick only the exceptionally long-legged can master. We tried going to the movies to cheer ourselves up, but I could not lift him out of the car when he was bad, and when we could get into a cinema, my eyes were so swollen and irritated I had to keep them shut.

When married couples can no longer communicate, and are not particularly friendly, there's still sex. In our case that, too, had gone. Impotency is hell. One of Matt's many sayings was: 'I'm a performance man. If I can't finish something I won't start it.' The problem was not to be discussed. Naturally enough that was one of the many topics I talked about with Dexter, and naturally enough he was concerned. When he began showing his concern in more ways than just verbally, I started hearing that Oklahoma jingle once again: 'I'm just a gal who cain't say no…' While I'd been in England he had unwisely written to me from his home near Palatine. My mother noted the, to her, unfamiliar handwriting landing on her doormat, misread the postmark and asked me who I knew in Palestine. Without hesitating I told her I must be having an affair with an Arab sheikh, at which we both laughed and dropped the subject. She knew I was joking, but was I even then trying to confess my developing secret? Once back in my own home I left enough hints around, semi-hoping Matt would challenge me so we could have a huge row, clear the air and start again. But no: there's none so blind as those who won't see.

The previous week carpenters had removed the old, unsafe balcony from around the second floor prior to renovating it. We woke early on Monday morning to the unmistakable dripping of water, landing some place it shouldn't. It was pouring in around the front door, forming a lake with a rug island; and on, through the floor, down into the basement. There it merrily poured some more, over and through still unpacked cartons, to saturate the wall-to-wall carpet. Frustration, anger, and dismay combined to fuel many hours of clean-up work. Every towel was used, plus mop and bucket and, eventually, fans to aid drying, once we'd rolled up the huge, sodden carpet. All I said was, 'Our old house never leaked', a sentence as heavily loaded as the carpeting. That October even more rain fell, the river kept rising and we had two further soakings to cope with in the basement, plus a number that originated in my heart.

Thanksgiving passed in a blur, and I wished Christmas had done likewise. It dragged on from December 12th when Jon, Kim, and their two little ones arrived. Roy returned having finished college early, and Sara and Mal arrived on the 22nd. I did my absolute best to keep everyone fed and happy, and the house looked as festive as I could make it. On Christmas morning Mal made breakfast of eggs benedict for all, before he and the others left to go to their mother. As the last car door slammed, Matt removed his 'jolly' face and retreated to his recliner, firmly shutting his study door. He'd had his Christmas with his family. So there I was, alone with mountains of washing-up and laundry, determined to keep cheerful for Garth and Kate. The three of us ended up watching television together. I frightened myself by seriously wondering about the gas oven, and how quickly it could inhale me away into black nothingness. Knowing I would never, ever, add any further distress onto my kids, on top of what they already had to cope with, rendered it a harmless thought; harmless maybe, but still frightening. Happy Christmas, everyone.

17

Officially the visits to Dexter continued, but the fees had long since been waived; perhaps I should just say the currency changed. There were unofficial visits too, whenever we could arrange them. Matt did ask at one point why I was still going and my immediate response came out sharper than intended: 'You never talk or listen to me anymore, so I'm reduced to paying someone else to.' Dexter had an office in his home as well, and I went there occasionally, or we met in the park, or walked down by the river. Sex was not the first priority. We spent happy hours talking and laughing, sharing deep thoughts and many similar interests and concerns. Sometimes we just walked hand-in-hand, silently, totally content. Well, not totally, because there was the ever-present guilt which would not leave me alone and would not stay buried. Rationalisation was overworked. Even when he spoke of things strange to me, such as hypnosis, and reincarnation (convinced we'd been married in a past life and the soul-mate thread never broken) I told myself it must be fine as he was meant to be a Christian. He obviously loved me, and I knew I loved him. He was my lifeboat on a wave-tossed emotional sea where the currents were strong and the undertow dangerous.

Clearly I had too much time on my hands. In the back of my mind was future employment, should I find myself on my own again. College beckoned. To earn an American nursing degree I'd have to produce a graduation certificate or take the high school equivalency test. They weren't interested in my English school and college achievements. So in January 1987 I became a student again, doing math and chemistry and creative writing. Insanity to think I'd be any better at polynomials, negative exponents or reciprocal inequalities than in my youth. The words sounded far better suited to descriptive marriage breakdown than algebra. I spent hours struggling with the homework and still had to fit in the usual amounts of domesticity. Pushing myself even further, I decided to tackle the decor of our bedroom. Hoping for some togetherness, I brought home wallpaper books to share with Matt and find out what he'd like. The cool response was a shrugged brush-off.

I knew he was feeling ghastly and preferred to suffer alone. I did try to be understanding and tactful. He had, at last, agreed to see an urologist, who sent him on to several specialists. He had to endure the most personal examination and tests. The results were good and bad. There was no cancer; but a new ailment, Peyronie's disease. It might respond to medication, but required surgery. If only he'd allowed the tests when the problem first became evident there would have been a greater chance of improvement, although no cure was ever guaranteed. We sat together uncomfortably in that specialist's office as he opened his desk drawer and pulled out several items of a pink, rubbery nature, lobbed them at me saying, 'You play with those and see which appeals, while I explain his options.'

Usually I am able to talk about anything with anyone, but that left me incapable of looking at either man. Equally incapable was I of selecting one of the penile implants on offer. It all proved immaterial anyway, because Matt refused to discuss any kind of surgery. When reminded about his yet untreated hernia, which could cover any other surgical procedure so conveniently, he still refused. To me, it could only mean he had no further interest in salvaging what was left of our marriage. It also surely meant that God must be pretty angry. I did try praying, but my self-condemned conscience kept getting in the way. Obviously my lifestyle prevented any chance of Divine acceptance, or help for the mess I was in. What it did not prevent was more awful headaches. While lying incapacitated I added a few more bricks to the wall shutting me off from God. I could never look Him in the face, so it felt safest to enlarge the rift between us; just like I saw Matt separating himself from me.

Well again, I made up for lost time: doubling my efforts in college, baking more cookies and bread, and spending lots of money on our bedroom. I worked obsessively on transforming it, and our bathroom, into a magazine showpiece. I used Laura Ashley's co-ordinating wallpapers and border, curtained the huge French window onto the balcony with matching fabric, and it did look lovely. Deliciously thick cream carpeting throughout finished it to perfection. There we lay, night after night, two logs either side of the vast king-size bed; a tight little ship of silence and pain adrift in a cold ocean of impersonal luxury.

For Kate's twelfth birthday she wanted a sleepover. A poor description as sleep is the very last consideration on such occasions. I let them loose in the kitchen to make their own cupcakes for a midnight snack, and ordered out for pizzas. They danced and sang to the latest music down in the rec room, and kept chasing Garth, begging him to dance too. At 11pm I went down to say goodnight and caution about noise. A three-storey house does have its good points. I did not hear them, although I did not sleep. Tornadoes were forecast and Matt was flying home. He eventually arrived at 3am having dodged a twister over Mississippi. He was giving his captains most of the trips, only taking a few himself, and those on nothing but will power and determination. At a high price too, as he suffered dreadfully for days after each trip, so therefore we did too. His medications got stronger in greater amounts, matched by his increasing alcohol intake. When it dawned on me that his slurred speech in late evenings and during the following mornings was not just the medication but whiskey and wine, I was shocked. From then on I never prepared nor offered another drink, nor bought any. I noticed he just drank more anyway, and bought more of the gallon jugs of Gallo wine and the largest bottles of Johnnie Walker.

He arranged a surprise birthday party for me. Lots of friends came, all bringing food and it was fun. He'd even ordered a bakery cake. Garth was the proud co-host and Kate was so excited that she'd kept

151

the plans secret. The play-acting was hard to endure, as he draped his arm around my shoulder, patted my behind and appeared delighted to be married to me. He needed public appearances kept up. His high-powered job driving high-powered people across the skies required appearances to be kept up at all costs. I honestly did grieve for him and tried to imagine his feelings, but being totally shut out of his emotional life as well as the physical, left me impotent also.

I'd asked for a rose bush for my birthday; he bought fifty. Beautiful, but it was such a job digging fifty holes; more of a punishment than a gift. The kids helped where they could, specially mixing in the over-ripe manure. While we were busy Garth observed, 'I wonder how Dad must feel when it used to be him doing everything like this and us just helping a little. Now we do it all and he can only fix sandwiches and lemonade, and can't even carry the tray out to us.'

Garth's sixteenth birthday was fun, and cheered us. After school he worked at Burger King till 7pm. always returning ripe with cooking fat. In his absence Kate and I prepared the rec room and welcomed in his friends from school, plus a few who already had driver licences and drove up from Zurich. He had met a girl who shared his birthday, and she brought three other girls. They all hid downstairs and then yelled 'Surprise.' as he arrived. Earlier I'd switched on the Jacuzzi (550 gallons take a while to heat) and the resulting conglomeration of teenaged bodies jammed into one hot tub should be in the Guinness book of records. That glass walled and roofed spa room was one of the features which persuaded Matt to buy the house: soaking in bubbling hot water is excellent for arthritics, but only works when they take the time to do so. It was still too cold to have the doors open much, so the steam soon filled the room as the decibel level escalated. Just two rules were set: all bathing suits must stay on; and Gracie must not enter the water. After the aquatics, five huge pizzas were demolished, and only crumbs were left from the double chocolate cake. At exactly 10pm Matt rang the cowbell and everyone went home. It was a school night and we'd stipulated 7-10pm. For once there was no taxiing for me, and Garth did most of the clean up. How lovely to have a good time with nothing to spoil it.

The slow horticultural transformations were a great delight for me, except the bout of poison ivy rash lasting several weeks. My efforts outdoors were starting to show – the beginnings of an English garden: the roses thrived, the seedlings bloomed, it was rewarding work.

For Matt's birthday I'd invited his good friends Don and Jenny to come for the weekend and surprise him, to which they'd agreed. In May there was a joint party for Dad's eightieth and Mum's seventieth birthdays. All the relatives and many friends, everyone, were there except me and my children. I hated not being there. I hated hearing later that as more and more people arrived, Dad kept hoping it would be me walking in, straight from the airport. I hated spoiling their day.

On June 1st Kate went to school, clutching her word list for the afternoon spelling bee. I'd arranged to meet her there to cheer her on, but I did not go. She said afterwards she knew at lunchtime that something was wrong. Then not seeing me in the audience she felt sick, but went ahead and won, becoming the school's top speller. Complete with trophy she returned home, racing up the driveway, starting to weep as soon as she saw my tears.

The 3pm call had been a shock. I took it in the kitchen and clearly remember sliding my back down the wall as my legs folded. Mum told me that Dad had been sunning in his garden chair but felt unwell, so made his way ponderously indoors. Resting in his living room chair he had a heart attack and died. I wanted to be instantly transported back home, and back in time, so I could at least say goodbye. Matt arranged immediate flights for all of us. That staggered me, I didn't want him to go, didn't think he should go, but he didn't ask what I thought; he was kind to me, briefly. The surprise birthday weekend had to be cancelled, both schools told, kennels booked and four cases hurriedly packed.

By 6pm we were in a limousine speeding to O'Hare. Soon after 9pm we were airborne on BA's night flight to London. Much of it I spent blocking out Matt's extra fussy demands. It was either that or locate the nearest exit door and shove him out. He'd been on at Garth constantly about manners, appearance, and even posture, until Garth donned earphones and Walkman, retreating into his music. Of course that infuriated Matt further, which upset Kate, and drove me deeper into isolated misery.

Arriving the next morning and meeting all the family felt so strange; my brothers and their clans, my sister and hers, squeezing into Mum's house – with no Dad. Tensions and emotions were rife amongst us. My brothers took on funeral arrangements and we girls took the kitchen. People came and went endlessly and the kettle was permanently on.

I was desperate to see my father. Everyone else had seen him well and happy at the party, some as recently as just days ago. It had been nearly a year since I'd seen him, and I needed proof that he was dead. Against advice I went to the funeral home. Yes, it was certainly the proof I required, but how I wish I hadn't insisted on it. What met my gaze in that hushed chapel of rest nearly did reduce me to a crumpled heap. In life he was a plain man, quietly placid, deeply tanned from maximum outdoor hours. In death he had been laid upon gold satin, ruched and frilled around him. His coffin should have been plain oak, but I saw shiny, gilded handles and decorative bits everywhere, glinting jovially in the candlelight. In place of tan his cheeks were rouged, and sunken due to the absence of his notably large teeth. It was vulgar and quite past bearing; I had to leave hastily.

Gathering at Amberley Church for the funeral was the point at which I could hold on no longer. So often the lament is heard, 'I couldn't cry because once started I'd never stop,' which is precisely what happened. Throughout the service my lachrymose contributions embarrassed me as much as others. Jonny turned a couple of times, looking back at me in wordless pleas for silence, then gave up, offering his silk handkerchief. Matt put his arm solicitously round me, which made it worse. If only they knew. Walking to the grave, he took my arm and seemed so supportive as the coffin went down. At tea in the church hall afterwards an aunt intended comfort, I'm sure, when correctly suggesting my tears weren't just for my father, but because of everything. The final blow came when we all dispersed to our temporary quarters. In the privacy of that little guestroom he turned on me with icy fire in his eyes. The loving, caring husband returned to normal. I was sharply criticised, told to pull myself together, quit snivelling in public, and not come out till I had. God had seen to it that there were not enough pills in my travel bottle, and highlighted in my brain that I could not abandon my children.

At the end of the week Matt and Garth returned to Chicago for work and for summer school. My sister and brothers took their families home, leaving Kate and me to stay on with Granny another ten days. It was a sad time, especially going through Gramps' belongings and finding the Altoids still in his pockets. Those extra strong peppermints were certainly his trademark, plus scraps of paper covered with pencilled numbers helping him keep his mileages and accounts in order. I had no doubt where he was. I knew we had only buried his body, and his soul had gone to heaven. As strongly as he believed it, I too believed it for him, that he was with Jesus, with whom he'd shared daily communication. That comfort evaporated when I turned the introspective spotlight around. I could not be so sure of my own final destination. His was a good life, full of unswerving faith and belief; mine was not. The obvious thing to do with thoughts like that is to shove them back down where they came from.

October brought surprising news from England. Granny agreed to an extensive travel plan to Australia and New Zealand after a five-week Christmas visit with us. Widowhood was not going to slow her pace. What nearly did tie her down in real devastation was the dreadful hurricane, known ever after as the Great Storm of '87. We saw television news flashes of uprooted trees and smashed cars and houses, but could not comprehend the enormous damage done to so much of the south of England. One paper claimed: 'Britain had seen nothing like that for three hundred years,' and estimated fifteen million trees were downed.

I'd struggled over giving up the college classes, determined not to because of all I'd taught my kids about not quitting when things get difficult. Yet common sense prevailed and I simply had to admit failure, again, which I hated. There was plenty to do in preparation for Mother's visit. 'Putting the yard to bed' for winter was a mammoth project including fencing in all those fifty rose bushes, then mulching them with umpteen barrow-loads of raked leaves. Indoors, each room to be spotlessly cleaned and all silver and brass polished to perfection. Meals were made ahead and frozen, likewise cookies and bread, as well as Christmas gifts made and bought. Still I strived for her unreachable approval. I knew Mum guessed my marriage was in trouble, but I also knew she needed some warning before she arrived. Firstly that Garth had retaken his driving test and passed, so was loose on the roads. More seriously, that Matt's condition had definitely worsened. The TENS machine (Transcutaneous Electrical Nerve Stimulation) sending high frequency little shocks meant to block pain was not helping, nor the ever stronger medication. The arthritis had settled in his hips, and replacement surgery had been agreed upon. He hobbled about using a stick, constantly feeling wretched.

Something happened that November that nearly made me cancel Mother's visit and, worse, break the one Commandment of the Ten I hadn't already broken. Matt, Kate and I were at home one evening, each in separate rooms as usual, doing our own thing. Garth had, with permission, driven Matt's car to visit friends in Zurich. I answered the phone to hear an unfamiliar voice checking my name, then asking if I was Garth's mother. My stomach leaped into my throat as the man continued, 'This is Officer Hall at Zurich Precinct. There's been an accident. Garth is alright but you'll have to come down here at once I'm afraid.' Surely not another call labelled 'every parent's nightmare'? Best if I went alone, but I couldn't leave without telling Matt the little I'd gleaned from the policeman. In the end we all three of us went, in my car, and it was a hellish journey. Matt drove, periodically hitting the steering wheel in anger. 'If he's wrecked my car I'll wreck him.' That was the least offensive comment.

The living nightmare waiting at the police station was worse than most suffered in sleep. Naturally I gathered my son into my arms, unspeakably thankful to find him physically in one piece. His shaking matched mine, and his apologies tumbled out through barely controlled sobs. Matt manhandled him away from me, snarling that he should stand and take his own punishment as he deserved. Garth repeatedly said how sorry he was, freely admitting it was entirely his fault, and promising to pay every penny he possessed and all future earnings to repair the damage. Matt kept telling him to shut up, and I got the same treatment. As the story unravelled it seemed like the end of the world, because I knew that my husband's reaction heralded the end of our marriage.

Yes, Garth had been extraordinarily stupid. He'd picked up a friend and given in to the temptation to show off. He lost control of the car, snaked across the road miraculously missing oncoming traffic, flipped over, rolled into a ditch and up again, knocking down a length of fence plus a couple of small trees, to finally halt upside-down with wheels still spinning, terrified but unhurt. Both boys hung by their seatbelts (thank God they'd put them on), then Garth elbowed out his smashed window, pulling his friend out after him, the only injury a cut finger. The officer told me they should not have survived it. He added, 'Somebody up there is looking after your kid.'

Once the paperwork and insurance was dealt with we were free to go. I considered asking the officer to accompany us home because I was very afraid of Matt's seething anger. Those fears were not unfounded. The return drive was even more hellish. Matt, who seldom swore and prided himself on being a gentleman, was a crazed madman, and more verbally abusive over the loss of his car than ever. When we got back he ordered us all to sit round the kitchen table for a family meeting, which was just a forum for him to continue venting his fury.

He made abominable comments about Garth's intelligence, and exactly where his brains might be, continually shouting down all the quiet apologies, attempts and offers to work to fix the fence and replace the trees. He also yelled out that he wished Garth had been badly hurt, totalled even, like his precious car. Then, he conceded, maybe he'd have felt sympathetic. At that, I noticed Kate staring in horror at me. It was only then I realised I'd left my chair and was standing against the sink, next to the cutlery drawer. Unaware of opening it, or of picking out a sharp knife, I found my hand gripping its handle as I stared at my husband's back..

God must have known the intention of my heart, a she-bear ready to kill to protect her cubs. He sent the guardian angel, already tired perhaps from saving Garth's life, to stay my hand and prevent further tragedy. It did not prevent an internal rage of loathing and fear, and a sure conviction I could not stay with this man so capable of emotionally destroying us all. How dare he treat my son so badly, when he was compassionate, long-suffering and forgiving to his own son when he wrecked a car twice? Some very bad days followed that dreadful evening, but we all made an effort to put it behind us and carry on. If Granny hadn't been coming, it would have been very different.

She arrived in time for Thanksgiving and stayed till after New Year and, generally, good times were had by all. I was past trying to cover our problems so was not too upset when Matt exhibited some of his obsessive behaviour. It was a relief for an outsider to see it, thereby realising I was not exaggerating, or imagining things to be worse than they were. He took Granny on the tour of his offices, hangars and planes, and she was duly impressed. He was justifiably proud of his aviation department, and showing it off was one pastime that did still please him. She and I enjoyed shopping and lunches out, sometimes with one or both the children. We went to the Chicago Botanic Gardens, and into Wisconsin, and good walks along the shores of Lake Michigan. Jon, Kim, Bridie and Seth came for their early Christmas with us and everyone got along fine. We took Granny to a tree farm where Garth cut the fir we chose, all struggling to hoist it onto the roof of my car, and home where all helped to decorate it. Mum was a bit staggered at the intensity of the cold but the only activity she declined was sledding. Soon it was time to return her to O'Hare for her long flight to Australia.

January's arctic cold increased with such ferocity that the inshore waters of Lake Michigan froze. As waves hit the freezing sand dunes they froze, creating amazing ice sculptures. Kate, Gracie and I walked and slithered over a large area of solidified water, thinking of polar bears. At home we luxuriated in the Jacuzzi's bubbling warmth, as Mum had loved doing the previous month, while looking out through festoons of icicles daggering down from the roof. Matt had his first total hip replacement surgery, and his recovery was quick and complete, marvelling at his new pain-free titanium joint. Manoeuvring a wheelchair around was a challenge requiring much tolerance, as was the use of crutches. The patient did not enjoy enforced inactivity, or having to accept assistance with daily hygiene. The patient's wife did not enjoy having to provide that assistance either.

The kids were both busy preparing for the spring musical, *Psalty's Camping Adventure*, at church. They both had big speaking parts plus all the songs to learn, and Garth did an excellent job as the main character. For Kate it had special meaning since her weekend away at youth group camp. There, on February 6th 1988 she was deeply moved by the speaker's description of Christ's crucifixion. She was overwhelmed by the sudden awareness of just how much Jesus suffered on the cross, the physical agony of it. At the same time realising that He did it for her, personally, because of His great love for her. The immediate response from her twelve-year old heart was to commit her whole life to Jesus there and then, to follow His teaching and obey His commandment Of course I was happy for her, but also anxious. There would be troubles ahead, especially at school, if she didn't curb her enthusiasm, but there was a good chance, I thought, that it would wear off. I kept thinking though, of that young man Scott, whose face shone when he spoke of Jesus. Nothing had worn off there. I was envious that my daughter had obviously found the certainty of faith that I still lacked, and from which might come that elusive inner peace. The whole performance of *Psalty* was a delight for everyone, and a credit to Howard who put it together while coaching the choir for another cantata, and still grieving for his beloved wife Sharon.

Matt had his second hip operation in April. It was equally successful, and equally challenging. Whenever possible I retreated to the light-filled, spacious spa room, not to laze in the hot tub, but to sit in my comfy wicker chair. From it I had an uninterrupted view across lawn and woods sloping down to open prairieland. Much contentment was found in simply observing nature come back to life after the long winter. Everything always seems a little better when spring comes.

There could be a few exceptions to that. When it was warm enough to dig out my roses from their winter wraps I was disgusted to find not only had my labours been in vain, but I'd provided first class accommodation and sustenance for all the local mice and chipmunks. Nothing to be done except dig them up and plant replacement bushes, and learn from my mistakes, and growl a lot. While I was working on the wooded slope in the back, cutting saplings and uprooting huge burdock plants, creating a pathway, Matt hobbled down to inspect my achievements and was surprisingly complimentary. I'd bought a park bench, assembled it, and placed it at the top of my path, for maximum view enjoyment. Unable to participate in choosing Dad's memorial bench at Wisley, UK, where he had done part of his horticultural training, I thought of my own park bench as my mini-Wisley, USA. Clearing such undergrowth requires a bonfire. Carefully observing sensible precautions, all was fine until the wind unexpectedly strengthened and changed direction. Flames shot everywhere, far quicker than I could deal with. I was thankful to see Kate. She noted what was happening and raced back to get help, dragging the hose as close as possible. Finally the flames were extinguished, and we soaked the whole blackened area. Coming indoors to wash my singed limbs, I discovered I'd lost eyelashes, brows and some hair as well. A cup of tea, actually a scotch, would have been nice, but I got a critical lecture on my stupidity.

Roy came home one weekend from Texas where he was learning to land bombers on aircraft carriers. He joined me briefly at mini-Wisley and actually thanked me for taking such good care of his dad. He'd not ever seen him in bad pain or so incapacitated, and realised how difficult it must have been. He hugged me, and said he loved me. Knowing him to be a good actor, I never believed anything he said, but that did seem genuine, and felt pretty good. A physiotherapist came to the house three times a week to make sure Matt exercised properly. He enjoyed those sessions, and she was pleased with his progress, soon pronouncing him well enough to return to work. He summoned me into his study, muttering pleasantries about my help during his immobility, then handed me $300 to go buy a dress or something. I couldn't have been more surprised if he'd smashed a fist into me; it felt the same. It could have been meant as a genuine thank you, but I've never heard of anyone paying a spouse in cold cash for nursing care. It painfully confirmed his opinion of my low, un-spousal status.

18

I spent a lot of time back in our old Zurich neighbourhood, and took the kids when possible to see their friends too. Howard and I shared much conversation, as well as our mutual delight in singing. He told me that the only way he coped with his wife's long illness and death was by walking daily hand in hand with Jesus Christ; being a Christian was the most important part of his life. That's nice, but privately I thought it a bit over the top, and rather embarrassing, like young Scott when he went on so about it. Walking hand in hand, for goodness sake. For some months my regular visits with Dexter had reduced. While still craving his attentions, I was starting to feel somewhat used, in that he and his wife were getting on better after a huge row. He'd confessed all, begged forgiveness, and their marriage was back on track. He was, however, more than happy to continue with me, and he still said he was a Christian.

That confused me, so he featured in my talks with Howard on the whole subject of Christianity and what it really means. Howard began seriously telling me I needed Jesus in my life. I needed to become a real Christian. My response was, repeatedly, that of course I was a Christian. He disagreed. He explained the difference between simply believing in God, doing good and being nice; and getting to know God personally by asking Jesus into your life. That meant then living by His rules, not your own any more. I knew all that stuff from my childhood and told Howard so, strongly suggesting he go away. Like a persistent mosquito, he hung around, and even when we were not together his words kept buzzing in my head. During May he was particularly pushy, asking why I wouldn't, or couldn't, answer his question: if I was so sure I was a Christian why couldn't I say yes,

Jesus is my Saviour and Lord? By then we were quite open with each other, so in spite of it being awkward, I told him. I knew if I asked Jesus to take charge of my life and help me live as He would like me to, I'd have to give up sexual freedom. Sexless marriage is grim, but if all chance of activity elsewhere is relinquished forever, that was too grim to live with. Possibly I could manage to give up Dexter, as he fancied his wife again anyway, but what if I met another irresistible man? Obviously I equated sex with not just fun but prowess, self-worth and value, none of which are easy to relinquish. Hadn't I had to give up enough in my life already? So it was reasonable to strike a bargain: *'OK God, I'll give You all of my life for You to be in charge of, except my sexuality. I'll hang onto that thanks: say 75/25%.'* Howard was even less polite to me than I'd been to God.

My friend was right: I realised an enormous truth, which had been in my head most of my life, yet never truly in my heart. I knew I must do what I'd been putting off. Stop running. Stop struggling. Stop the desperate search for happiness, love, approval and acceptance in other people, and that elusive peace. I needed to start looking at Jesus, let Him prove all those promises in the Bible, and offer Him 100% of me. At the last minute my independent streak asserted itself defiantly. Did I honestly want sudden, total dependence? My reasoning self reminded me that so far, my being in control had shown disastrous results. Wasn't it time for a policy change? Inner turmoil continued. Knowing I wanted to make the decision, I knew also it was not to be undertaken lightly. I was scared.

About midday on May 20th I silenced the phone, shut myself in my little sitting room where, pacing back and forth, I began a tentative conversation with Jesus. I couldn't use the formal Thee and Thou of remembered church prayers. I just talked. Awed by the staggering awareness of Almighty God, Creator of the universe, listening to me, I sank to my knees beside the end of the couch. There I voiced out loud the fears and anxieties, about not only what I was giving up, but my inability to stick to any new resolutions. I admitted huge embarrassment even trying to talk to Him, let alone look at His face, because of ignoring Him for so long or only paying Him lip service. So a lot of apologies came too. Remembering a verse learned in childhood, I pondered: '*If we confess our sins, He is faithful and just and will forgive us our sins and purify us from all unrighteousness*' (1 John 1:9). Did that seriously mean even my promiscuous sins forgiven, with purified protection for the future, even for me? Somewhere in there I heard the unmistakable voice of Jesus assuring me that when He died on the cross it wasn't done partially, so that merely 75% of my stupidity, anger, nastiness, that is to say sin, could be washed away and forgiven. It had been a freely, willingly given 100% for me.

Then, through copious tears I was able to see clearly that I did want to proceed. In dedicating the rest of my life, all of it, in every area, to Jesus, I was amazed to realise I wasn't feeling the anticipated grimness about giving up certain pleasures. Instead, I knew as I got up from the floor that a weight was off my back, I felt clean, light-hearted and far more than just happy: there was a bubble of joy in my heart, and, yes, I felt peaceful. I also sensed the moment was not simply a conclusion of my earlier struggles, but a beginning, no doubt of new struggles, and the start of a new journey. It was so much deeper than just turning over a new leaf: more of starting a new life under a new Master. There were no lightning flashes, drum rolls or pealing bells, but I knew it was the most significant day of my life. Later, on the phone with Howard, he said there were angels rejoicing in heaven over my decision, and I wondered if it was all those guardian ones who'd so often taken care of me in the past. I rather wanted to dance with them, so I did, then felt silly and glad no one was home.

One of the first things to be seen to was long overdue anyway. I went to Dexter in his office when I knew he'd be alone. While driving I asked Jesus to go in with me. It was funny how it didn't seem over the top now to include Him in everything. Believing I was now a gal who could say no was relatively easy until I heard his lovely voice, saw his lovely face. As always he invited me round to his side of the desk, looking surprised when I declined. Somehow I told him it had to be goodbye. The words kept sticking in my throat. He got up and came towards me but I backed away, knowing if I felt his gentle touch I'd melt. In a rush I explained that Jesus was now in charge of my life, and I was allowing Him to guide my thoughts and actions. Dexter's response was unexpected. His face took on a sneering cynicism, as did his voice. 'If you think finding religion is the answer, then you need a psychiatrist more than ever.' Was it a game called Retaliation? He didn't need me after repairing his marriage, so I was now saying I didn't need him, and he did not appreciate rejection. I loved that man. Ending it was like surgery without anaesthetic. Much later I saw it as exactly that, under the hand of the Great Physician, a major amputation of a bad part of my life, in order to promote healing of the whole.

I woke heavily on June 1st, achingly aware of it being the first anniversary of Dad's death. One of the hymns he'd played on his keyboard that last time was, 'On Christ, the solid Rock I stand, all other ground is sinking sand.' I wanted him to know that, at last, I had found the solid Rock, and was no longer scrabbling about in sinking sand. After my family left for their various activities I cleared breakfast and drove to a favourite haunt, Lake Michigan beach. There I walked a long way before settling on an old tree trunk to pour out my pain to God. I begged Him to erase the still vivid image of Dad lying there in the funeral home. Looking up, I noticed the puffy cumulous clouds shift and divide, though there was no wind. Gradually the blue space grew, and into it I clearly saw Dad's face, and next to him, Jesus. You may well be thinking: 'Good gracious, this I do not believe; she must have been drinking or fallen asleep.' If I had not seen it I'd have a hard time believing it too. Dad's face was healthily tanned and radiant. His words, deep and mumbly, were straightforward: 'Yes darling, I'm here, I'm fine, and happier than ever.' Jesus' smile confirmed it just before they faded from sight. Blinking several times, I kept staring at the place, only seeing more clouds lazily hanging around, nothing else. It made me sing. I stayed sitting on the log quite a while, feeling like a song thrush, but not sounding, I'm sure, anywhere near as lovely.

After discussions Garth decided he would go with the youth group on a Project Serve trip to St Vincent. Sponsored by Youth for Christ, they were to help build a school on the small tropical island. While packing, Garth glanced at the suggested list and scoffed at the first three items: Bible, notebook and pencil. He was quite happy to go dig, and heave bricks around, but wanted no part of any 'religious stuff.' Having so recently heard of first his sister's and then his mother's new-found spiritual enthusiasm, he sought life on his own terms. His departure was backed by quantities of prayer, unknown and doubtless unwanted by him. During the first night of his absence I had a dream. I could see inside his cabin, in the compound cleared in the trees close to the foundations of the school. The dark interior was lit by a sunbeam draping the shoulders of my kneeling son. Feeling like an intruder, I couldn't look for very long, but I knew when I woke that Garth had also heard Jesus calling him, and had responded.

During the next ten days I often doubted my dream, thinking it was just what I so hoped would happen, and too good to be true. Little nudges came, as reminders about my prayers. At the airport, immediately I laid eyes on him, I knew it was true. After hugs and suitcases were sorted he said, 'Hang on Mum, before we get in the car I've got something to tell you. Right at the beginning I became a Christian. I wasn't going to at all, but Jesus came to see me in the cabin.' More hugs, and tears too, and all I could say was, 'I know, I know. Thank You Lord.'

An intriguing talk I'd heard on Moses and the Red Sea, a story I thought I knew fairly well, came alive with new meaning for me. God's words to Moses were also to me: 'Wait, obey, and I will'. Already tormented by the marriage problems, those words helped me bear a cutting letter from Matt. Sixteen angry pages of accusation of it all being my fault, with great avoidance of truth. A choir song about troubles kept ringing in my ears, with a chorus of, 'Where could I go but to the Lord?' Taking another beach walk I sang that over and over, pleading for clear guidance.

Garth was trying to sort himself out and make plans for the future. Having been turned down by the military because of his asthma, he cheered up realising he couldn't get drafted either. One more strike against him, in Matt's eyes; those feelings are easily read. He considered art schools in England because having an English parent entitled him to the 'Right of Citizenship' added to his passport. The problem was obtaining the natural father's signature. It was hard to accept, a man who has blatantly ignored his son for years being credited with such importance. Garth wrote a polite and mature letter to his father, including a stamped, addressed envelope, and prepared to wait.

Life at home shrivelled although we all remained civil and behaved decently. That play-acting was dreadfully like living in my old, surreal nightmare where all is illusion and off balance. Discovering a highly recommended lawyer, I went to see him, just to find out where I stood and what my options were, if any. We talked of divorce but I made no official statements, and signed nothing.

November brought the four-day war, a particularly hellish time of angry silences and angrier outbursts. Garth was not home but Kate witnessed more than any child should ever have to. At the end Matt got on his knees and beseeched me not to divorce him. That was the only time I ever saw tears in his eyes. He asked, 'What do you want me to do? I'll do anything to help, anything.'

He agreed to go with me for counselling, and see it through, and promised to try to accept us as family instead of an irritating trio he was obliged to support. I desperately wanted to believe him, and clung to those promises as an exhausted climber clings to a finger hold. Garth asked a lot of questions; I answered those I could. He'd been spending his free time with friends to avoid the tension and stress at home but he was very loving, with understanding way past his years. It was difficult to bring Jesus into the conversation because I was so worn down, and he was sensing that drinking beer with his friends helped more than going to church. I know I failed him there.

Oh God what must I do to undo this mess? Is it fixable? How can I ever feel any hope? How can I love the man when he is slowly destroying my children, having already finished me? I will not crumble, I will not go mad, though most days it feels as if both are imminent. How can I live right when I don't want him in the same house with me, let alone the same bed? What's between us now is a cancer, growing darker, sicker, all the time. Oh God, I cry out to You – show me the way.

Up till then I had merely jotted bits and pieces down, but gradually began writing more. Talking to God in written prayer seemed to be strengthening our communication. The kids and I went to Des Moines for a weekend; we committed the journey to God then saw His protection clearly when we were nearly sideswiped by a huge, silver tanker truck at 60mph. Garth was driving and did not lose control, handled it excellently, pulled onto the shoulder to recover afterwards. *Thank You, Lord.*

Back at home at Thanksgiving we'd all agreed to make an effort for the evening, going out to eat at the Country Squire, where Garth worked. He and the other waiters were exceptionally busy that night, and their black trousers, white shirts, red braces and bow ties added to the festive air. Even with that cheerful interlude it was hard to summon much enthusiasm for Christmas. There was no cantata to sing as Howard was taking a well-earned break. My usual trick of immersing my mind in good books was helping, and I found I wanted to include the Bible. That came as a surprise because most, if not all, of my reading of that book had been out of duty. Gradually I found I wanted to read it, wanted to discover what it really meant, and I started to see, slowly at first, what a wealth of advice, wisdom and comfort it contains. In a very different book I found descriptions of a married man so like Matt it was as if he had written it himself. That man claimed to love his wife but admitted to knowing he was not doing so. He knew he was making her isolation unbearably miserable as he excluded her from his heart while play-acting affection in public. Although not at all nice to read, it was somewhat comforting to to think my situation might not be as uniquely abnormal as it felt.

Looking inwards from the outside rather than remaining entrenched inside, can be a great help and bring clearer understanding.

Have I been idolising all the wrong things in my life? Doing exactly what the Bible warns not to do? Worshipping the creature instead of the Creator? It's taken me over forty years to figure out. So God had to allow me to go through all that stuff in order to see this great, obvious, illuminating truth that just hit me at 6.15am today – there's always been something other than God that I've been concentrating on; either me, or food, first marriage mess, sex, money or lack of, then barging into another marriage and so onto my burdens, my unhappiness, affairs, problems etc. All that had to come and go in order for me to see my way clearly to 'the liberating, loving power of the one true God', that only God is worthy of worship.

Kate got miserably sick again, this time with pneumonia. Fortunately my hours working at Nanny4Today, the hospital agency, were flexible enough to let me stay home and, while Kate slept, I talked to God, begging Him to show me what to do. As if in answer Matt rang, requesting an hour of my evening to talk; and almost at once the verse, 'be anxious for nothing', filled my mind, pushing out panic. It was a long day, waiting and wondering. The talk was good, though so sad. From the man who had boomed, 'There will be no divorce,' there now most likely would be. I wrote:

I shall not barge into or out of any major decisions any more without seriously seeking God's will. I goof up too badly on my own. I promise You

Lord that if I am freed, and end up alone with my children, and after they've grown and gone, I will have a house full and spilling over with Your love and I will not be ashamed.

We had a quiet Christmas; it was very cold with lots of snow, and a fair bit of frostiness around inside the house too.

1989 was bleak, though not without its highlights, one being my growing friendship with the Miller family. We knew each other from church but Ann and I met at a school functions also. Her daughter Kerry and Kate were already good friends, her husband Bill, and their two younger children, Doug and Julie, were equally welcoming and we enjoyed each other's company. I liked the happy chaos in their home and she loved the quiet spaciousness of mine. Much of the winter went on officialdom. Letters and calls to and from the British Consulate in Chicago, and repetitious signing and mailing forms. The object was to obtain dual citizenship for Garth before his planned departure for England, and for Kate also just in case. Bureaucracy will not be hurried. Nor will ex-husbands who appear to have lost interest in their offspring. A tense time, but with less than a week to go, all was signed and sealed. Matt did pay for both sets of paperwork, for which of course I was grateful, even if he saw it as an eventual way of getting rid of us.

For months I'd been thinking about baptism and its symbolism. The church the kids and I attended had a baptistery under the floor up at the front, and I'd seen a good few people taking the plunge, and heard their testimonies of the difference Jesus had made in their lives and why they wanted to acknowledge Him publicly. Both my children had done this. The desire was growing in me as my own relationship with Jesus Christ was growing. The main battle was physical. I hated my head being under water even briefly, or then to climb out and have wet garments cling. *Sorry Lord, I can't.* The more I pondered all that God had done, and was doing for me, the more my battles shrank. Then I understood another part of the amazing mystery which is

Jesus walking beside every one of His children, yes, hand in hand even. If I agreed to stand up in public and tell the congregation that Jesus is my Lord and Saviour, I would not be alone. He'd be right there beside me, and if I agreed to being dunked under completely, thus symbolising washing away my sins, death and burial of my old life, resurrection into the new, He'd be there too and I would not drown or feel embarrassed. I'd be doing it not only for Him, but with Him. So I did, on May 20th, exactly a year since I became a real Christian.

Garth put more energy into his job and social life than school. I think he cut more classes than even I knew about. He had the use of Roy's old car, and it was good that he had to earn his own petrol money, though hard to overlook that those rules had not been enforced for his stepsiblings. Kate put much time and effort into her graduation speech, while Ann and I did likewise making dresses for the girls' leaving junior high ceremony. Leaving high school was not particularly special for Garth, just a relief. He won a scholarship to an art school, presented on Awards Night. His actual graduation ceremony, in the football field on a hot June day, was meant to be carried out with military precision and marching. My son was not the only graduate to flaunt sunglasses, chewing gum, and a less than serious attitude, using the bright blue cap and gown to add dramatic flair and plenty of smiles.

Believing God knows best, there were still many days when I simply couldn't pray, couldn't seem to get through to Him at all. The most recent family meeting had been another of Matt's out-of-control rampages. His face was contorted by derision, revulsion, ice, anger, uglier than I've ever seen it during one of his 'sessions' with us. The handsome blue eyes were quite obliterated by bulging, black psychotic pupils, ashen face, mouth a bitter, tight line, hand shaking so badly he had to use both to take a sip of tea; no booze this time. Garth was exemplary. I was so proud of him and amazed by his calm maturity. As Matt flung out blame, accusations, ridicule and threats of punishment, Garth took only what was deserved, apologised (e.g. for not cutting the lawn too well the last time), refusing to accept he'd done it on purpose to annoy. It was a copy of many past episodes, but by far the most abusive. When we were dismissed, Kate went sobbing to her room and Garth was ordered to the bank for his money for his car insurance. I then verified by calling Sara that her dad had paid for her insurance until she was twenty-four, Roy's till he was twenty-three.

Then the towel rail incident. After I'd finished stripping and re-wallpapering the guest bathroom, the last room in the house to be decorated, my husband insisted on taking off, then putting back, all the woodwork, cleaning everything I'd just cleaned, and adding another mirror and extra towel rails. Quietly asking him to stop as the room was tiny and they weren't needed only made him angrier. He drilled several holes in the walls, 'looking for studs', which he'd always found before just by knuckle-taps, put up all the rails plus mirror, drilling more holes as he worked, leaving the walls looking like Swiss cheese. A maniac with a power drill is not someone to argue with.

Three letters came with good news. An article I'd written for a magazine after a writers' conference at Moody Bible Institute in Chicago where I'd met a dear friend, Marla, from Tennessee, had been accepted for publication. A job offer had come from the chiropractic clinic where I'd been going regularly for headache treatment. The third was from the British Consul giving Garth an appointment to sign and make his oath – exactly as I had done at Grosvenor House, London, twenty-three years earlier. He chose to go down alone, and managed just fine. Once the copies arrived he would be free to go. There were moments when all I wanted to do was pack up Kate and myself and go with him. In a long letter Marla wisely cautioned against, 'submitting my blueprint plans to God and asking Him to bless them, rather than patiently waiting for His blueprint plans for me'. Good advice, but, *'Oh Lord, I'm not good at waiting. Let me be still and quiet enough to hear You'* became my frequent prayer. I did see gradual change occurring. No longer was I so totally wrapped up in desperate co-dependency. I began to realise and accept a deep, secure knowledge of God's continuing love and concern for me, His guidance available as long as I'm willing to receive it.

I arranged to see Rudi, another counsellor, this one also highly recommended, but on the phone I explained my hesitation due to past experiences that I had no wish to repeat: *Did I say that? Was it me saying I no longer wanted to jump into any available bed? Wow, Lord, You are working in me. Thank You.* Before going to him I prayed for guidance and wisdom, to prevent any: 'Thy will be done. Then go ahead with my will anyway,' sort of attitude.

Nothing had come of Matt agreeing before Christmas to get help. It took all my courage to ask, for the third time. We so desperately needed a mediator or I knew it'd be over. I had to give him that last chance (again) before returning to the lawyer. I dreaded any sort of confrontation with him, but to my amazement he agreed to call for an appointment with Rudi. Our rib dinner was delicious but consumed in silence, and I went to bed shortly after. He knocked fiercely (I was sleeping in the downstairs guest suite) and barged in announcing that he'd rung but the man had not returned his call. He did not like being kept waiting, so maybe he just would not go, especially since I was hostile again. I responded with a sigh, 'No. Not hostile; just sad,' to which he snapped, 'Well if you're sad that's too damn bad.'

For a couple who recently attended a seminar on improving marriage, that was not an example of good dialogue. We had heard, taken notes, bought the books and reckoned the speaker, Gary Chapman, made a lot of sense. Any time I referred to what we'd learned, it was greeted with silence or, if pushed: 'I went to your wretched seminar didn't I? I took more notes than anyone else. What more do you want?'

That last question was not one he wanted me to answer. In another solo visit to Rudi I told him of my confusion while listening to some Christian friends saying divorce is not an option, and my own fears of utter breakdown if I stayed, unless I was murdered first. I knew God was there to help, but wished He would hurry up. Immediately I sensed Him chiding me, then I knew for sure that He had led me to Rudi and was helping me, and Rudi's words shed a lot of light. I saw the need to drop the heavy loads I'd struggled with for so long; two dead marriages, dysfunctional family, my guilt, and two non-fathers for my children, my lack of growth and progress as a Christian. Then I saw that God's mercy, love and forgiveness, and upholding strength truly are new every morning. At home I told Matt I could do no more. If he wanted it fixed he'd have to fix it. Officially separated, I stayed in the guestroom, and tried to be no longer so intimidated by his anger. *Lord, if I'm scared, worried and hurt, he must be as well, maybe more so. Please help him too. Lord, do You have some surprises for me way down the line from here? Please help me to be receptive and ready for whatever Your plans are.*

Garth had several farewell parties, one of which extended to the actual departure lounge at O'Hare Airport. I could well imagine how he must have been feeling. Seeing him go was a huge wrench, made worse by not knowing when we'd next meet, and far worse by knowing he must have been thankful to get away. He planned to live in Kent with David and Jan, finding work till he could start at the American Art College in London, putting his scholarship award towards the fees, the remainder promised to him by Matt. There was so much I wish had been different in Garth's teenage years. He'd had a very rough time in most ways, not least spiritually, and I failed him so often, and not fully equipped him to face life head on. Rather like David Copperfield's mother, unable to stand up to her new husband and divert his unpleasantness from her young son. With Garth gone I thought Matt's attitude might improve, but to my dismay, he started on Kate.

My new job as a chiropractic assistant was great. Although part-time, it tired me out, and I loved it. Learning new skills birthed a tiny drop of confidence. The two doctors and four other girls and I made a good team, working well together. I got to know the patients, looking forward to their return visits. The doctors saw each person, took x-rays and treated any subluxations, and we then followed up with the physiotherapy machines. I also had to master the reception desk and office work, multiple phone lines and computers. My confidence grew in discovering, after all the years of nannying small children, that I had a real rapport with hurting people of all sorts, particularly the elderly. While easing physical pain, I found by simply listening and asking a few key questions, I could also help to ease emotional pain, which in turn eased my own somewhat.

God… I'm sorry I'm such a slow learner. Thank You for being patient with me. Thank You for that recent sermon when the chap alerted us to listen for prods, or phone calls, from You. Back on May 20th last year it was like putting my whole life on the altar for You, like Abraham put his son Isaac, willing to sacrifice even him, but what I keep doing is taking bits off again, if I don't think You're acting fast enough, or to my liking. Lord I'm sorry, I want to hand everything back to You and just wait, and be ready for Your calls.

Matt and I did go together to Rudi. Some revealing stuff emerged about his parents' inability to show affection, or confront each other about anything, and I had to say that anger was not acceptable in my childhood or ever dealt with. The next visit there was equally hard, and deeply interesting. We learned more of co-dependency, interdependency, and symbiosis, and I went home with a headache plus a little hope.

Lord, all I ever wanted is a real marriage, a real partnership, a happy home. I don't need a mansion – a tent would do, as long as those in it love each other. Surely that's not too much to ask? The more I try to grow and learn the less he wants me. Lord, Your steadfast love is dependable. I'd be lost without it, thank You.

Predictable, and in a way understandable I guess, Matt soon refused any further help from Rudi, denying any further need. None of his promises made in November 1988 had been kept, except the counselling, but that only lasted a month, so in November 1989 I returned to the lawyer and started proceedings. Only people who have sat trembling at a lawyer's desk and said, 'I have to divorce – again,' can know how utterly awful it was. Civil, quick, painless – I don't think so.

Kate, caught in the crossfire, was thrilled to go to England for Christmas, and wanted Kerry to go too. I was glad to think of both my children together, away from my husband, and with my family where they'd be well looked after and loved. It was tempting to quit then and there and go with them. The Millers invited me to spend my free time in their home over the festive season. At work I'd increased my hours, not only for financial reasons. I coped better by being extremely busy and could sleep a few hours at night if sufficiently exhausted. I was still very afraid of Matt's anger when fuelled by alcohol, which was every evening he was home with no early flight next morning. Quite often I brought dear Gracie's bed into my room, and always barricaded the door. Thankfully the guestroom had its own bathroom (not the ruined woodpeckered one) all on the ground floor. One day when alone Grace went in there, then my door must have banged shut, trapping her. She charged about, up over the bed, onto the windowsill and to the door, again and again. Grace was not young. She broke several claws scratching chunks of wood from the door and skirting board, and was only semi-conscious when I found her. She got cuddled and gently rocked as I wept over her.

Soon after that the vet told me what I already knew. There was no more that medicine could do for her. Matt loved that dog but was not around enough to care for her, and I was away more and more, so I had to do the deed. Again, only those who have taken a beloved pet for its final injection can know that heartache. Dragging or carrying the unwilling animal into the place they all instinctively dislike anyway, up onto the cold metal table. You hug and hold tight, look into the trusting, loyal eyes for the last time. With a sigh the velvety body sags against yours, the breathing slows as the legs fold. You wait till you know it's over, then leave, wordless and weeping.

19

The days were a blur of work, which was positive, pleasant and quite often fun, and visits to the lawyer, which were not. There were calls to and from England where everyone seemed to be having a marvellous time, and said sweet things about missing me and wishing I was there. I wished I was there too. When the girls returned there was, with the welcoming excitement, an awareness that things had not gone altogether smoothly. Many stories of Garth's escapades emerged, how he'd found a job as a hospital porter, 'borrowed' a hospital car one night, returning it via a thick hedge. His adapting to the strength of English beer and walking at night in pitch darkness, badly frightened by a chance meeting with a badger, plus his efforts at buying a very small, very old car. More eventually came out about Kate's unbearable turmoil, which naturally tore me apart as I thought she'd be happier there. Tensions between us grew worse as the palpable fear, anger and stress in the house became too much to deal with. On February 25th 1990, her fifteenth birthday, Kate left. My son gone, my marriage going, my daughter gone. I had no home. A house still, yes, but no home to insist she return to, and I could quite understand, or so I thought, why she'd gone. Kate also had good friends at church, and was very fond of one of the youth workers, Shelly. She offered Kate sanctuary and I knew she'd be safe there but hated her being away.

The following week I made a similar move. With no children or dog to need me, only icy silence or violent anger, there was no point in staying. A couple offered me their spare room, so I packed a few essentials and went. My hosts could not have been kinder, and the room was large, bright and comfortable. Shelly rang several times, asking if the three of us could meet to talk. At first she irritated me, but in hindsight I have frequently thanked God for her. Having listened late into many nights to Kate's distress, and seen the need to tackle me, she did. Straight to the point, gently but firmly she opened my eyes to what I'm ashamed to say I had not seen. For too long I'd been confiding in Kate, inappropriately dumping my emotional baggage on her, adding impossible loads on top of what she was already carrying of her own. It had to be faced, and apologised for. It was very difficult. We shouted, cried, hugged and prayed together. Fragile shards may be glued back together, but they do not gain former strength right away. The Millers helped again by inviting both Kate and me to move in with them, which was truly noble as their house was overfull with the five of them, plus dogs, gerbils and bird.

During the winter my gentlemanly husband aimed some extra low blows. The way to get to me is to get to my children. Matt suddenly announced he would no longer pay Garth's London college fees. That was bad. I certainly couldn't afford it, nor could any of my family, so I had to ring Garth and tell him. In looking back I can understand more of Matt's point of view, but at the time I saw it only as the end of any future education for Garth. He'd seen the art college as his big break, then seen his stepfather remove all hope – an angry puppeteer cutting the support string because the puppet's mother didn't dance to the right tune. I tried to persuade Garth to stay in England anyway, aware of the possibility that Kate and I might end up there. Although truly appreciative of all his uncle and aunt had done for him, his friends had been persuading him to return. It was of course wonderful to see him, but awful not to have a home to welcome him back into. I will always be grateful to his best buddy and parents who took him in as another son and helped him tremendously. Still scattered but at least I was once again in contact with both my children.

It was a tight squeeze at the Millers, but we managed. We kept to organised schedules and took turns in the one bathroom, starting soon after 5.30am as Bill drove the girls to school on his way to work at 7am. We all ate breakfast together and committed each day to Jesus, asking for and depending on His grace and patience. I'd been gradually losing weight, quite unintentionally, but it started accelerating, and other worrying symptoms appeared, as well as the increasing migraines. A specialist and some nasty tests proved it wasn't cancer, thank God, just extreme stress. The pounds continued disappearing and other than feeling permanently tired, I didn't mind at all. At church the flourishing youth group, The Crossing, took up most of Kate's free time. At Easter they put on a mime play, telling the crucifixion and resurrection story most powerfully without words. Kate played Mary who met Jesus in the garden early on Easter morning. The entire performance was excellently done and extremely moving. Garth drove up to see it and was warmly welcomed but could not be persuaded to return to church at all. He was working hard at two jobs and proving his independence.

The divorce legalities dragged on, my lawyer assuring me he was doing all he could, and that it was always Matt's lawyer causing the delays. It was so utterly sad that we could not talk to each other as two human beings any more, only through legal mediators. I'm quite sure that side of things is worsened by the system, the cash-hungry lawyers carefully adding every call, every letter and every court appearance to their bills, not concerned how long it takes. After several cancelled hearings, and two preliminaries, our time in court came towards the end of April. It was a long day of red tape, paperwork, signing, exiting to confer, re-appearing, oath-taking, adjournment for lunch, but who could eat? I don't suppose I looked good, but Matt's face was ice-hard and menacing. He shook his raised fist at me across the room, loudly vowing to make me regret it, threatening to make me so broke I'd have to crawl back to him for money. The judge conceded that since his earning power was so much greater than mine I would be awarded a larger portion of the estate. None of that could happen, however, until our house sold and since Matt intended to remain there, it could take a while. The best part of that day was when it was over. It is a fact that in reality divorce is never over. In death there is the bereavement and time of grieving, and a body to bury but then it is over. Divorce is never final because that other person to whom you once were joined is still out there. When all legal strings are neatly tied the emotional ones are left to fray. Many years would pass before I realised the major part forgiveness plays in the healing of those frayed ends.

I had to produce a comprehensive list of everything in the marital residence considered mine and, subject to his agreement, I could then remove those items. I only listed what was mine, leaving anything of ours, or unknown origin, to save any further trouble. When I went back to pack he was there watching, hawk-like. Bill and two other men from the church returned with me the following weekend, plus some of the youth group in a convoy of small trucks, to help move my belongings out, to be stored in the Miller's huge three-car garage. For that project I had to switch off every remaining emotion and coldly go through each room until it was stripped of me.

Shortly after that was Matt's birthday, so I baked a farewell cake and took it round, intending to have one final check on what was left of my house and garden. The absence of his car told me I was at least temporarily alone. My garage opener did its job, but then the door from the garage into the house would not open. Checking my keys, I went round to the front door with the same result. What a nasty jolt to realise he'd already had all the locks changed. So that was that. Goodbye. I left the cake on the garage step, knowing it wouldn't stay edible for long in the heat, but its cover would prevent consumption by furry or feathered intruders. As I went slowly down the drive, noticing my roses budding but with no heart to pick them, there was sudden shouting and yelling. Roy appeared from nowhere, leaping at my car in full marine attack mode, leaning in through the open window trying to grab me. Clearly intending harm, his angry swearing and shoving was frightful, but definitely another guardian angel time; somehow I was able to accelerate, heave him off me, dislodge his grip on the door, and race away.

Life continued fairly smoothly. Naturally there were tensions now and then between so many people living in such cramped quarters. One of the main problems was the weird phone calls, mostly just clicking off as soon as answered, and the distinct impression of me being under surveillance. If it had been just me who felt it, I'd have assumed my mental state was worse than it was, but each of us was very aware of it, and unnerved. After getting the telephone number changed, adding considerably to my burden of indebtedness, the calls ceased, but the surveillance didn't. No proof that Matt was responsible, but we had all witnessed enough irrational behaviour to make it probable.

An example was an earlier occasion when I could have been killed, and believe that was his, or possibly Roy's, intention. Even after Matt and I parted he still maintained all the cars for a short time. Nobody was a better mechanic, or more meticulous about insurance payments. Driving to work, joining the main stream of traffic from a side road, I suddenly heard loud grinding, scraping noises as the steering seized up. Going so slowly anyway, I inched along and turned off again into the very next side road, an office parking lot. The car was not driveable so I found a phone, rang work to say I'd be late, then rang Matt who said, 'Too bad. I'm not interested any more. You'll have to get a tow truck, I guess.' I didn't expect him to care if I was stuck, but I was surprised at his lack of concern for a car of his fleet. Having arranged towing for the car and a ride to work, I was further surprised by a summons to the garage, 'to see something'. I went, totally unprepared for the shock awaiting me. Up on the racks was my car, exposed to public scrutiny. The garage owner asked me to look carefully at the main coil spring holding the left front wheel to the axle. It had come apart, wrapping itself round the inside of the wheel. He pointed to the break saying, 'It's been cut.' I felt sick. He continued, 'The other three are in excellent condition, and so is this one except for that smooth cut. Those springs rarely wear down. Somebody planned a nasty accident, and if you'd been travelling at speed it would've been very nasty. Somebody up there is watching out for you, lady.' I told him I believed that, thanking God audibly but shakily. In contacting the insurance company to foot the considerable bill, I had another bad shock. Nearly six months earlier when the policies were due for renewal, Matt had paid fully to renew his cars but had paid nothing on mine. I'd been driving for half a year totally uninsured. His decision not to pay for me was I suppose understandable, but not telling me was not.

Certain the poor Millers wanted their house to themselves for a break, and if I was to contemplate moving permanently back to England, a trial run seemed essential. Was I too Americanised to fit in? Was there too big a gap between me and my family? Would they accept me back? Could I make yet another complete cultural changeover? Naturally I included Kate, and was not prepared for her abject refusal and lack of interest. So I booked my own flight for July 29th for three weeks, saying no more about it but striving to write a preparatory letter home including Kate, still hoping we'd go together:

Please try to understand, this is just the tip of the iceberg for me; juggling reality and caution. One cannot enjoy the prospect of leaving a country after more than twenty years and all the friends gathered along the way, any more than one can enjoy alienation from family. There is so much about America that I love just as there's so much of England I've missed. Even if I were childless it would be a hard decision but considering G's and K's feelings also makes it seem impossible. They both want to continue living as Americans in America, I want to return to England – I think. Heartache of some kind seems to be my permanent companion. We're praying the Almighty will clarify the questioning soon. I know He has a plan for me and will show me in His time (not soon enough for my impatience I'm sure). I'm not asking you to treat us with kid gloves, just to understand, be loving and supportive and uphold us in your prayers as we struggle with the shreds of family life in our own different ways and attempt to regain priorities and values, wherever that best may be done.

I continued driving to work – in my properly fixed and insured vehicle – and it was during the evening return journeys that I spent much time crying out to God, and singing to Him also. I'd learned a lot of new songs and sang my heart out, not caring how choked up it sounded. Most days I had no words to pray, but knew I was connecting with Jesus, as if He rode in the car with me. I always felt encouraged and strengthened. Now and then I asked Kate again and each time received the same negative answer, until precisely one week before I was to leave. She wasn't enthusiastic but did grudgingly agree to accompany me. Thinking it must be far too late I prayed all the way to the travel agent, *Lord if You want Kate to be with me please make one seat left on that plane.* There was just one seat left. *Thank You Lord.* I didn't realise at the time that we each had such different agendas for those three weeks. She was happy to see everyone and enjoy Sussex briefly before returning stateside, back to her friends and preparations for her sophomore year at high school. My need was to continue asking the Lord for guidance as I tested the waters. It was strange to be home again but in circumstances so different this time. Each of my siblings and their families, plus Mother, outdid themselves in being welcoming and lovely, each pointing out the benefits of settling in their part of the country, and offering every kind of help.

With Granny we did the well-loved Downland walks, tea in the garden, fell in love with a house for sale, and toured a school Kate would attend if we lived there. We went by train to Somerset to stay with Jonny and family, including infant Miney who used to nap contentedly in the ironing basket. Back to Sussex with Alison and family, and Claire made a cake with 'Jeremiah 29:11' written in icing for us. We went on to Kent, staying with David and his family, where Garth had so recently been living. The heat had turned most of England's green and pleasant land to arid brown acreage resembling Arizona.

Kate and I walked through stubble in a recently harvested field. We'd been discussing the pros and cons of coming to live in England permanently, each adding our own particular needs, fears and hopes. The three weeks were nearly over and a decision had to be made. We sat down in that field to pray, both very aware that our own ideas might not match the plans God already had for us. As much as Kate was sure she wanted to live in America, I was sure I should be in England. Earlier, on the same subject, she had bravely and defiantly stated she was going back whether I stayed or not, and she would make her own way in life just as Garth was struggling to do. As we prayed the Lord was speaking to both our hearts. It wasn't till later I fully appreciated what that agreement cost Kate. Her determination to hear and follow God's will for her overrode her own strong need to return to the life she knew, far from ideal as it was.

We did agree that Lewes seemed the best place to settle. Both the town and church were full of teenagers, and the school sounded good, so we went there for detailed planning of the two-year GCSE program Kate would have to slot into, then to purchase the uniform, a major adjustment for her, and my finances. I had to fly back to finalise my job and our belongings and Kate had to stay to start the term at her new school. Trying to get a refund on her return ticket was nothing compared with having to leave her where she didn't want to be. Alison was great. She signed a legal document taking full responsibility as Kate's guardian in my absence, and rearranged her home so Kate could have the attic bedroom as her own domain. It was small, with a small window, but wonderfully wide views of the Downs and the sea. I had enough money left to buy Kate a good radio/tape player, and order a flower basket to be delivered on her first day of school.

Somehow my legs got me onto that plane at Heathrow and off again nine hours later at O'Hare. I felt utterly fragmented and very wobbly, not just physically. I believed I was doing the right thing, but what if not? Again I had one child on each side of the Atlantic. I had a job, a car, no home but plenty of dear friends in America. I had no job, no home of my own and no car, few friends but a large family waiting for me in England. Had I really heard God? Was it just me who thought

I'd prefer England? Did I trust God? Did He care enough about me to have a plan individually tailored for me? If so, was that plan to finish in the States then turn back home once and for all? *O God, help, talk to me, tell me what to do please. What about the Gulf War? What if, as threatened, domestic flights are curtailed and I can't leave America? Lord, where are You? Please speak soon. I desperately need to hear You.*

With the Millers again, I was at least temporarily secure, although a great many things started happening quickly. Bill found a buyer for my car when I was ready to sell. The Gulf War intensified, causing frightening headlines and news bulletins. Kate's friends were dismayed she wasn't coming back, and not best pleased with me. At work everyone was sweet and my boss wrote me a glowing reference. In church one Sunday my mind was leaping back and forth across the Atlantic, as the pastor announced his sermon from Deuteronomy. It sounded boring: who reads that book of the Bible? I sure didn't. Finding chapter eight we followed as he read. What I heard was so powerful, so clear, so individually meant for me, that I knew God was talking to me, just like I'd asked Him to. Aware of Revelation 22:18-19, my intention is certainly not to rewrite Scripture but just to state what my ears heard that day:

Remember the way I have guided you these forty years, mostly in America, that I might humble you and test you, to know what was in your heart, and whether or not you would obey Me. I humbled you and let you hunger, and fed you with manna which you didn't know, so that I could make you know that man does not live by bread alone but by every word that proceeds out of the mouth of the Lord. Know then that the Lord disciplines you, so you shall keep My commandments and walk in My ways. For I am bringing you into a good land, a land of brooks and water, springs flowing forth in valleys and hills, a land of wheat and barley, where you will eat bread without scarcity, in which you will lack nothing. You shall bless the Lord your God for bringing you back to England. Take heed lest you forget Me and My commandments. Lest, when you have eaten, and have a home to live in and a job, you become proud and you forget the Lord. The Lord who brought you out of Chicago, out of the house of bondage, who led you through the terrible years; the serpents and scorpions of divorce, the thirsty ground of a home without Living Water. The Lord who brought you water and fed you manna at Lakeland Church (which your fathers did not know) that He might humble you and test you, to do you good in the end. Beware lest you say in your heart, 'my power has gotten me this wealth.' You shall remember Me, the Lord your God, for it is I who gives you this power. I solemnly warn you this day that you shall have no other gods but Me, and shall surely perish if you do not obey Me.

The most un-boring sermon I've ever listened to, it was direct confirmation that I had got it right, and a direct answer to those desperate prayers. Immediately my questions started again. When should I go, and how? What will I do when I get there? How will I live, and where? I can't stay with my sister forever. Wait a minute. Hadn't God just answered the first main question: go or stay? Surely He'll carry on answering the rest soon enough, maybe I should shut up and listen. That required faith and patience. *Lord, please grant me plenty of each.*

Garth came over for a barbecue, and a haircut, and we had a good chat. He was so sweet and maturely supportive, encouraging me to go and not worry about him. At nineteen he was an adult in the eyes of the law, quite capable of looking after himself, but I agonised over abandoning him. With friends and girlfriends he would not starve, and as long as he worked he could pay his rent, but I cringed when thinking of his non-existent family life. I'd be leaving him where he had only a father and a stepfather, neither of whom were interested. Matt prohibited his own family from any contact at all with me or mine. Such a pity, and so very shortsighted. Because Garth was used to it didn't make it better.

When not working my two weeks' notice at the Clinic, I was in the Miller garage. My stuff had been hurriedly thrown into boxes for the removal from what had been my house, now every item needed sorting and repacking. Dear Jeannie drove up from Zurich on the hottest, most humid day to help. We didn't dwell on the reason, just kept busy. Anything electrical was excluded because I'd never afford enough transformers once in the UK. Dishes, cutlery, pictures and small treasures, antiques, photo-albums and books were all padded and wrapped in bed linens, towels and winter clothes, and re-boxed. Each item listed and carefully marked, taped and labelled to meet the required specifications of the shipping company. Unknown to me, Jeannie wrote little notes, slipping them in amongst the things she packed, tear-jerkers and smile-producers for me to discover when unpacking later on. What a blessing dear friends are.

The divorce judge had waived any alimony or child support, rendering me dependent on my portion of Matt's pension fund, and when the house sold, part of that too. On August 30th the first of the two promised cheques came. I was thankful, but still wondering how to manage. My seasonal allergies were bad, turning tiredness into exhaustion, so I went to bed soon after 9pm. Sleep eluded me and at 1.30am I was still awake. Not good. Work loomed again in a few short hours and the edges of panic were creeping in, so I prayed. I should have done it sooner. I heard His un-ignorable voice: I want to talk to you.

O Lord not now, You've just made me sleepy. Let's talk in the morning.

I want to talk to you. You wanted to talk to Me; now I want to talk to you. Get out of bed and listen to Me.

(Later my son asked if I heard that with my ears or in my head. I think it was both, but there was no mistaking it, and no doubt Who it was, so out I got onto my knees.)

OK Lord, here I am, too tired to think straight. I've got to pack, sell my car, figure out how to get home...

Sshh. I want to talk to you. Take a boat.

What? Oh Lord, You must be kidding me.

Take a boat.

Lord, You know me. I get sick on a dock. Don't make me go on a boat.

Take a boat.

It's too expensive.

The cheque arrived today.

It's selfish to spend it on me.

You need a rest.

My allergies are too bad.

There is no ragweed, nor air-pressure to hurt your ears, on boats.

What about my medication?

Go check. You have just enough left.

When do boats go? How long will it take?

My timing is perfect. It will be five days of peace and quiet for you to spend with Me, to relax and refresh you before starting again when you get there. Oh and one more thing: I want you to tell people what I've done for you.

Lord, You can't mean it. Isn't taking the boat bad enough? You know I'm dreadful at speaking to anyone about You. I stutter and mumble. Please don't ask me to do this.

And you can start with the ladies of Lakeland on Tuesday.

That was the Bible study group I attended but never felt worthy enough to mix with, as they were such super-spiritual types. I realised I'd simply have to do it. Not only go on Tuesday, but say something too. There wasn't much time to digest all that. It was soon 5am and the Millers were waking. The temptation to tell no one was strong, but I couldn't possibly go to work as if nothing had happened; and I didn't need a mirror to show the effects of the night. I rang to excuse my absence that day. Ann's early morning enthusiasm was a help. As I sipped coffee she was already arranging Tuesday's meeting. There was a strange unreality yet, at the same time vivid awareness of the absolute reality of the night's conversation. Hardly a case of wishful thinking nicely masked with a smug, 'Oh, God told me to,' when both boats and public speaking were abhorrent to me. Walking with Him, hand in hand, like Howard when I thought he was way over the top, using weird language for his relationship with Jesus – thanks again, Howard, for persisting. It's all true, and very wonderful. That night I was conversing with Almighty God, the Lord Jesus Christ, and I wasn't even very polite. It was a truly awesome experience.

By 8.55am I was at the door of the travel agency, without a clue what to say, feeling sure it wasn't usual to announce that God had ordered the journey. The agent of course was keen to arrange it all, telling me that the QE2 would sail from New York on September 15th and there still were a few berths available to Southampton, most surprising at the late date. I'd have time to take the Amtrak train overnight, Chicago to New York, stay with Doraine another night, and she'd take me to the docks on the 15th, arriving in Southampton on the 20th. The agent then told me about the share-program: the fare is halved if you're willing to share a cabin. My smile alerted her to snip, 'Same sex sharing only', to which I agreed, paying a small deposit. On the way back to Millers I fervently prayed for dead calm seas and no roommate, or if I had to share, then please no cigar-smoking, overly friendly type.

Ten days left. The huge truck arrived on schedule, reversing up the driveway to position the container doors nearest the garage. I'm forever grateful for all those friends who showed up to help load earthly possessions into the metal container perched on the flatbed truck. My stuff plus both children's childhoods neatly packaged. Ninety-one boxes in all. I could hardly speak that day. I stood alone in the empty driveway hearing his engine revving right down the street. My container was to join dozens of others on some enormous vessel crossing the Atlantic, then meet me in Lewes many weeks later. The couple who bought my car were happy to let me keep driving it till the last day. Such a help. The money went to the travel agent, as did the little bit I got from selling my rings. The sad part was confirming my diagnosis, made within a year of the wedding. I'd spotted a crack across my diamond very soon after Matt gave it to me, but didn't mention it for fear of reprisals, which came anyway. So when the jeweller told me it was worth almost nothing, I knew he was not trying to con me. I'll never know if Matt was duped into paying a lot, which he told me he did, for a poor quality stone, or if he knew perfectly well, thinking it would do for me. It took a long time before I could tell myself it doesn't matter anymore.

Tuesday came quickly but went extraordinarily slowly. The Lord was good to me, and so were the Lakeland ladies. Nearly ill with nervousness beforehand, I was conscious of Jesus providing strength way beyond my own capabilities, enabling me to walk to the microphone and use it to tell what He had done, and was doing. I did cry a bit, not near as much as I was afraid I would; and how incredible to see others dabbing at mascara'd lashes as more and more tissues were put to use. Those frighteningly holy women were with me, we were together in spirit. I was not up there in freakish isolation. Thank You, Lord for that unity which set such an example for the future. They were wonderfully supportive and kind and encouraging. They gave me a book which most of them had signed and written nice things in, but the title did cause me an inner groan or two: *The Pursuit of Holiness*. They would pick a book of that nature, something quite unattainable for ordinary people like me. Then I realised it's unattainable on my own strength, yes, but anything's possible with God. Before we parted those women prayed so beautifully for me, specifically that I would have the cabin to myself and that there'd be no storms as I crossed the ocean.

Garth came over late one afternoon and we had such a good time. We went to the movies and enjoyed vanilla malts before and after the film, and laughed a lot. The last days at work were fun too, as well as sad. Linda gave me a poem, possibly never realising how much it would be used. The poem is about Jesus teaching us to ride a tandem bicycle through life, allowing Him behind at first, then alongside, and eventually up front, steering and guiding. More hugs and tears on the last Sunday at church, and so many uplifting and lovely prayers. Last farewell phone calls to and from those I could not get to see, final hugs with those I could, then it was time to go. Parting is such sweet sorrow. Garth took time off to go with me on the train to Chicago, then cross-town to the Amtrak station, and I'm so very glad he did. That parting, accompanied by whistle shrieking, door slamming, and a kiss blown through a sealed window, remains in my heart.

At the docks Doraine and Jen took me to the embarkation point where they could go no further. We agreed that as I followed the crowd on board and found my cabin, they would go back outside, along the quayside, to wait till I appeared on the top deck. It took some time because the Queen is like a small city herself, very easy to get lost in, umpteen different decks with miles of walkways in between and stairs everywhere. It took ages to find my cabin – nobody else in it yet – then back up again. I was sure they'd have left, but there they were, two little miniatures way down below, looking up and waving madly. As we parted they thrust a package in my hands, containing, among other delights, a pair of boy's underpants, brand new, for me to wave, as they used an identical pair to wave to me. We certainly had no problem identifying each other. The reason went back about fifteen years to when Garth absent-mindedly used to wave his underwear around when he couldn't remember if he was supposed to be undressing or dressing. It was a great idea of Jen's and it sure helped turn tears to laughter.

Leaning on the railing looking down at them, I had to keep waving as long as they were willing to stand there, everyone shouting ribbons of words that mixed with all the others evaporating unheard in the breezes. The minutes seemed like hours until at last sirens and horns heralded departure, confirmed by slight juddering coming up through my feet and a weird sense of very slow movement. The great ship and I appeared to share an unwillingness to leave. Painfully, heart-wrenchingly slowly we dragged ourselves loose from secure moorings and began the eastward journey. My dear friends shrank to mere specks then vanished altogether, but I stayed, still leaning on that rail, watching Manhattan's vast skyscrapers also shrinking, down to Lego-land buildings until I could no longer see one from another. The Statue of Liberty smiled a sad farewell as we slid past her, and the shores she guards so faithfully became just part of the horizon.

Dear God, please, please keep this ship afloat the whole way to England, I am picturing Your hands underneath holding it up. Underneath are the everlasting arms. Please hang onto me too, and please Lord let me have the cabin alone, and I will try to behave myself with all these interesting-looking men I've already noticed all over the place, and not think (too much) about dancing under the stars with some of them.

I found my way back to my cabin in the lower quarters and there was no other luggage but mine – thank You, Lord. I couldn't decide if it was a good thing there was no porthole or not. Would I want to look out and see water, possibly very close? With plenty of time to explore before dinner, I went to make the most of it. Several times I nearly lost my balance, wondering at the strange feelings, apparently known as 'getting your sea legs.' Later, while queuing for dinner, I sensed my sea legs weren't coping well, nor the anti-motion-sickness skin patches. Seated at a round table with five others, I tried desperately to be charmingly sociable instead of nastily sick. Passing the menus around, chatting about food, smelling the sizzling, spicy selections, I happened to look up and saw the horizon at a different angle to the wide window. It was then that the man next to me said, 'Oh dear, you don't look well. Did you know the nurse is on duty and she can give you an injection? You may sleep a while, but you'll feel better.'

Leaving apologies beside my crisp linen napkin, I fled to the medical office. Situated in the very bowels of the ship, it was easy to locate due to at least twenty other greenish-faced fellow sufferers waiting outside the door. My ears were popping. Surely the ocean heaved just the other side of the wall. I half expected to see wet carpeting. That nurse was not gentle. Her vicious needlework propelled me upstairs and thankfully to bed.

Fourteen hours later I woke feeling absolutely fine and relieved to note there was still no one with me. *Thank You, Lord.* After a little sustenance came lots more exploring. What a place! A daily walk around one deck was good exercise, but if insufficient, there were two swimming pools, cricket nets, a mini-golf course, aerobics classes, and a variety of films to watch. There were also restaurants, bars and dance-floors on every deck, and enough shops to fill Woodfield Mall USA and Meadowhall UK. Down near the nurse's office I discovered the gym, with saunas, whirlpool hot tubs and massage rooms. I splurged on a full massage. Quite an experience, followed by an invitation from Pete to return at 8pm for more. Tempting, but dangerous. Day three encouraged laziness so I took my journal and found a quiet spot:

Here I am, sitting on Lido deck, just over half way across the Atlantic. Wow. It's foggy and I'm wrapped in a blanket like the old biddies around me. It is chilly but invigorating and the sea is calm. Not millpond flat but the swell is only tipping and rolling slightly, and I'm fine, not sick any more. Wonderful food always available but I can't eat nearly as much as I'd like. Have met and chatted with some nice people, over 70s mostly. As for the men, all these hunks everywhere, well, Lord, You sure do have a sense of humour. Yes, I admit, I was hoping for a fling, albeit a brief one, but You know me and took care of that temptation nicely, didn't You? Not one man has shown the slightest interest in me, and it didn't take long to figure out why: they're all too busy kissing each other. I've never seen so many males arm in arm, holding hands. I came across one pair behind a lifeboat this morning. It does make a girl feel unnecessary. Lord did You have to put me on this particular boat? Yeah, I guess You know what You're doing!

Thank You, Lord for this rest time, time to think, and to talk to You. You seem very close here, Lord, when there's nothing but sea and sky to look at. I do trust You because I know You keep Your promises and will never let me down. Lord, I don't want to let You down, but I'm scared I will. When I get to England please guide every step and show me clearly what to do, and please go on helping me control my old habits, and changing me so I want to do what You want me to do. Please lead me to a job and somewhere to live so I don't outstay my welcome with Alison, and Lord, I won't forget my promise to You – when I get a home it'll be Yours.

Our final full day, September 19th 1990, ended with another delicious dinner, after which I sampled the variety show as invited by my table companions. In hindsight I'm thankful, because being alone down in my cabin when the freak wave knocked us sideways would have been even more frightening. It was quite bad enough surrounded by many other passengers and staff all enjoying the musical entertainment and dancing, until everything started tipping.

Following instructions on the last morning we, the passengers, glad to be alive, assembled at the correct spot on each deck in preparation for disembarkation. Five days of living the (supposedly) high life in the lap of luxury concluded in an extremely long wait. With no fanfare whatsoever we processed out onto an insignificant gangplank, down onto very ordinary concrete, into a draughty shed, past an unmanned Customs signboard, out into a car park. Wandering around feeling very strange, I suddenly saw Jan, full of smiles, waving me over to her car. I was not exhilarating company, feeling oddly ill at ease, nowhere near brave enough to start another new life – just as on the very first page of this story. At Alison's house a big welcome meal was prepared, and everyone was sweet and kind. The spare room was ready for me, and Kate was well settled in the attic room above. I will never fault my sister's hospitality and eagerness to help, but there must have been times when she wondered what she'd let herself, and her family, in for by giving us houseroom. I tried so hard to fit in, determined to be supportive and understanding of Kate struggling similarly.

20

I walked all over Lewes looking for a job, into every shop, offering to work at anything legal. Discouragement abounded: 'Don't you know there's a recession on?' and 'I can't take on staff now, certainly not an American.' As advised, I applied for income support. Acceptance was slow, followed quickly by rejection, setting a pattern of frustrating delays and aggravation. I borrowed cash and bought into a small, failsafe business selling cosmetics, which promptly failed, but at least I met lots of nice people through it!

Weeks rolled on with no word from the shipping company, feeding the grim image of my container having fallen off the boat unnoticed, the ruined contents decorating beaches around the globe. On November 1st 1990 I wrote:

Still living out of suitcases in someone else's home – altogether eight months now – no job, no money, no home; very alone and very wobbly. Where are You, God? If this is a test I'm failing it; and I'm angry at You – there – I've said it. OK. I see: I've been trying to manage on my own, leaving You out. I'm sorry. Right, I'll go read Deuteronomy 8 again, and I won't be too busy to hear the next 'phone call' from You.

Finally an enormous truck arrived outside my sister's house. The swarthy driver heaved my life out of the container in far less time than it took us to fill it. Packing up our American life was so hard, but here it was, safe and dry: *Thank You, Lord.* We cleared out the garage and stacked it to capacity, then the playroom, hall and landing. It is one thing to give two relatives houseroom, but to accommodate their belongings as well is enough to try anyone's patience. We were excited and thankful to have our own stuff around in spite of having no place of our own yet to put it, or even space to unpack it.

Alison took me to the appropriate council offices to get on the housing list, but we received only a frosty glare from one whom we named 'Twinkletoes', who looked as if she'd never been free from the discomfort of large feet squashed into very dainty shoes. She shot questions at me without listening to the answers, announcing I had no points and no chance because I'd made myself voluntarily homeless by exiting the marital residence. Clearly she'd rather I'd stayed to get killed. Further hunting produced nothing but sore feet for me too, until suddenly, *thank You, God*, both home and job materialised. Both brought unimaginable problems, further frustrations with joyful times interspersed.

At the hospital I took the offered part-time auxiliary nursing post, not sure what it entailed, just thankful to get work. I wanted to avoid two moves, but still no money came from the settlement in America so I had to rent first. Very few unfurnished places were available, but there was one, and I tried to sign on the dotted line at once. Silly me, to think anything could be that simple. The unaffordable rent forced me to return to Twinkletoes in search, this time, of housing benefit and the answer was first yes, then no, then, much anxious waiting; later, yes again, naturally with the required red tape and form filling. Next came the lease, and while dealing with those papers, this conversation with the prospective landlord ensued:

'Ah, Americans.'

'No, I'm English. I've just lived there a while.'

'Why hasn't your husband signed these forms?'

'I haven't got a husband any more.'

'Ah. American, was he?'

'Yes. My daughter and I just want to sign the lease and move in.'

'Ah. Daughter's a teenager. We don't want no trouble, drugs and the like. I'll have to have her checked; you'll have to wait.'

It was infuriating, insulting, and impossible to get around. His concerns were understandable after previous student tenants wrecked the place, but the lengths he went to checking our credentials were incredible: passports, papers and driving licence; he rang the school for a character reference on Kate who'd only been there a few weeks; and the hospital for what little they knew about me; plus contacting my family and our new doctor.

My first nursing auxiliary day was just one shock after another. I tried not to think of the individual en suite rooms in American hospitals. So grateful to have a job, I tried not to be critical. I was told to shadow Ann and learn how things were done on the ward. We gathered the first patient and her toiletries into the room with the hoist bath, then Ann went, leaving me to undress and wash the patient. That one looked as if any breath might be her last. I'd been told she was unable to see or hear much, and I prayed quickly she'd be unaware of my fumbling efforts. Somehow I got her into the tub, relieved that she still seemed alive. I've always been completely comfortable around babies so I coped by thinking of her as a rather large, ungainly infant. Each day going to work my heart sank and my feet dragged up the hospital driveway.

Once finances were sorted, and Kate and I sufficiently vetted, the lease was signed, we got the keys, and on December 15th we moved in. *Thank You, Lord.* We got a little potted live Christmas tree, and found the box of those gingerbread-men and Santas. The fridge fitted, but with no cooker, we ate lots of sandwiches – as in Deuteronomy 8: 'a land where you will eat bread without scarcity'. *Well, we're next door to a bakery, and they sell day-old bread at half price. Thank You, Lord.* Mother came to stay a couple of days and bought us a couch, two chairs and a single bed since my bed didn't fit up the stairs.

Shortly before leaving Alison's home her phone rang at 2am. It was my second ex, well aware of the time, telling me my first ex had died of a heart attack. My annoyance at him for deliberately waking the household with news that could have waited soon turned to guilt over lack of sadness, though I did feel sorry for poor Florida Grandma.

Kate and I were thrilled with our new home, but there still were plenty of black days. London hospitals were put on alert, ready for Gulf War casualties. I agonised over Garth, and kept praying for him, then feeling guilty for not praying enough. It got so bad I could only weep instead of praying. I missed him dreadfully, wondering constantly if he was all right. *Lord,* please *keep him safe.* A new friend, Prilla, was particularly helpful and understanding, having three teenage sons herself. She thoughtfully offered to pray daily for Garth for a while.

Oh Lord, it's so easy to wallow in the old feelings of anger and hurt, plus worry about Garth. I do want to go Your way, but WHY is it so d... difficult? I want to trust You completely, in everything, so why do I mess up so often? I am sorry. When I ask and You answer, I still find myself doubting — it could be just a coincidence — how can I be sure? You've given me good friends when I was scared I'd never find friends like those I had to leave behind. My precious son — Lord how I hated leaving him too — Oh God please watch over Garth, keep him close to You; let him be that one sheep that You'd delay the other ninety-nine for while You go hunt for him; treasure him Lord, and hold him in the palm of Your hand.

On my next day's Bible reading notes was a sub-heading: 'Pray for teenagers: God has long ropes; sometimes our teens' pilgrimages will take them far away, but we must set them free to go if they are to be free to return.' Yes, indeed.

21

In March we went on a church weekend to Ashburnham, near Battle, a peaceful place in beautiful gardens. We learned a lot and I enjoyed the talks. I believe that the phrase 'all I can do is pray' should not be used; prayer is the most effective tool at my disposal, the most important way of helping others and myself in every situation. Pondering the enormity of the crucifixion, I read where Jesus said His soul was overwhelmed with sadness. That brought alive to me His real ability to understand, and His willingness to join with us in our phases of sadness.

My birthday celebrations lasted over a week, and they were wonderful. Lots of post from both sides of the Atlantic, and phone calls too; the first being at 4.09am from Ev shortly followed by Garth's dear voice at 6am: 'Happy Birthday, Mom: see, I didn't forget.' Kate had festooned the kitchen with paper streamers and balloons, and fixed breakfast, and written me a very special letter. Inundated with visitors, both family and friends, bringing treats and treasures, I loved every minute. Some of Kate's friends popped in with cards and hugs in their lunch break, then more after school. Palm Sunday was marked by a lovely visit from Jonny, Miriam and family who brought champagne to celebrate my birthday, the new home and our return to England. A month or so later I wrote:

There is much to thank You for, Lord. Warm sunshine today, and such contentment here, even in the simplest things, having family around, and dear friends. Last Sunday's phone call to Garth for his twentieth birthday was so good, and he was awake and just going off to Willow Creek church. Oh God, bless him and keep him safe. Thank you for young Daniel's total immersion baptism service and for Songs of Praise featuring the new Archbishop of Canterbury, George Carey, who sounds good. Lord, that Celebration evening at the college – Steve Chalke spoke excellently. He said You not only died on the cross to save me from eternal death, but to save – release – me from all the damaging things done to me, and from my stupidity, and from the dreadful years of hurt and unjust awfulness to me and to my kids, specially the pain of Garth's UK incident. Oh Lord, You do care, don't You. You do know and understand what it's been like, don't You. You don't doubt my words, or say it's just my hormones. Oh Lord, You did die for all that stuff to be lifted off me. Thank You so much.

It was cold, wet and windy for weeks. I longed for sunshine. I also longed for fewer headaches and more cash. Yes, sometimes I longed for sex. God was keen to sort that one out too. Every time my yearnings threatened insistently I prayed, reminding Jesus I'd given everything into His control on May 20th 1988, and that He'd have to help as on my own I'd be in trouble very quickly. He did, help, every time. Usually by ensuring I was so physically tired there was no spare energy for sexual thoughts, never mind activity, but more than that, by filling my mind with His love for me, so totally satisfying – and I do mean totally.

Another prayer was answered one morning as I walked to the shops, worried about finances. *Lord, please, how can I make more money?* Stopping at the notices in the newsagent's window I saw items for sale and situations vacant. One wanting domestic help announced 'no children, no pets, not too much mess', which amused me as I walked on. Suddenly I stopped, clearly hearing: *I just showed you something and you went right past it.* I went back to the newsagent's notice and wrote down the number as a battle raged in me. That's being somebody's cleaning woman – I don't want to do that – my, how the mighty are fallen. *Lord, do I have to do this?* To which I felt Him smile and remind me of Who is in charge, and to trust Him. I rang the number and arranged an interview, asking the speaker her name and hearing in crisp tone, 'Lady S'. I found her in the sunroom at the back of her elegant house, and we liked each other at once. Terms and conditions were agreed and I started the next week, two hours a day, three days a week, depending on my shifts at the hospital. There began not only a job, but a friendship which continued to be mutually beneficial for years.

My nightmares and some desperate calls from Garth resulted in me raiding my paltry savings to send him a ticket, and he came for three turbulent weeks in June. We had some great times together, and good talks, but oh how hard to feel your own son almost a stranger. His excessive drinking and smoking was dreadful. Honest and open as ever, we talked of spiritual matters, paternal likenesses, and cheque scams. He said Christianity is too restrictive and he wants to have fun. *Lord, You protected me all those years I ignored You, please do the same for my son.* We charity-shopped, showing him the bargains to be had, and he wore his 'new' grey jacket daily. He got on well with Kate's boyfriend, enjoying a day on his farm. How I love the photo of my boy in borrowed wellies, cloth cap and shepherd's crook. We were all intrigued with the antiquity of a flat for sale, and I knew I could fix it up, but the survey showed massive decay and structural damage. *Lord keep me trusting You, not only for G's welfare, but where K and I will live when the lease is up on our flat. Lord, about this divorce settlement money – when will it be here? I'm sorry for being impatient but it does feel desperate some days – yes, I will remember 'be anxious for nothing.'*

A plea was made in church for a family to accept a sixteen-year old Eritrean girl for a month who would pay for her keep. Kate and I reckoned we constituted a good enough family, and she could sleep on the foldaway bed in Kate's room, as Garth had done, and yes, the money would help. So Ergaalem arrived, bringing a lot of history and beauty from her culture as well as a lot of very normal teenage behaviour!

It was deeply interesting and moving to hear her speak of the troubles in her country, and to listen to her amazing singing, sometimes putting herself into a semi-trance. Her music was unwritten, handed down the generations, pouring out verbal traditions, histories of wars and famines, bereavements and loves, in a strangely tuneless yet musical manner. One day when suffering bad stomach cramps, she fixed a remedy for herself that her mother always offered, a mug of warm milk with a lot of salt stirred in. Copied, she said, from the ancient remedy of bloodletting cattle for a healthy tonic.

My dear Dutch friend Trudi came to England with her young son, and wanted to stay a few days after Erga left. Her widowhood was hanging heavily on brave shoulders. I think we were able to cheer each other up.

The on-going house hunting took most of my free hours although the money issues remained unsettled. Was my ex-husband deliberately stalling, even actively not selling 'our' house? Or maybe he had sold it and managed to prevent me getting my share of the proceeds. My attention was drawn to Psalm 65, all of which is comforting but especially verse 4: *We are filled with the good things of Your house.* We had many good things, but oh, so many bad things too: frustrations, delays, hold-ups, cancellations, the lonely heartache of missing American family, friends and lifestyle.

Yes, Lord, I am satisfied with the goodness of Your house, but still aching for so much. July 29th: one year ago today we left the States. I picked the neighbour's roses growing over our wall and gave them to Kate with a letter of congratulations and thanks for adapting so well. Thank You, God, for my lovely daughter, and for keeping us both mostly sane this year; for the sun drying our laundry outside on the line; for the freedom to walk up on the Downs whenever, enjoying fantastic views all round. Lord, I've put an offer on Hope Cottage – scary but exciting – if it's right I trust You to help us proceed.

The agent drove me to see several houses each time we went, any of which would do, but none grabbed me. If within price range they were

certainly small, some just plain pokey, some with staircases so narrow
I knew my American furniture would not fit. Some had no garden or
yard, two had stunning views but one bedroom, and so on. Sensing I'd
had enough that one day, the agent suggested we omit the last on his
list, saying it was derelict and I wouldn't want it. That made me curious
so we drove past just to look. The narrow street was full of tightly
parked cars, overshadowed by a high concrete wall, and very close to
the prison. Glancing up I saw a stone plaque set above the door, with
writing so weathered it was barely readable. Announcing proudly that
the little end-of-terrace home was 'Hope Cottage 1881', I stood
rooted, quietly stating what I knew to be the truth, and a Bible verse:
'My hope is in the Lord.' Yes, this must be the place. The mystified
agent asked what I'd said but still gave me strange looks. He was right;
it was derelict, dark, dank and dismal. It had character and a charm
that refused to be hidden. I saw how it could look, how both the tiny
house and garden could be brought to life again, restored, loved back
into healthy, happy use. It began to feel personal – just as I had found
hope for my own renewal and repair, knowing it would be a long, slow
process, now I'd found a house needing the same – *Lord, with Your
help, I can do it.*

*Lord, it can't be wrong to be so sure of something while still praying 'if it be
Thy will', can it? Thank You for that bank teller explaining improvement
grants for properties over 100 years old. It looks like I can get a mortgage
and income support and the grant, but it's so scary and I don't know what
I'm doing, or ought to do next. I am sorry for moaning; I know Your timing
is perfect and You are in control, but Lord it's all taking so long and I'm so
tired. Please continue reminding me I've prayed to be and do only what You
want – especially when I can't see what that is. Were those three months
living with my sister a lesson in patience as well as invaluable shelter when
we had none? It seemed so wrong to rent at first, and there is still four
months left of the lease. Mr and Mrs Elchak need to sell and want
Christians to buy their house, and now at last the money has come from*

America – Thank You. – it all seems so right, but where is the mortgage/sale document? Why another delay? Are You testing me some more? I know You don't play games and wouldn't bring us this close, dangle this under my nose then whip it away – Lord, I love and trust You – please help me hang on.

My heart was made heavier by the death of a very special patient on my ward. I'd become very fond of Elsie during her final weeks, and the last evening shift when we knew she would soon slip away was terribly sad. None of us wanted to leave. When I was interviewed for the nursing job, one questions had been, 'Can you handle death?' How do you know until you have to? Death is absolutely part of life. One good thing to come out of Elsie's death was her wonderful funeral at the Baptist church, where I was made so welcome, and Kate and I started attending there regularly.

I spent an hour talking with Mr Elchak from whom I was trying to buy Hope Cottage. It's probably safe to say that no other house can ever have changed hands under such unusual circumstances. It was on the market for £59,950 and, remembering what I'd learned bargaining for small antiques and collectibles, I offered £45,000 – laughingly low, but believing the necessary manoeuvring would keep the house within my range. I was extremely nervous, and found him to be even more frightening than I'd imagined as I laid all my cards, such as they were, on his table, waiting for him to show me the door. He did not go back on his acceptance of my very slightly raised offer, though still far lower than he wanted. He and his wife were kindly willing to wait however long it took to organise the American finances, sure that God would sort it. Philippians 4:19 was alive in my head: 'And my God will meet all your needs according to His glorious riches in Christ Jesus.'

Two other jobs I'd applied for turned me down: the lesson in humility was clear. I had to eat humble pie, and apologise to Jesus for arrogance. My return visit to the council offices was dismal. That day cigarette smoke created a foul haze through which a pallid toddler screamed incessantly. My patience dwindled with each tick of the clock. Anger took over when I saw an unfamiliar face at the glassed-in desk, meaning I'd have to repeat my story yet again. Feeling I could soon murder the child, or better, its mother, I begged the Lord to step in and do something. He did. Getting quickly to the front of the queue I received a smiley greeting: 'Oh, you're a Christian too. (there was a tiny gold fish on my collar) So am I.' Instantly my ire melted and I was able to be calm and patient, and remember what I was there to do. The DSS will now pay the mortgage interest. *Thank You, God.* The long, uphill walk back to the flat couldn't stop my heart smiling.

On September 20th I wrote:

Today is Dexter's birthday. Thinking about men in his category – sorry Lord but I do get lonesome – what did I read this morning but Your promise in John 14:16 to give me another Counsellor, one who'll stay forever. What a timely reminder – thank You, Lord. It must be You who keeps my belief and trust alive, as I honestly can't claim any great efforts to do so, specially as things are pretty black again. I'm so tired. Thank You for protecting that spark and gently fanning it, even when I do nothing to help. I'm gratefully amazed You haven't given up on me, and that You still answer prayer – like last week when we thought the Monday group had died yet seventeen kids showed up. As I walked past Hope Cottage (will I ever be able to call it our house?) the other day there was the surveyor busy surveying, so things are moving. Later an open-air service seemed to feature divorce and the divorced as if we're some wretched breed apart, and I got pretty steamed, but Prilla and Richard, sitting next to me, sensed it and he put his arm round me. So many blessings from You, and I'm being such a poop. Sorry, Lord.

Right after that entry, when I was struggling to smile a bit more, there came a bad call from Garth, in trouble again. Trying to be firm yet gentle and agreeing with James Dobson's ideas of tough love does not make it any easier to administer from far way:

207

O God, he's my child, heart of my heart: I ache and long to straighten out all his troubles but I know even if I could I mustn't; he's got to learn to handle them himself. The agonies of guilt sometimes suffocate me: if I'd not divorced, Garth could be in college now; if I'd not abandoned him over there maybe he wouldn't be in this mess now; if I'd not come here then Kate wouldn't have had to uproot. God I'm sinking into a black pit of 'what ifs'. There I would've stayed if You hadn't sent an angel in human form to come and pray most earnestly for me and my children. It was such intense prayer I felt like an intruder at an intimate conversation between You and her. Amazing! You were right there in the room with us, Lord, and I could only weep.

The next blow was the surveyor's chilling report stating far too much work needed to be done at too great an expense, that there was no hope for Hope Cottage, and strongly suggesting that I proceed no further. A pity, as the day before I had arranged with the builders that they should start the following week. I'm quite certain the Lord's perfect timing arranged all that so when the surveyor's report came it would only feel like another setback, not a mortal wound. I'd just read 2nd Chronicles 20 and knew I trusted God to fight for me. However, another migraine wiped out the next several days. I am not good at pain. I feel miserably, pathetically alone, and all God's wonderful promises are fine for other people but they don't reach me: *I need Your help with this, Lord.*

Instead, Kate and I had a fight. She hated it when I was ill (not as much as I hated it) and this time we'd been going somewhere and I'd had to back out. We sorted ourselves, exchanging lots of apologies, and she went off happily. When I got back to bed there was a note under my pillow: 'You are a fantastic mum and I love you.'

Lord that note was such a gift, such an unexpected delight; it showed me how You must feel when one of Your children praises You. So I did, and it was joyful. Lying there singing away, knowing it was pleasing You and realising it was making me better, physically as well as spiritually – thank You, Lord.

Walking past 'my' house was elation cloaked in uncertainty and anxiety wrapped in trust. The day the agent finally replaced the For Sale sign with a Sale Agreed sign was a happy one. I stared, pinching myself as a neighbour came by saying, 'I've been watching for this. Someone must be very pleased now,' at which I burst out, 'Yes, it's me. As it isn't completely sorted yet, I'm trying not to get too excited.' She introduced herself and her small white dog, and another friendship was born. Dealing with plumbers, electricians, builders, lawyers, and carpenters; getting estimates, and juggling huge amounts of money on paper was very scary and nerve-wracking, especially when my incoming salary cheque was small enough to need a magnifying glass to see it. Securing the mortgage seemed impossible without the promised help from the DSS, whose vital letter still had not appeared. Returning to the hallowed halls of the legal people, gliding up wide, curving stairs into tastefully decorated offices, I signed terribly important papers with a golden pen and a reverent air. But those papers were no more important than the ones thrust at me under the protective glass at the social security office. 'Except the Lord builds the house, those who build it labour in vain,' keep repeating in my thoughts. Still there was no certainty of the renovation grant, without which I couldn't afford a can of paint, never mind a new roof.

Christmas came and went, with much fun and luxury at David and Jan's house.

They are so generous and sweet, Lord. I want this season always to be real in my heart, not just a few days in mid-winter. Today is the anniversary of my marriage to Kurt: what memories and legacies I have from that union. I was glad to hear his ashes were sprinkled somewhere in the Shenandoah Valley; he'd have liked that. Good stuff's been happening and I thank You, Lord. Thank You for continuing to put up with me and my mercurial moods — throughout which You remain my rock, my constant, my anchor. Jesus Christ, the same yesterday, today and forever. You are literally raining blessings down on us and it's so exciting and amazing and humbling all at the same time. Can I write Hope Cottage is ours — Yours, mine and Kate's? My hand is shaking — the mortgage is signed and sealed, and the insurance and the renovation grant contracts promised.

22

In the Daily Bible Reading Notes, January 14th 1992 was an interesting title: 'Hope Restored', so I cut it out and pinned it on the hallway wall of Hope Cottage. There it stayed throughout the restoration, getting daily more tattered and torn. It announced to builders, the council inspector and everyone who bothered to look that 'the Lord upholds all who fall, and raises up all who are bowed down... those who believe in Jesus have every reason to hope; no one is hopeless whose hope is in God' (Psalm 145).

Two more promised dates come and gone, with nothing. Preparing to blast angry frustration down the phone, I found a crumpled paper in my pocket on which I'd written ages ago: 'trust in the Lord and lean not unto your own understanding,' so I did, said nothing, and now suddenly, the grant is approved. Paid the builder his first instalment. Nearly six months waiting and now things can get going, thank You, Lord. I've never owned a home; it's so scary and exciting. Work at the hospital is slightly less awful, which helps. Lord, I've met a lovely man and keep bumping into him in the town – he is married – it's fun to dream but oh, God, keep me walking so close to You that I never stray down that path again. In fact, Lord, please help me to stop even thinking of him: it's too dangerous.

Every spare hour when not at work was spent in the house, scraping off old glue and carpet backing, stripping layers of old dark green paint. As I worked I pondered the house's history and those who lived in it. With the living room floor up for joist repair, I poked about in the cobwebby crawlspace and discovered a leather boot, feminine and slim, and a china doll head dated 1909. How I'd love to know their stories.

Victorian wallpaper with roses still pink was revealed behind the cupboard.

It's so wonderful, but Lord I'm so tired, remind me to pace myself, and get my priorities right and never let anything, even Hope Cottage, come ahead of You in my life. Please help me too, to be a better pray-er; either I fall asleep or my mind drifts off on umpteen other tangents, which must seem so rude to You.

Kate had her first driving lesson on her seventeenth birthday. We pushed forward on blind faith there too. In spite of the expense I was sure it was right for her to learn. We were trusting God to provide a car if we were meant to have one. We met our soon-to-be immediate neighbours, and some others further down the street, all welcoming, friendly and helpful. At work in early March, while lifting with four colleagues a grossly obese patient, I damaged my back, requiring more time off. For the first few horrible days all I could do was sit still, with a heatpad. Enforced rest, though obviously necessary, was so difficult because we only had six weeks left on the lease and would have to move then whether Hope Cottage was habitable or not.

Walking along 'my' street again, I saw a scaffolding truck blocking traffic. Two young lads were speedily erecting a skeletal frame around 'my' house for the roofers the following day. That roofing team worked – and whistled – well, retiling the house and outside loo and shed in one continuous, neat watertight covering. Through many rainstorms I thanked God for their workmanship. They agreed to leave the scaffolding up one more day for me to climb up and paint below the guttering and the outside window frames, impossible to reach from inside. Up there I leaned out over the front door to delineate the stone plaque, only just able to stretch far enough with a long paintbrush. That had to be done with eyes nearly shut for fear of seeing how far there was to fall.

March 24ᵗʰ: Good morning, Lord. Thank you for the wonderful birdsong and sunshine today. Why do my emotions get in the way of facts? I know You love me and have forgiven me and will steadfastly continue so to do, yet on days like yesterday I can only think how fed up You must be with me. Thanks for Your patient reassurances. Last night I was done in, aching with tiredness, back still sore, and fearful of all the bills, then I read in Hebrews '... keep your mind free from the love of money... be content with what you have... for God hath said He will never fail you or forsake you...' and now the other promised cheques are in, so I can buy a microwave, and pay for the carpeting. Thank you, Lord God. Before leaving for school Kate set out a lovely birthday breakfast with flowers and the week's horded mail. Later D and J arrived bringing Arthur's (J's dad) old Triumph Acclaim for us to drive for a couple of years. Lord. I will acclaim all Your triumphs. Thank You so much.

Friends from church came round to help strip paint, sand, refinish, or repaint. I was encouraged and cheered with so much assistance. I had to force myself to take time out, to sit quietly, even for five minutes here and there to remind myself Who is in charge, and stay in close contact with Him.

The final verses of Zephaniah 3 became favourite reading. What wonderfulness, what peace within the turmoil. That illusive peace I'd been hankering after for so long, merely the lack of stress and trauma, pales when compared to the peace I discovered on May 20ᵗʰ 1988. The peace Jesus Christ offers isn't illusory at all, it's the only real, lasting peace there is: peace and joy come not with the absence of trials but with the presence of God.

It was exquisitely wonderful to move in to Hope Cottage at long last.

April 11ᵗʰ: Oh Lord. How majestic is Your Name. We're in, and so tired and happy. So many friends came to help, some in the flat to load and some in the house to unload, that it was all done in two hours. You provided perfect weather for our picnic in the junk yard that will be a garden. Sue made up our beds before she left, then we went along to see my new friend, the owner of the white dog, who asked us to supper. So many blessings and kindnesses: Thank You, Lord. 'As for me and my house, we will serve the Lord.' Yes, indeed, Heavenly Father, please bless this house and bless us in it. Please keep complaints, jealousy, gossip and greed away, but draw people here and let it be a haven of peace for all who enter. We are rich because of what we have in Jesus Christ, not what we have in the bank.

April 20ᵗʰ: On the 16ᵗʰ, Lord, it was Maundy Thursday and I thought how You must have felt so vile, waiting, knowing what was ahead for You. Thank you, Jesus for going on with the agony and shame of that unimaginably awful death You died for me – without You there'd be no light to lead us out of the darkness. No amount of thanks is enough, let me live out my thankfulness. Now we rejoice the world over; Christ is risen. Yesterday was lovely. Kate and I were welcomed into Baptist membership during the morning service, and given Isaiah 43:18, 19: 'Forget the former things, do not dwell on the past. See, I am doing a new thing! Now it springs up; do you not perceive it?' We feasted on tacos for Easter Sunday lunch in our new home, then went to Alison and Chris for tea. Happy twenty-first birthday, Garth. My son is twenty-one on the twenty-first and I cannot hug him. I hate separations. Lord, I ache and yearn over that boy so deeply, please continue protecting him.

Coping daily with settling, unpacking, and rearranging, as well as school studies and exams, my nursing plus cleaning for Lady S., making curtains, and gardening, was very tiring indeed, but most days fine. Fairly often I sank into seething anger at Matt for getting a far greater proportion of the divorce settlement, in direct opposition to the judge's initial decree. The only way for me to fight that was to return to America and drag him back to court, something he knew I'd not do. What I got was just enough for the Hope Cottage down payment, and for that I'll always be grateful. Even more so for the infinite patience and steadfast love of Jesus helping lift my eyes innumerable times from the depths back up to His face. It's never easy being a Christian, but always rewarding. After one awful day I scribbled across a page: *Please Lord, over-rule my anxieties* – and the next day's suggested reading notes proclaimed this verse: 'Thou wilt keep him in perfect peace whose mind is stayed on Thee'. *What an answer: thanks, Lord.*

I was gradually learning that the more baggage from the past I could let go of the more room that allowed for the Holy Spirit. I was also learning that God's Holy Spirit has a lot more to Him than I'd ever heard or imagined. By then I was quite comfortable and familiar with two out of the three members of the Trinity, God my Heavenly Father, and His Son Jesus my Saviour and Lord. It was exciting to realise just how much more there was to discover. Two verses given by American friends kept coming up, reminding me of the Lord's challenge. There was Joshua 1:5,6 AMP: '…As I was with Moses, so I will be with you: I will not fail you or forsake you. Be strong and of good courage.' And Mark 5:19 RSV: 'Go home to your friends, and tell them how much the Lord has done for you…' Also, a chorus kept popping into my mind, as a catchy tune often does, but these words could not be sung unless meant: 'Lord prepare me to be a sanctuary, pure and holy, tried and true; with thanksgiving I'll be a living sanctuary for You.' Although it felt scary I truly meant it; but I'd done the scariest bit already, coming back to England. That's a risky line to take; God often has something far scarier up His sleeve. From then on most journal entries had something such as: *Lord, I'm sure You are preparing me for something. I want to be willing and ready. Is it talking to people casually, or writing, or speaking publicly?*

Kate and I missed having a dog so went in search of potential adoptees. Before you could say Jack Russell, Kia jumped in the car with us going home. For the first few days she appeared to be desperately awaiting her former owner, who, we'd been told, had had to move into a nursing home. We loved her to bits and did all we could to ease her transition, and were well repaid with loyal adoration for

215

many years. What a treat to have a dog well trained by someone else. Just occasionally I called her a pest, when she barked suddenly without cause, when the floor was covered in hair, and when rabbit obsession got the better of her. Mostly she was wonderful and we told her so often. Wasn't it good of the Lord to select Hope Cottage for us from the thousands of little homes locally, for not only was it two minutes from my job, but in less than five minutes we could be up on the Downs with the freedom to walk miles. Kia and I spent many happy hours up there in all weathers.

Kate started the autumn term at a tertiary college for A level studies, and I too enrolled for a one day a week AMSPAR course for medical receptionists. Having done that work in Chicago and loved it, it was hard to accept I could not do it here without a piece of paper pronouncing me capable. So I set about procuring the qualification, determined to do better than my previous college attempt, and not be an embarrassment to my daughter if we met between classes. The hospital did allow me every Friday off but I continued my twenty hours a week, plus the three housekeeping sessions for Lady S, plus studying. Very tiring; but some nights I still craved male companionship. As long as I remembered to talk to Jesus about it it was all right. *Lord, help, You know what I want, what I miss so much. Please remind me how much You love me and that I can trust You completely, Lord, without You I'd be lost, and back into so many disasters.* Invariably after praying like that, the next thing I knew it was morning. I found a helpful prayer in a magazine and copied it into my journal:

Lord with You there is
Joy without guilt, freedom without fear,
Satisfaction without sordidness,
Purpose without confusion, friendship without compromise,
Forgiveness without penance and fulfilment without frustration.

November brought a wretched three-day migraine with different, worse pain going right through my chest. Tests, an ambulance to Brighton hospital, many more tests prodding and poking through that crushing pain: pancreatitis again. People were so kind but it was good to get home. Physically, a bleak time; emotionally also as the two are hard to separate, and together they tend to overpower. Therefore it is due to God's grace – and I said I would acclaim His triumphs – that I survived, able and willing to sing His praises. Not singing all the time. There was considerable blackness, along with: *This is so unfair, I can't take anymore; I hate hurting. God where are You?* No sense of being a 'good Christian' at all, but wallowing in miserable self-pity and anxiety. Yet at the end of the month this came out of my heart via my pen:

Oh my Father what a lot I've seen of You and learned in the last few weeks. Please forgive my stupid doubts and fears; the ease with which I move away from You, then wonder where You are. I have met You face to face in others recently, heard You speak, seen clear glimpses of what it's like to be close to You, sort of in a higher place than usual. So amazing to be able to see through the bad stuff sometimes while still in it, out the other side, see You beckoning, leading, guiding and calming. Your timing is perfect, and leaves me humbled, grateful, amazed. You have filled me with such peace and calm assurance that You are in control at all times; I don't have to understand Your reasons and plans, just trust and follow. I feel so blessed. Please keep this vision of how You work always in front of me, so even in dark times I'll remember this inner rejoicing.

Great good came out of that bad time, as God promises, but as we can't see till afterwards. Garth rang to tell me he was doing better, had a new address, new girlfriend and new job. The paperwork for my family credit benefit was finally processed, granting me a little more help each week. Thankful for every penny especially as it meant I could give up the cleaning job. Lady S urged me to continue visiting now and then as we had become firm friends, but it was so nice to be released from the drudgery. Somehow there was always just enough money; often I was counting out the last coins for one more meal when an invitation came to share someone else's. There was never extra, and we did have to live very frugally, but that's manageable. Several times an anonymous cash gift arrived of the exact amount needed to pay a bill or buy a necessity. 'And my God shall supply' – *that's pretty amazing Lord, thank you.*

Two people who came to see me while I was in hospital were Pastor T and Kath, angels again in human form, of that I'm quite sure. We talked a great deal and they invited me to their Eastbourne ministry centre. Nervousness threatened to head the car away but prayer got me to ring the doorbell. Almost at once I felt comfortable, soon realising the initial chitchat was drawing things out of me I'd thought I could not speak of. They talked as much to Jesus as to me. It was a safe place to let go, to stop having to cope and be brave and strong. It wasn't just me dumping on them, then feeling better; they were the facilitators enabling me to let out a lot of the blackness of rejection locked deep inside, and give it to Jesus, asking His forgiveness for my part in the mess. I apologised to God and asked His forgiveness for mucking about with the occult. When first challenged on that subject of course I said no… then I remembered… years ago in New York we did play with a Ouija board for fun; I allowed myself to be hypnotised a couple of times to see what that was about, and I used to read my stars in magazines. For a while I was quite interested in subliminal messages, reading books full of channelling and self-fulfilment and similar 'new age' ideas so easily inculcated. It was a shock to learn that all those 'harmless' occupations are in fact an abomination to God, detestable in His sight, provoking Him to anger as in Deuteronomy18 and Leviticus 20.

Later, in the privacy of home, I asked the Lord to help with listing each of the men I have been with. Could I not do it out of shame or because not remembering was safer? Remembering would make me want, and in some cases, fear, again. Having sex with someone outside of marriage, even only once, whether it's terrific or forced, carries consequences. How I wish I'd known this earlier. I did know that nice girls shouldn't, but nobody ever said why not. Two become one in more than just a physical way; there is long-term emotional bondage, usually negative, because God designed His great wedding gift of good sex between one man and one woman within their marriage for long-term positive emotional bonding. Illicit bed hopping simply cannot be shrugged off; it is unhealthily dangerous in every way. Writing each name I prayed for them and for me to be forgiven and then for the will to forgive, thereby releasing us from one another and cutting any remaining emotional or spiritual bonds. It is hardest to forgive yourself and accept God's forgiveness. Then I burned the paper. Guilty but now redeemed.

More stones, more layers, so I ventured back a second time. Then more weights such as anger, grief, fear, remorse and humiliation were let go of and handed over. I felt spring-cleaned, scrubbed of the blackness, free of cumbersome baggage, making room for the Holy Spirit: 'Fill my cup, Lord, fill it up and make me whole.' Then Pastor T surprised me by quietly apologising to me on behalf of all men who have in any way used or abused me. A wonderful gift, then followed by a lovely hug. Words of a well-known Wesley hymn suddenly took on new reality:

O for a thousand tongues to sing my great Redeemer's praise!
The glories of my God and King, the triumphs of His grace.
Jesus the name that calms our fears, that bids our sorrows cease,
'Tis music to the sinner's ears, 'tis life and health and peace,
He breaks the power of cancelled sin, He sets the prisoner free.
His blood can make the foulest clean, His blood availed for me.
My gracious Master and my God, assist me to proclaim,
To spread through all the earth abroad the honours of Thy Name.

As I came across more of God's promises in the Bible I was also experiencing them, particularly seeing good come from bad situations, as in Isaiah 45:3: 'I will give you the treasures of darkness... that you may know that I am the Lord,' and more good news for me in Isaiah 61 about comfort, freedom and release from darkness. Then from verse 3NAS... giving them a garland instead of ashes, the oil of gladness instead of mourning, the mantle of praise instead of a spirit of fainting. So they will be called oaks of righteousness, the planting of the Lord, that He may be glorified.

Over the years I'd built up a fairly strong pile of evidence that all men are liars. Then I found those very words in Psalm 116:11. I was learning not to take just bits here and there to suit, because out of context the meaning can be very different, so I read again the whole psalm. I read, '...And in my dismay I said all men are liars.' Then on to verse 16 to read: 'I am Your servant... You have freed me from my chains.' This showed me that yes, many men (i.e. mankind), and women, are liars, but I cannot dislike men because I've known a few rotters and been disillusioned and let down by several more. Yet it has to be said that I did find nursing men of any description extremely difficult. Each one stirred up huge emotions I had to struggle with while doing my best to be charitable and caring, remembering that not one of them personally was anything to do with my past. That was some of the 'stones' in the heavy backpack I'd let go of. Having experienced God's freedom it was up to me not to go picking up and shouldering that weight again. Some days this was easier said than done.

The college course included six months of work experience which needed interviews, funding, phone calls and schedules to be arranged. The local GP surgery agreed to show me the ropes as I attempted to fit in while learning about patient-doctor-staff interactions. I couldn't possibly pay for the course, and right after the work experience was set up it looked as if I'd have to cancel. At the last minute I met a wonderful person who provided a bursary so I could proceed. Yet again I was seeing the truth of God's word. He promises never to fail me, and to supply all my needs. I was also learning the difference between my idea of my needs and God's idea of my needs. There were still black days then too. I seemed to be always tired with too much to fit into each day. Knowing that eventually I'll be able to look back and see God's plan unfolding, bringing good out of bad, does help.

23

Early in 1993 I spotted this descriptive paragraph in a magazine: 'Jesus was chipping away, preparing me by smoothing my rough edges, like the potter at his wheel. He has to smash down the clay when necessary to repair cracks and other damage, to remove air bubbles and impurities, continually re-starting and re-shaping for improved use.' Flashback to my childhood, using modelling clay to make sculptures, and realising it's what Jesus is doing to me. Does it have to hurt so much, or be such hard work?

When not at my job, and not in pain, I was fine, singing even, sometimes, but pain nearly destroyed me. Mostly it was the crushing, breath-stopping, inescapable pancreas pain. When that was stabbing at me I could think of nothing else. I didn't stop believing or loving God, nor did I blame Him. All I could do was roll about moaning to Him to take it away. On January 27th it took me back to Brighton hospital for three days of tests that lasted instead for five days, then a further three locally to recover. Jo Paley stayed with Kate and lots of dear people visited and wrapped us in prayer. It was odd being a patient in my own hospital, but I was treated surprisingly kindly.

What intricacies, O Lord, in these human bodies You make, and how we do take them for granted. Thank You for medical skills, thank You that I'm not dying (though it's felt very close recently). Whether chronic or acute, pancreatitis is treatable and I'm thankful for that. I don't fancy the regime of pills and further tests yet to come but when it's not hurting I can cope with anything.

We all looked forward to Kate's eighteenth birthday, and it didn't disappoint. Careful planning, saving, organising and telephoning paid off and we had a wonderful party, managing to cram eighteen relatives plus her good friend Andy under our roof, utilising every inch of space including the stairs. It was a wonderful evening, followed by a pizza party in Brighton with her friends.

One of my scans showed pancreatic cysts and a bifurcated duct. Before returning for the repeat scan it had been my turn to host our house group. Nobody minded playing sardines squashed up beside the log fire. Those dear friends prayed specifically that God would heal the cysts. It was hard waiting for appointments and results.

April 2nd: After today's scan the doctor announced I have a beautiful pancreas. Duct is still distended but no sign of the cysts; and it's been nearly two weeks without pain. Wow. Thank you Lord.

April 4th: Lord God I know You don't play tricks but WHY such pain last night? I thought my pancreas was healed? Thank you for the Pastor's phone call and prayer but, what's happening? I'm confused and I hurt. Please help. I need grace and patience, and relief. Please hang on to me in my doubting and, yes anger, that makes me turn from You. Haul me back, Lord.

In May there was an article in the *Independent* newspaper that gave me a jolt:

Fifty hurt as freak wave hits QE2. A 30ft wave hit the ship off Land's End on the way to Southampton from New York, sending it into a deep roll. People were thrown across the floor and a grand piano skated away after breaking free from metal fixtures. If anyone doubts what I described earlier, here is proof that our little island is surrounded by temperamental waters, and my voyage of three years before was hit in the same terrifying way.

The summer raced by in spite of many headaches and pancreatic bouts, both usually occurring during days off from work. I did manage to finish the AMSPAR course (and passed with Credit) and the

223

obligatory work experience, after which I was not offered a job at the surgery. It was a blow to my pride, but in hindsight a great relief; another demonstration of God's plans being so much better than mine. When the new post of hospital Ward Clerk opened I applied for that too (no rubber gloves needed). Unsuccessful again, my complaints to the Lord increased: *why God? Aren't You hearing me? I hate this miserable job; I need something better. Surely I deserve something better?* Grumble, groan, mutter.

We had a lot of visitors, the first being my dear old friend and ex-neighbour from the Woods, Jeannie. Noticing her American-ness made me see just how British I'd become once again. We had such good times: one day in Brighton we had to stand back as a Girls' Brigade band came marching by and Jeannie got out her camera, convinced it must be the Queen! She simply could not believe the quantity of pebbles on the beach, or that anyone willingly walked or sat on them.

There was a reunion with the girls from Wellgarth College, and Cassie – of the Cornwall trip – and I had a hard time accepting how we'd each changed so much, while both enjoying Jo and John's excellent hospitality. I also had a hard time keeping envy at bay as I admired their beautiful home and rose-filled garden. Doraine and her family brought lots of laughs and happy memories from New York; shortly followed by Garth; and then Ela from Germany. Finances were incredibly tight and I had to be so careful. Our guests contributed petrol money and frequent meals out, and we had countless invitations from kind friends too.

Early in October the pain was dreadful again. Despite quantities of medication it just kept hammering away at me over the weekend, dragging me back into Brighton hospital. A further scan showed absolutely nothing. *What is it Lord – what's going on inside me?* Recovery is such a blessing. Still no answers as to the pain's cause, if indeed the pancreas was healed; like migraine, though, once it's truly over, you feel wonderful again. Kate and I joined most of the congregation for another church weekend at Ashburnham, and that was great. For me there were deepening friendships, discovering a lot in common with several people I'd only known at face value. Listening to others' troubles always helps put one's own into perspective. And just knowing you are not alone with some of your deepest feelings really helps. The communion service on Sunday morning was wonderful. There was no sermon because the singing and praising brought us all not only closer to Jesus, but closer to one another too, real communion… and that led to soul-searching, facing issues long ignored or avoided and seeking and accepting forgiveness. Putting matters right between friends, or un-favourite people, and with God where necessary; made it a very special time. One thing clarified there was the vital importance of listening. Every person has a story and wants to be heard

Prilla and I began praying 'with intent' as regularly as we could for an unspecific goal, just to be ready and available. Little did we know what those times would lead to. The more I prayed the more I learned about prayer, discovering not only the wonder of seeing answers, but the calming, restoring power of communicating, with or without words and with or without answers, but just 'being' with God. It is about deepening our relationship with God far more than getting our needs met. We also attended a couple of training days put on by Christian Viewpoint. I found that the more time I spent with God the more I 'paid for it' by increased enemy attack. Often it was sudden bad pain again, or worrying money troubles, or just feeling wretched.

In a dream which went on for months in one short night, I was having a breakdown, calmly knowing all would be well eventually. Fragmented bits of me were lying about on shelves in the room, but no progress was possible until they could be slowly collected and put back together. Aware of several different levels at once, I woke praising God for the power and complexity of the subconscious as well as thinking of a nursery rhyme. Divorce is a life-shattering experience, making us wonder if the pieces can ever be put back right. All the king's horses and all the king's men couldn't put life or Humpty Dumpty back together again, but the King of Kings can, and He will just as soon as He's given all the broken bits. As a child holds up a broken toy to his father and says 'Daddy, fix it', I say: *Oh Lord, my King, here are all my broken, shattered bits. Please go on putting me back together.*

Over Easter 1994 Kate went to a conference in Swanwick, and I went with Jill to Spring Harvest. Another totally new experience for me, and I was only able to go thanks to a friend's generosity. It was fantastic. Skegness, as a place name, does not ignite interest, but it was great and can rightfully boast one of the best beaches in England – miles of lovely sand and interesting shells. It's not possible to attend all the seminars, but we did a good job, absorbing much good teaching.

In early May I was woken about 5am one Sunday to hear 'Happy (American) Mother's Day, Mom,' fast followed by an apology for waking me. I don't sound great at that hour but I never mind being greeted by my offspring. It was close to midnight in Chicago and Garth was keen to tell me about the great evening he was having with Crissy, then put her on the line. I guess she was a bit more prepared for the conversation than I was, and she sounded sweet, but when we'd hung up I wondered if I'd just spoken to my future daughter-in-law. I tried to imagine what she looked like from her voice, seriously hoping she wasn't doing the same about me just then. A couple of weeks later I wrote:

Lord, I'm useless at this. Why do I think I can manage, then wonder why I get wobbly? There isn't ever a time when I can sit back successful; it's a daily battle – I'm so glad You're in it with me. Thank you for yet again drawing me back to You – the Source of all I need. Augustine was right: 'Our hearts are restless until they find their rest in Thee.' Thank you for all the people down the ages who've discovered that truth.

When raging to God one night instead of getting to sleep, I found myself kneeling by my bed, suddenly wordless in front of Jesus who was right there. Also wordlessly, He responded by putting His hands on top of my head – I could feel the warmth and pressure on my hair. Utterly calming and reassuring, it was lovely and I didn't move a muscle until I felt Him lifting His hands away. Then I ran my fingers through my hair as you do when you take off a hat, got back into bed and slept soundly till morning.

When all benefits were cancelled my first reaction was fear, but it was short-lived; there was a quotation on my kitchen board for that: 'Fear and faith cannot keep house together, when one enters the other departs'. Before I became a Christian I was afraid of a lot of people, and generally anxious. That has not disappeared; the difference is I know what to do with it now: *Lord, I'm scared, anxious, worried, please help...* and He does, every time, not often by removing the object of my fear, but by removing the fear and replacing it with His peace, that peace which passes all understanding. Fear of bad pain seemed to be in a different category. That year there were many days when all I could write through my tears was *'I hate pain'* across the page. *Lord please help here, I need You to help me control this and to put a stop to it controlling me, but that's easy to say when I'm not in pain. It seems the more time I spend with You the more pain comes afterwards.*

The garden blossomed that summer and was a quiet haven for me, and Kate, and many others, especially Australian Jude, who often came to visit. In the autumn, in another lovely call from Chicago, Garth told me he and Crissy were engaged and he was so happy the words came out jumbled up. We chatted briefly and I was glad I was more awake than before. They planned to marry in a year's time, which I felt was an excellent idea.

Oh God, my son wants to get married, so fantastic after the rotten example he's had from me, thank You so much and please bless them as a couple and individually, protect their hearts from hurt, keep them honest, open and united – I'm so excited for them; teach me to be a good mother-in-law.

Exactly four years since the terrifying freak wave nearly drowned the QE2 I realised the significance of that occasion. On September 19th 1994 the Holy Spirit wakened my thoughts, showing how, as Christians, we obey God, follow His leading as things go smoothly along – until a sudden major upset. Then do we still trust Him and believe Him to be there, in control? When the crisis passes, we move on, till the next big problem, an endlessly repeating pattern. I saw that day that if I remain totally committed to Jesus He will, as He promises, never fail or forsake me even in the roughest, most unexpected storms. A letter came inviting me to be a Christian Viewpoint speaker, in spite of what I felt was my pathetic effort at the training days. Before self-adulation could replace surprise, the Holy Spirit highlighted the story of the burning coal put on Isaiah's mouth. I knew instantly that my lips could not be used any more to speak publicly about Jesus until they had been privately cleansed by Him, I needed to repent of bad language and lack of control; something I've had to do many times since.

In November Ev came from Iowa and what a time we had! As well as local delights, we went by train to Cambridge, guidebook in hand, and loved every minute; especially evensong at King's College. That was spectacular. She too sent some lovely photos after her trip. Prilla, Anita, Becks and I were busily preparing for our first Supper Party on December 5th, which turned into a wonderful evening despite our nerves. We invited Jesus into the room as the first Guest, before anyone arrived. The food was delicious and most of the women invited showed up. Shaking with nerves, I gained strength from the words in John 7:18, especially when I altered the pronoun: '(S)he who speaks on his/her own does so to gain honour for him/herself, but (s)he who works for the honour of the One who sent him/her is a (wo)man of truth.' My God did assist me to proclaim the wonder of how we met and the changes He's bringing into my life.

24

In February a group of friends and I went to hear John Arnott at Brighton's Church of Christ the King. They were holding a God Party and that's the first time I've ever queued to get into church! The music was like an exhilarating jazz festival, and the sermon was on freedom and joy in the Lord. Until John suddenly paused, seemed to look directly at me and began talking about forgiveness. The hundreds of people around ceased to exist and I knew I was being challenged. Then and there I was enabled to let go of and forgive the man who kidnapped and attacked my son, The next morning, walking on the Downs, I found myself praying for him, even feeling compassion, seeing him as an abused little boy helplessly growing up into an abuser.

Over Easter I was invited to a Swanwick conference. My plan while there was to ask God for the specific gift He knew I wanted. His reply was to show me His more-needed wisdom: understanding the greater importance for me in not straining to reach goals before the journeying. What I needed was 'impamba', a Rwandan word for 'a little food for the journey'. In other words to learn contentment where I was, being happy with just enough illumination on the path for the next few step, as in Psalm 119:105 rather than expecting the whole path lit up. He had something else to show me after that. Kate had been away for nearly five months in Scotland with YWAM: Youth With A Mission and it was quite an adjustment for me to be living completely alone. Naturally I was longing for her return and when she did come she brought half a dozen friends with her, all needing food and a few feet of floor space to unroll sleeping bags for the night. It was wonderful and I loved having them. God spoke so clearly while I cleaned up after that whirlwind visit, replaying in my mind the moment I picked Kate out of the crowds and we ran towards each other with open arms. Her clothes were rumpled and dirty, she was weighed down with baggage and really tired but what mattered to me was the joyfully deep happiness I felt seeing my child so pleased to come home. I knew then just a fraction of the joy Jesus feels each time one of His beloved children, prodigal sons and daughters with filthy clothes and accumulated baggage, returns to Him.

Two more speaking engagements came and went, with much prayer and encouragement, as did more bad days and nights of pain. A further summons back to Brighton Hospital for more horrible tests resulted in being pronounced fit with no need of further tests – *thank You, Lord.* I wanted to spend more time in prayer. The very next day, on a picnic, I twisted my knee and tore the ligaments around it, so I could hardly walk on it, never mind kneel. Those of us preparing for the first Alpha Course were experiencing such challenges, knowing that 'Satan trembles when he sees the weakest Christian on her knees,' and we were all feeling pretty wobbly at starting such a ten-week responsibility.

In August I couldn't help thinking of Matt on what would have been our seventeenth wedding anniversary. *Lord, is it just me who thinks of him? Does he have only angry thoughts, or none at all about me? Is he well? Is he still flying? Is he happily married? What of his kids? I would like to know he's OK.*

In September Jude drove us up to Sheffield to settle Kate into her new room at the Medical School, an epic journey in many ways. Almost too much time to dwell on upheavals, adjustments, great excitement and not a little trepidation. Any parent who's taken a child to university for the first time will know it exactly.

For a while I slid deeper into craving silence and time alone, turning away from the One who knows, the Source of all comfort – why am I so stupid? As more tears flowed out so I turned inward. It was a big jolt when someone asked if I'd been depressed like this before. Depressed? Again? *I'm sinking Lord, help, please rescue me. Get me back to the truth of the City of London's motto: Domine Dirige Nos: Our God shall direct us.* He does: Garth and Crissy rang to say they'd cancelled their honeymoon plans so they could come to England for Christmas for a week; and thirty minutes later he rang back having found a cheaper deal and asking if they could stay two weeks instead! Then I was given a mini-vacation at a Christian Retreat Centre over the wedding weekend, a time just for me to be refreshed in the comfort of that peaceful place. *Thank you for both those gifts, Lord, and* that my unconventional first-born should agree to a conventional ceremony with all the trimmings. They both struggled through many hours of overtime and second jobs to finance their big day, and even got a video organised, changed from PAL to VHS for me.

Oh God, I know You allow things to happen to test our faith, and that You bring good out of even the bleakest situations. Well, I have to say, this one feels very bleak indeed. I know faith is useless if it only sustains in the good times. Thank you for many praying friends, and for this wise saying: you can't control your circumstances but you can control your reactions. I want to get better at this Lord.

The kids sent a bouquet: 'from Garth and Crissy – wish you were here'. When it was over a call came from the married man himself: 'Hang on Mom, I'll have to put the phone down, my arm aches, there's this great band of gold on my finger and I'm not used to the weight.' He told me everything went perfectly, and that plus news of reconciliations within the wider family filled my heart with joy and, yes, my eyes with tears too.

Hardly able to contain myself in anticipation of their visit, I got busy arranging time off work, and tickets for all of us to spend Christmas week in Ireland with David and Jan plus as many family members as possible. A friend kindly drove me to Heathrow. Seeing Garth stride through the crowds, proudly introducing me to his wife was a moment never to be forgotten; I already loved her so we just needed to get to know each other better. That was accomplished in some unplanned ways, such as plumbing disasters of various kinds. My brand new daughter-in-law cleaned up and coped with everything. Later we revelled in wedding video and photos: such a great time together. New Year often brings reflective mood, whether resolutions are made and soon broken, or not bothered with. The evening of December 22nd 1995 was treasured, all three of my 'children', Garth, Crissy and Kate, gathered under my roof for the first time, and we sat chatting in the firelight, Christmas candles adding their flickering glow.

Weeks climbed into months and they sped by. Somehow there was time for continuing Alphas; speaking engagements, and my unpleasantly wearisome job. I so wanted to be able to echo Paul's words in his letter to the Philippians, knowing what it is to be in need and to have plenty, he had learned the secret of being content in any and every situation. But I couldn't quite echo yet as I lost sight of contentment fairly often. Also in Rom.12:2, 'Do not conform any longer to the pattern of this world, but be transformed by the renewing of your mind.' Mine still needed a lot of help.

A couple more years passed with no new job opportunities.

Lord I do try to obey You. I do not like wiping bottoms for a living. I keep praying for change, and even that it might begin with me. OK, I'm truly sorry. I'll stop moaning & begging for a better job; I'll stay on at the hospital, as You obviously want me to; I'll stop fighting against it... and You. I am sorry.

Remarkably soon after that things began to change! The nurses became kinder, nicer to work with (or possibly it was me who changed), more shifts were bearable and I was actually praised occasionally and my abilities called for in some surprising areas, as well as bedside care of the dying.

One sunny afternoon stands out as an oasis of peace when I

returned to the Quaker meetinghouse we attended as children. That visit strengthened links with the past; back beyond my childhood, to generations of my forebears who worshipped God under that same roof; and the odd sensation of being a child again; and of my ancestors being children there too but now outside lying in moss-covered rest. Another generation was starting then in1998 as I eagerly awaited my first grandchild's birth. Wandering through the graveyard I found the old family names, most just still legible. We're created and born, we live and we die, all so different yet starting and finishing the same; every one of us, past, present and future, ready or not, will stand before the judgement throne of God. When I die I hope someone will read out what was read for my grandmother, 'She really has gone Home.' At last I realised there was no need to fret about on which side of the Atlantic I felt more home; the confusion of divided loyalties can be gently let go. Being a 'resident alien' anywhere is actually no bad thing because 'here we have no continuing city'; and in Eph.2:19, 'Consequently you are no longer foreigners and aliens, but fellow-citizens with God's people and members of God's household.' That means I'm a citizen of Heaven already and when I actually arrive there it will be my true Homecoming!

25

Crissy's pregnancy progressed despite being considered 'at risk'. Having to miss the wedding, I determined to do everything possible to get there in the autumn, overcoming the many obstacles, to see that precious infant.

Three summer months got squeezed under a blanket of grief. Our dear pastor became suddenly ill and after brain surgery he was a patient on my ward. Cancer is vile and the fast-growing, vicious astrocytoma surely is among the worst kinds. Gently nursing that lovely man was a privilege, but heartbreaking. In hindsight his Homecall came mercifully quickly, unlike the weeks leading up to it.

'Mom, we have a daughter, Elizabeth. She's fine, beautiful, everything's Ok. Six pounds seven ounces, and perfect.' The call came on September 16th, and caused me to praise God, weep, and ring family all at once. Then up into the attic to sort through Garth's baby things; I considered making a pink jacket for Peter Rabbit but knew he'd be re-loved just as well in blue. Grateful for financial help from the family, my October trip was sorted, but what would it be like to return to the States, even for a short visit? On departure day this was the reading in my ancient copy of *Daily Light*:

The Sovereign Lord is my strength. He enables me to go on the heights. The Lord shall be thy confidence and shall keep thy foot from being taken. I sought the Lord and He heard me and delivered me from all my fears. The eternal God is thy refuge, and underneath are the everlasting arms. Blessed is the one who trusts in the Lord. If God be for us who can be against us?

And my spirit heard His voice: You will go out with joy and be led forth in peace.

Thank You so much Lord.

That flight started so smoothly but didn't stay that way, bringing the humiliating use of the paper-bag provided. A doctor, called for over the PA system, insisted on the oxygen mask I could not keep up and pills I could not keep down. Naturally I wondered bleakly why this had to happen as I'd prayed specifically for it not to.

Emerging at last to see Garth waiting beside his wife holding their pink bundle was so wonderful. The relief of getting there, almost migraine-free but still perfumed with dried 'eau du vomit', brought chuckles through the tears. We stayed up late (after I had showered) opening the baby things I'd brought, enjoying getting re-acquainted, gazing and marvelling at the velvet newness of that precious infant.

One day at the Pickle Barrel for lunch, one of their friends said, 'Well, Ma'am, you have a truly beautiful granddaughter an' her dad ain't so bad either!' We went out a lot; met up with friends and with Crissy's family too; browsed for country antiques, and ate at Applebee's. I was able to take care of my daughter-in-law when she got sick and we joked about paybacks as she'd looked after me three years earlier when they visited me. There were only brief quiet moments, usually early in the morning, to chat with Jesus, reconnecting with His peace and gaining strength for the day. It was enough, enabling me to just *be,* savouring each moment and not fussing about schedules or different ways of doing things. I studied my grandchild, heart of my heart, inhaled her loveliness, cherished the ability to do so, aware of having little time to spend so wondrously. Several old friends rang for lovely long chats, Mary even flew in from Massachusetts for a few days, and Ev and Tony drove down from Sheldon.

Liza's christening day was memorable. Florida Grandma came to join us with her remaining son Bud, and we all got on so well, happily agreeing to drop the 'ex' out of 'ex-in-laws'. Having not seen Bud for over twenty years and not knowing quite what to expect from my former brother-in-law, it was very special to hear him say, 'Did you honestly think we thought it was your fault? We were just so mad at Kurt for letting you go. We've always loved you and it's so good to be with you again.'

Acknowledging and reconciling past hurts, I trusted this trip would not disrupt settling back into England. Actually being in the great US of A again, I was keen to let go the bad stuff and enjoy the good while accepting that I live in the UK. With the Lord, 'home' really is where the heart is. That helped with the Iowa farewells.

In Chicago Jeannie drove me through my old neighbourhood then up to the Miller's Wisconsin home where we all shared much laughter, good food and memories. Early the next day Ann, Jeannie and I walked along the shore of Lake Michigan; they knew it was one of my favourite places. I found there a smooth pebble with a perfectly defined smiling face one side yet a sombre, mouthless reverse. It is still one of my treasures. Glad to get out of the biting cold, we dawdled over brunch in the shoreline restaurant before heading back to O'Hare. Thank You Lord enormously for all Your care, Your blessings and journeying mercies.

Back at work, into the daily grind, which was much improved, a restlessness was growing. Change was in the air. *Lord? Are You going to move me now to a nicer job, just when I'm doing better with this one?* A few doors of opportunity seemed ajar but when hesitantly pushed on, slammed shut. Kate went to spend Christmas in Romania as part of her medical training. I wondered whether to move up north to Sheffield where she was so happy and houses were so much cheaper. Were all the years of singing and praying 'Lord, prepare me to be a sanctuary' about to ripen? A friend lent me a sermon tape on the work with street children in Ukraine, commenting, 'It's all the same in that part of the world so you'll have an idea what Kate's doing.'

In January Garth and Crissy brought Liza to England to meet the rest of the family. We made the most of it, revelling in togetherness again. I found myself telling them I was going on a mission trip probably to the Ukraine. Was I? Did my heart know it before the rest of me? Chernobyl, the very place I never wanted to be, was surely not safe?

Assurance of the rightness of this, of doing this weird thing, grew stronger. One Sunday a visiting preacher was hardly riveting until he talked of the work in Ukrainian prisons, orphanages and amongst street children. I could almost hear the Lord grin as I got the message; and then several amazing things happened in quick succession. A video explained that age is no barrier, nor language, as there are plenty of interpreters. Unsolicited offers of financial support overwhelmed me. I spent a day in Southampton meeting the people who head the work, and discovering mutual friends. Most incredible of all was obtaining unheard of time off work, the full month. Initially the request had been ridiculed, then stalled, debated and stalled again. It was granted at the last minute, and one nurse present told me another had said: 'It's something to do with God; we'll have to let her go.'

My scribbled journal of mid-March to mid-April 1999 turned into quite a number of typed pages. Discretion demands that only the highlights be reproduced here, and none of my conversations with God, but there were a lot of both. Descriptions of food and cultural differences are meant only to enliven the whole experience, not cause any offence whatsoever. Most names have been changed.

It was an easy flight, Gatwick to Borispol, Kiev, where I met more of the team in the hour waiting for the minibus, then a three-hour drive on either side of or down the middle of the pot-holed road. The flat, straight, tree-lined tarmac helped delineate the way through horizontal snow. Most vehicles had at least one light, in use only once it was really dark. I was thankful for no motion sickness and the warm welcome at the Cherkassy Refuge. In the morning we were driven to the charity's base, Big House, truly a mansion beside local dwellings. A team meeting in the top floor offices stopped at 11am for a working lunch plus the unexpected perk found in the basement office: email availability. The dearest couple, house-parents Lisha and Mena, had a lovely flat on the middle floor and were wonderfully hospitable. They gave us another lunch and later tea also. It was warm tea with no milk, or warm water with a spoon of jam. Then it was upstairs for a lengthy English class, taught well by Katya. Beginning with much prayer in Ukrainian, Russian and English, the young people were enthusiastically determined to become fully fluent interpreters.

The days were filled with visits to outlying villages, overabundant meals in cramped rural homes, much larger homes of officials, or community gatherings, sometimes three in one evening. People were amazingly generous and keen to watch us consume every morsel. We spent time playing with many of the rescued orphaned or abandoned children, saddened by stories of those who ran away back to the 'freedom' of the streets. Out in the marketplace the divide was clear between rotund, sack-clad babushkas and the taller, elegantly fur-clad wealthy. Plenty of gold teeth were evident although few smiles to be seen. All available food was bartered for by rich and poor alike: offal, chunks of pork fat, *sala*, cigarettes, jars of greeny-brown things, sausages, mounds of sugar. Getting these items to and from the open stalls was usually done by wheeling, pushing or dragging varieties of ancient containers such as carts, enamel or plastic buckets, sleds, and over-laden mule and human backs.

One evening we drove over or around extra cavernous potholes to Huteri for a meal with Anatoli and his extended family. A wonderful welcome from lovely people who prayed beautifully before presenting us with mashed potato, cold fish, beetroot jelly, bitter cheese, tongue, juice, coffee and cakes. We continued on to Maximum Security Prison 62 to meet Governor Saraseinki. Being checked and rechecked, having to relinquish passports, we went through further security and a corridor enclosed in barbed wire through a courtyard where inmates clutched the wire and stared at us. My knees shook. In the chapel we faced about three hundred men, many with grey complexions, awful coughs and much snorting but all with a united desire to praise God in singing and prayer. Prayers got interrupted by more prayers: one young chap could only repeatedly sob, 'Mama'. A few of us gave brief testimonies or read from the Bible, after which some prisoners gave gifts they had carved. Mine was a candlestick. Feeling threatened at one point I edged closer to a guard as an inmate, an angry-looking sumo wrestler, pushed his way to me. He knelt, gently took my hand, weeping while thanking me for bothering to visit one such as him. What a stark reminder from the Lord not to judge appearances but to look on the heart as He does.

Equal hospitality was always shown us in homes whether rich or poor. In one village we struggled through mud-filled potholes, loose chickens, stray dogs and broken fencing to reach a dwelling little more than a hovel. My heart tore for the woman who welcomed us with tearful smiles as she scuttled about wiping children's faces and adjusting her headscarf. Her one-room home was dark and dank with a ragged curtain trying to hide the sagging bed. Many years ago she had tacked a variety of multi-floral papers to the walls, perhaps to try cheering the ravages of her husband's vodka habit. We were expected at two more families several hours driving apart, Vladimir and Larissa, then Sasha and Svetlana, where we were fed over-abundantly with beetroot in many forms. Sasha owned a business, had a fine apartment, a bodyguard and a car; such a contrast to the morning visit.

More snow had fallen, beautifully blanketing much of the unpleasantness of another market. One seller, dressed in three buttonless coats belted with string, was hunched over her stall noisily sipping something hot and brown from a jar held in filthy hands. She presided over enamel dishes containing piggery of all sorts: hearts, livers, snouts, ears on half heads, trotters, and slabs of rank *sala*. Further on was the opportunity to buy milk if you had brought along a container. A grubby hose shoved into the bottleneck directed most of the flow from a rusty oil-drum perched in a wheelbarrow. Beside it were more jars and bottles of milk in all stages from liquid to solid via rancid. Other tables displayed an eclectic mix of chocolate, pens, boots, soap, old war medals and uncomfortably thick, clearly second-hand undergarments.

Happy hours spent with the young interpreters nearly always included singing, food, car journeys, and crowded meetings where we were expected to speak. Snow, potholes, or vehicle insufficiency never seemed to spoil any plans. Crossing the great Dniepr River it was hard to tell if the van or the bridge was rattling more. The river is partly dammed to make a reservoir, but plenty of hopeful fishermen crouched on ice floes or over holes they cut in the ice, undeterred by the knowledge of many drownings each year or the radiation from Chernobyl. They have to eat something. In Luka Remand Home, with far less security than at the prison, we were ushered into their newly built chapel, complete with fancy chandeliers. Faith-filled Ukrainians are willing to live in abject poverty if necessary, as long as the places they gather to worship God have the best they can provide, especially sparkling light fixtures. Also, all married women always wear headscarves or hats in church, and usually everywhere else as well.

After the three-hour drive the girls and I were hoping for a break in the lengthy service – three sermons are common at such gatherings. We had been warned, as the 'home' was 'only' for teenage boys, but, needs must. The toilet had another glass door, but we were given a guard to stand facing outwards, so in we went. One of the girls was promptly sick; then lit several cigarettes at once. There was literally shocking neglect of hygiene basics for three-hundred and fifty detained boys. Cracked and broken urinals, basins with no running water, obviously used for anything but hand-washing, open drains blocked solid. Up two steps, set into the floor, were two chipped enamel bedpans. One was full. In desperation I simply had to use the other. Each had a rusted cistern suspended above with no means of flushing, but rust dripped onto my back. Truly thankful for tissues in my pocket, I battled foot slippage, and exited fast.

The service was tremendously moving, with powerful testimonies and joyful singing. Those boys were in there for petty theft or fighting. The few murders had been in defence of beaten-up mothers. At nineteen they had to move on into prison to finish their sentences. We felt encouraged by the statistics: 100% of those who become Christians are followed up wherever they go after release, and 95% never reoffend. That day six lads came forward to repent publicly and commit their lives to Jesus, and three of their mothers sobbed out thanksgiving. The Governor spoke of his recent conversion to Christianity, and the very trendy resident psychiatrist said she was constantly amazed at the radical difference Jesus Christ makes in the lives of believers.

A uniformed woman then handed each boy his meal of a large chunk of bread from their own bakery. We saw this bakery next. Rich, enveloping yeasty aromas had to suffice until we had a surprise stop at a restaurant on the return journey; the gesture nicer than the meal. We each received, served on several tea-plates, wet spam with coleslaw; small bits of cold fried fish on large bits of grey bread; then cold, rubbery ravioli swimming in oil. Each little pale pasta pocket, initially tasteless, released unbearably strong gristly offal from something long dead. Next came slices of warm tongue still retaining shape and, if you listened carefully, conversation also. Oh, how we welcomed the chocolate cake and warm coffee.

One early evening we were taken to a restaurant with some very nice food, plenty of fresh orange juice, champagne, and excellent coffee. There was much teasing from all the team members returning to England the next day. They told me that would be my last good food as I was going to stay on, but out in the villages. I thought they were joking. Communication generally was not great, and I did know I was expected to help with more language classes during the following days, but surely not alone. For the final service in Mantsievki we arrived through crater-like potholes full of rainy twilight. A clearing in the woods showed the church exhaling welcome and inhaling people. Again, we were ushered up to the front, but I was personally overwhelmed by too many hugs, too many demands to meet my hosts,

241

and to promise how long I would stay. Something else clutched at me, something similar to panic.

Wisdom suggests I should ease over the dreadful embarrassment when a 'helpful' team member announced I would not stay where there was no indoor toilet, and sweet Irina quietly telling us no one in the village had such a luxury. And the meal in a cramped, stuffy, upper room: I managed to nibble on a bendy biscuit and sip strongly fermented blue-grey 'juice' tasting of aspirin, drawn from silver-birch trees. My teammates did leave for Kiev and their flight home. Had I ever agreed to stay on? I felt decidedly unchristian. More communal singing plus a mild chastisement from a pastor: 'You not like us? Indoor toilet not everything in life. You pray, England people pray you, we feed you, you be happy and learn us English. We hold you up. You be so very good for us, please?'

The farmhouse to be my home for the duration took some getting used to, but my hostess Lessyna's welcome was genuinely, graciously warm. The main (only) bed was for me. The bathroom was not plumbed: the pink washing-up bowl on the floor was the loo, to be emptied into the bath, whose gaping drainpipe led outside to the chicken yard. There was also a 'long-drop dunny' out there, with no paper, no roof, and walls which only started about a foot off the ground, offering free range to the animals. That dear family provided a feast in my honour, after which I was ordered to rest, with Lessyna resting in a chair next to me. Then we walked miles through the woods to class.

The sandy paths past small homes and farms reminded me of Germany. Although very different from Cherkassy, the rural youth were equally keen to improve their English. Returning through the darkening woods with Lydia and Katya, the youngest students went on alone to their farms, fearlessly and safely in the moonlight. A whole boiled rooster awaited us. 'He big bird, many muscles for you, good fat skin.' I longed for sleep, thankful for bedtime when Lessyna banished her husband Stus out to the barn, but then she settled into two chairs this time, right beside me.

Breakfast 'tea' was interesting, made from the first spring flowers; a walk was planned, 'only' about four kilometres, to the big forest where they grow. Olya and Leesa were my guides but not a lot of conversation happened, despite my best phrasebook efforts. Snow still lay in the shadow of the fir trees. Huge mistletoe balls hung from every non-evergreen tree. Farm wives each had their precious cow on a chain after wintering them in the dark sheds. Eventually the tiny blue flowers were spotted and Olya began picking energetically. They must be pulled up slowly to include their long white underground stems for tea making. Leesa managed one bunch then found a log to lie upon. Other folk arrived in cars, and I fondly hoped we'd get a lift back. Lack of sleep and long walks don't mix well, and my headache was worsening. Somebody's relative nearly ran us over with his ancient Lada, engendering great hilarity, then drove us to his house. Slavic made us a piping hot drink of sugary black tea before driving us back. He had been fishing the previous week and part of his catch, newspaper wrapped, was still in the car, and the windows did not open.

Once back at Lessyna's home I had to refuse her borscht lunch and go to bed. The dear woman brought her neighbours in to confer, sit with me, stroke and kiss me, deciding it must be salmonella. The pink washing-up bowl joined us. They urged me to chew a handful of black peppers, and drink a steaming hot purple liquid. The geriatric bottle it came from had a barely legible label: potassium, or magnesium permanganate. Soon most of the English class came to me as I was unable to get to them. One brought a small hot-water bottle with a long nozzle and demonstrated its use to relieve symptoms. There were many other helpful suggestions and offers. I was even accompanied outside to the dunny. Privacy and personal space became a priceless, unattainable dream. The migraine did lift and I was thankful for some sleep: *Slava Boghu – Praise God.*

My friendship with Lessyna increased. Early each morning she went to market, bringing back a speciality for me, and she baked treats in her primitive kitchen. Kafir, a liquid yogurt, carrot juice, a variety of buckwheat which she boiled into salty porridge, and her famous bread rolls stuffed with either cabbage or sugar. She asked about English tea. Hearing of the milk, she grabbed my hand, took me out to the tethered goat lying in its own muck. Unearthing its udder she wiped off manure and straw to aim a liberal squirt into my mug: a proudly radiant gift. Had I asked for her one dress, or the woolly hat she never removed, she would have been as quickly generous. In the evenings, if her work was done, we practised each other's language, and she gave me many of her embroidered cloths. Women seemed to be always working in farms and fields, but men seemed to loll about a lot, presumably because there were no paid jobs for them. Stus presented us with a live, still flapping, whale direct from the Dniepr. His wife gleefully started hacking it, de-scaling and gutting it into – yes, the pink washing-up bowl. Cats and hens came running to help, pulling out and fighting over entrails. I just knew that fish was going to be my lunch too. It was. Served lukewarm in a basin of sea, with most of its tail over the side as a handle. Stus got its face as another handle and obviously thought he'd won the prize. The *sala* eaten with this had raw garlic embedded inside for an extra treat. Each afternoon we walked to the church for language class then a lengthy service, and that day supper was fish chunks in congealed sea jelly.

26

On Sunday I enjoyed warm kasha and milk before the three-hour church service. They may be 'very farm people' but oh, how they love to praise the Lord with their exquisitely harmonious singing and deeply prayerful worship. The sermon was short, only ninety minutes, as the children were practising Easter songs such as Khristos Voskres – Christ is Risen – and there was a birthday celebration for two youngsters, a grandfather, and me! Another English lesson followed for the many children who live so far away they walk once to church, stay all day then walk home after dark. A communal lunch was great fun with Igor and Helena, Sergei, Slavic, Lydia, Volic, Delfusa plus baby Anastasia, and Sveta who'd cycled nearly an hour to be with us. During the evening service Lisha, Mena and family came from Big House to see me. It was a happy reunion and I wanted to return with them, but knew I should stay; the truly harmonious a cappella singing was reward enough. There were early Monday morning farewells with the girls who walked those four kilometres to school every day; we had grown fond of each other. Lessyna kept hugging me weepily while we waited for Victor to collect me. They had all been so kind but it was good to get back to Big House for a long hot shower, clean clothes and one blissful night in a clean bed by myself.

Next day's journey was to the distant village of Chiyevka to visit Sveta, taking my last gifts of tea and Easter eggs. Securing a promise from Victor to come back for me in twenty-four hours, it was still rather un-nerving to see him drive away. The place looked extremely un-prosperous, especially the school where Sveta taught. Paraded like royalty, I was shown into each classroom, given every child's name, plus that of two other teachers who spoke a little English. Each child stood to ask or receive information, or raised a hand with elbow still on the desk, all impressively quiet and polite. They had no computers, only shared pencils and thin exercise books, with torn maps on the walls, and outdated worn readers in very stilted English. There were no RE classes, and only Orthodox ideas. I was invited to explain about Easter, and tell my story, thereby connecting the two – what a privilege; then tell about my family and everything English I could think of.

It was a long day but one of the best. At home time Sveta sent a young lad ahead, carrying my bag, while we stopped at the only 'shop'. It had almost nothing to sell but Sveta bought lemonade and two tired pastries. Her house had several rooms, as befits a schoolteacher, albeit one without salary for the previous five months. I met her elderly parents and found they were younger than me, also her aunt, plus her ninety-year old incontinent grandmother who slept out in the chicken shed. Possibly why the fine Iraq wool carpet hung on the wall and only rag rugs on the floor. Sveta's parents took her little daughter to their house overnight so we would be free to talk. Talk we did, about orthodoxy, Russia, Jesus, her communism, my Christianity, husbands, Baptists, and Ukraine life. She popped out to milk her goat; we drank tea and ate those very dry pastries. Then she surprised me with news of a meeting that evening led by Pastor Anatoli, to which she'd never normally go but was willing to take me and be my interpreter. A fantastic sunset enriched our walk along sandy paths through fields, greeting neighbours and admiring a *leleka* (a stork) circling, then roosting in its messy nest atop a high pole.

Although a bit late we were loudly welcomed – almost as if they'd been praying we would show up – and ushered to the front seats in the unusually large room of an important villager's home. Without a church building, the people often gathered there, happily crammed onto extremely hard benches. In between more lovely singing Anatoli spoke, and asked me to. As Sveta interpreted she kept stopping to exclaim that what he was saying was just what I'd been saying, then and in her home earlier so maybe it was all true. The Pastor drove us back telling me he'd been praying for my dear interpreter for years and for someone to whom she would listen. Quite possibly she was the main purpose of my entire trip.

Back in her house Sveta warmed up soup and meat patties while we continued talking. As I stirred my soup a fly came up, but there was plenty of warm goat milk, and in my honour she strained out the hairs and straw through a well-used cloth. Our conversation rolled from communism to atheism to baptism, from the Trinity to personal belief in Jesus, why He died, how He rose again, and the almightiness of God. We shared laughter and tears and the milk. Around midnight we heard increasingly loud male joviality outside, and I felt rather exposed in the un-curtained window. Up till then it had been a silent, moonlit night, tranquil and delightfully rural. Sveta's reaction was disturbing, her fear and apologies increased as she whispered: 'Oh this is bad, so bad, I can do nothing, there is no lock on my door, they have come for you and will come in.'

We turned off the one light and moved into a smaller, curtained room where she explained that her whole village knew I was there. To them UK or USA meant wealth; the men had been drinking and intended big trouble. The only other people who knew my whereabouts were thirty minutes away by car. We had no telephone, and there was just granny in the chicken shed between us and those charmers circling the house in shivery, silver shadows. My poor hostess whispered, 'You are a Christian, yes, perhaps you'd better pray to your God.' Seldom has an assurance been more heartfelt: 'I am.'

Knowing you can do absolutely nothing but pray makes prayer even more extraordinarily real. Probably we will never know if the men simply wandered off, or if they encountered angel hosts surrounding us, but certainly my prayers were heard and answered. As I breathed out thanks to my Lord, I believe my friend did too.

In the re-established quiet we gradually relaxed, staying on the floor in that little dark room, talking about Jesus for as long as she still had questions. Eventually we both needed the outhouse but neither was willing to venture to it across the field. I was offered an indoor convenience, a bucket in the front room. There were six in there, containing such staples as potatoes, twigs full of dried berries, pickles, and grain for porridge. Finding the empty one had become vital. Sveta slept the moment she lay down. I did not; I was not alone on my couch and soon began itching. Suddenly, a truly awful clatter – surely the men had returned? I stopped breathing. Sveta hardly stirred. The metal curtain-rod, perhaps unused to being used, left its brackets and crashed to the floor. Nothing else happened. Dawn was slow to arrive.

We did just manage to get to school on time, for a day very similar to the previous one, except for the headmaster's anger. Religion is not permitted and I had told children about Jesus and Easter. Sveta tremblingly spoke up, asking why he had listened outside doors rather than coming in to classes, and reminding him that he had set the theme of Easter: all she had done was bring in an 'expert'. *Slava Boghu* again, *Praise God*, all was well; we were smilingly invited to join headmaster's lunch. I had to use the one school loo, thankful for a certain dexterity acquired with those outdoor squatters. Slowly walking back to Sveta's home we were greeted by her aunt in a great state. While she was working in the fields, gypsies (perhaps some of our night visitors) had gone into the house. It would have been slim pickings if it was my stuff they wanted, but all seemed undisturbed. My hostess consoled us with bottled apples, not pickled but delicious in a nectar like juice. Her little daughter played in the hard-packed dirt with the chickens, and old granny babushka dozed in the sunshine, leaning on a stump.

I was looking forward to my 5pm pick-up time but it came and went. Sveta sat with me on the bench outside her roadside fence, contentedly chatting while we waited. Her father drove up in his battered red 'machina-car', with his supper of vodka/silver birch juice in a jar between his legs, plus a lump of pig lard *sala* in a grubby bag, urging me to share with him. Such a friendly chap. After another lovely sunset we chivvied chooks and granny in and went indoors ourselves. Ukrainian mode does help one remain unflustered, especially when punctuality was so hoped for. At long last Victor did come for me, and it was good to get back to Big House.

Several days were taken up with business planning meetings, more language classes, and very pleasant interludes of home life with Mena, Lisha and their children. Meals often were a surprise, both in timing and content: one lunch was liver chunks cooked in with buckwheat *kasha*; a breakfast was sandwiches of raw bacon. My favourite, that which caused the least internal unrest, was *khleeb* and *maslo* – bread and butter. On Good Friday, or Willow Weekend, Mena took me to her family's home and introduced me to Papa. Oh, how my heart heaved to see that dear man, totally helpless since a stroke five years ago. Someone had got him an English Kings Mk5 hospital bed, but he needed hospital care, rather than slowly rotting behind that curtain. He groaned and sobbed as I held his hand, the once great preacher and shepherd of his flock. A tram ride back allowed time for me to take a walk by myself for some much needed prayer space. Finding an old rugged cross in the corner of an overgrown cemetery, I sat for a while reading Max Lucado's *Six Hours One Friday*. Lisha and Mena's family prayer that evening was most special, for even the youngest child prayed and all joined in beautiful singing. They gave me typed translations of each song.

Sunday morning's church was joyfully loud, packed full, and very hot indeed. Ksenyia, another lovely student, returned to her seat beside me whispering, 'Excuse me, too heat. I was sicking.'

During the third sermon a woman ran weeping to the front and knelt with her face touching the floor. The preacher abandoned his message to lift her and pray with her and telling us: 'This is Margurite, who has just opened her heart to Jesus.' The congregation sang a welcome song similar to 'Happy Birthday' but before it finished four more adults and one small boy went forward. They all wanted to repent of going their own way, and give their lives over to Jesus. It took ages for them to get back to their seats due to so many hugs and handshakes in the aisle, and receiving new Bibles. People are created to hunger for God and there, uncluttered by materialism, they hear Him and naturally respond. They found what so many haven't even started to look for yet. What an honour to see it happen and to rejoice with the church family.

Late evening supper and prayers at home highlighted more Ukrainian ways and extremes. Devotion to God and great love was demonstrated by all to all, with real togetherness. There were interesting or non-existent table manners, but one burp and you're banished. Independence was encouraged, there were no set bedtimes –little Roma fell asleep while singing – and absolutely no bare feet allowed.

My final few days were busy with more classes, some painting of the newly completed rooms, some gardening, and a little help with wedding preparations for the sweetest couple, Katya and David. The girls, Anna, Ksenyia and Katya, prepared a feast of murdered chicken with beetroot and tapioca salad, plenty of champagne and chocolate cake. There was a violin concert; and a communion service in a monumental thunderstorm. That church too was packed, and I was moved by the array of male hats and caps adorning each wide windowsill, piling up as the people crowded in. It was good to recognise some familiar faces and to be greeted by so many afterwards. Pastor Vladimir prayed beautifully before handing out the bread and wine. The reverence of his words needed no translation. It was hard saying goodbye to the Saraseinki family, and several more who could not visit again before my departure. These were sweetly tender farewells.

Mena and Lisha honoured me with the gift of a boxed chandelier, a small version of the kind hanging in most churches. Mena also gave me six traditional Ukrainian necklaces she had painted. Victor invited us to his home so I could meet his beloved Ruta and their magnificent family, including granny. They had a three-room flat in a concrete high-rise and it was a joy to be there. Two teenage girls played piano and sang beautifully for us as we drooled over the newest addition, baby number nine, named Princess Diana. A table set up in the boys' bunk bedroom was laden with quantities of food, plus tea from the blue forest flowers in an elegant china teapot. Nothing was touched until after many prayers, and still not touched by any of the children until after we had eaten. Eight pairs of hungry eyes watched us in silence. It was stern discipline, but wrapped in obvious vibrant love and a great deal of fun.

Pastor Anatoli visited and brought me a bag of Lessyna's cabbage rolls plus more of her superb embroidery. Her generous giving touched me deeply; she has so little to call her own. He took my poem for her and one for Sveta, and letters to the students, which he promised to hand-deliver. He kept thanking me for spending time out in the villages, but I kept trying to tell him it was me who was thankful, for those dear people had given and taught me so much. My heart was full.

The final goodbye in early morning chill was mercifully brief. Victor was taking some students for a day in Kiev. Mena got up with me and waved us off in the minivan. The Dniepr was dazzling with the first slanting sunbeams. There was no ice that day but many fishermen. For miles of mist-ribboned flatlands we were stuck behind a rickety vehicle held together with string, like its passenger's sack coat. She sat precariously amongst her night's baking, trusting her man to keep the truck on the road till they reached market. Would she make enough kopeks on each loaf to buy fuel to get them home and bake the next batch? In contrast, once in the city we had time to look around, and go in the gold-domed Orthodox cathedral. No cameras allowed, or postcards, and yet stalls filled the dim interior selling candles, crucifixes and icons. Amazing gilded paintings on every inch of wall and ceiling made an exotic gallery of artistic religion, or was it religious artistry? People queued to kneel and kiss glass-covered saints' remains, while bearded, black-clad priests with silent footfalls intoned dirge-like chants. The gold and silver trim around their robes seemed a bit ironic.

251

The oppressive opulence and mix of incense with candle smoke hastened me outside to find a seat in the sunshine. There I nearly stepped on a young mother cradling an infant, with a toddler tied to her leg, counting on churchgoer generosity. Beseeching eyes sunk in filthy faces under matted hair; that little trio was amongst a number of similar heartaches on that sidewalk. Many were genuine, but some, surely, were actors taking advantage of a likely spot to milk the tourists. I've seen the same in other big cities; Kiev wasn't so different. Cynicism always argues with compassion.

At Borispol an airport official shouted instructions to me in Russian then suddenly exposed several gold teeth saying: 'Entjoy your fliiight!'

27

How good it was to be home – yes, even though that meant returning to drudgery and bottoms at work. It was quite surprising to find it was still 1999, as I felt I'd been away a very long time. There was unexpected interest in the trip from my colleagues which brought about some interesting conversations. Things generally were improving (including my attitude) and I found small encouragements hugely helpful. Seeing I did have real worth, unlike the kind mentioned in earlier years, an ability to be a blessing to elderly and frail patients.

Spring and summer settled into pleasant routines with enough free time to enjoy getting the garden looking its best, as I felt the house already was. There I thought I'd stay, until Garth and Kate had to decide 'what to do with mother'. Except I had a continuing sense of something going to change, which fuelled my frequent prayer to be ready, willing and able to know God's will and do it. Suddenly, one rosy June day, I believe He showed me I had become too dependent on independence and asked if I was willing to give it all up, firstly by selling the house. Initial reaction was not polite. How could I continue telling others about trusting God completely if I wasn't doing that – trusting even when it seems crazy? No answers to my many questions would come until I responded. So I agreed. Scary but exciting too, as God stuff so often is. I prayed for the new owner to find it a safe haven, as it had been for me. Someone came in to view it saying almost immediately, 'Oh this feels like a safe haven.'

All signed, sealed and sold in eight days. Right, what next? In July a friend rang to talk about Bible College again. Previously I'd ignored her and changed the subject, but suddenly I knew I needed to pay attention; this was it. *Er, Lord, seriously, do You mean it?* He did.

August was my final month of nine long years' auxiliary nursing. In those last few weeks two favourite patients died; my elderly, beloved dog had another fit and had to take a one-way trip to the vet; and I had to deal with all the legalities of selling a much-loved house and buying a car. All of it happened quickly, while I was once again giving away, selling or packing belongings into a friend's kindly offered garage. Since giving my life over to Jesus I was always aware of a small bubble of joy and real peace; both received many a battering and were frequently put to the test. Would it last, was it genuine? Or was it just the proverbial 'pie in the sky' only for the good times? Making radical choices often causes raised eyebrows, veiled and not so veiled comments, even opposition and ridicule. In this case, unhelpful predictions of disaster also. Plain indifference would have been preferable. Encouragement was treasured, especially by one who in younger years knew nothing about choices of any kind.

September 3rd was not my best day: my first one as a fulltime residential student, still thinking I was too old, too divorced, and not nearly holy enough. Surely I would find super-spiritual types lurking in linoleum corridors, ready to pounce on every sin? The place was full of inescapable kindness, but escape felt necessary. Having no home anymore, there was nowhere to run to, and I knew without doubt that God's timing was, as always, perfect and His plan had me there for a reason. Learning to survive and even enjoy community living, with a variety of age groups – thank you, Ukraine. Coping with a classmate who mirrored an ex-husband; dealing with things I thought long since dealt with; discovering that my brain could still work hard: all extracurricular lessons just as important as the scheduled ones.

We were not simply instructed in Biblical content and meaning in order to regurgitate it into essays, scrape through exams and gain a diploma. We were exhorted and encouraged to memorise it, apply it, live it, and so be able to pass it on to others, while growing towards deeper dependence on the Holy Spirit to accomplish all that. When God promises to do more than we ask or imagine, that doesn't mean make us more miserable than we already imagined. When He asks for commitment and faith enough to say 'yes' to follow exactly where He leads, however unlikely it may seem, He does provide the ability once He sees willingness (which doesn't have to be enthusiasm). He changes negatives into positives, He is faithful, He will not forsake, and He does know what we need. He poured more grace into my heart as He continued renewing my mind and reviving my soul.

The College exterior may have looked like the Dickensian poorhouse it once was, but inside it was a goldfish-bowl. As we got to know each other, multi-faceted individuals in a family group, it was often confrontational, always hard work but very rewarding. Living life like that, even for a few years, challenges, changes, turns you inside out, shatters, and puts you gently back together piece by piece by peace. Much grace was needed and much was freely available. God had to take me out of all known comfort zones into a place safe enough to see myself clearly. I have long been a nurturer of others; there I had to admit to starvation: a deficit of personal nurture. Vulnerability that weighty can be unkind.

Many days I simply did not feel up to the challenge, although continuing to eat up the lectures and thrive on the frequent discussions. Studying, finding answers, digging into Scripture, starting to understand so much more was sometimes difficult, but such a joy. It was hard to believe I didn't have to rush off to work – that this *was* my work. I needed to earn some petrol money, so I squeezed in as many hours per week as possible nannying for a married student with a baby, and also dog sitting occasionally. Someone's else's baby, however adorable, is not the same and I felt that keenly as my second precious granddaughter was born five thousand miles away; a huge welcome to Catherine!

In most classes different opinions were raised, and even lecturers did not always agree on interpretation detail. We were encouraged to spend much time in the library researching thoroughly, reaching informed conclusions, and remembering always that God is committed to His Word, not necessarily to one's own interpretation of it. Of special delight to me was reading a familiar verse or chapter and suddenly seeing new meaning, both of the original text and its application. Those revelations were my 'wow' moments and there were lots of them. Learning some very basic Greek and Hebrew also opened my eyes to so much more; as did comparing the many different Bible translations.

Naturally I wondered what it was all for, where it would lead. Mostly I turned those thoughts into thankfulness that my nursing days were over, while admitting that I'd learned a lot in that hospital, being stretched into new growth in some surprising areas. Also I thanked God for the many opportunities for public speaking, in small Alpha groups and larger Christian Viewpoint meetings, all hugely helpful when having to stand up in class, in chapel, or in local churches as a trainee preacher. Much to re-learn, but so much was new to me; so many topics both historical and relevant were dug up, expounded, expanded, and understood. I was completely sure that I was where I was meant to be. The One Who so clearly directed me and opened all necessary doors to make it possible, would continue to sustain me then show me the next step at just the right time.

However, even with that certainty I was not immune from struggles with lesser thinking. Any major life-change takes a while to get used to, at any age, as I well knew, but at over fifty all adjustments tend to be tougher. Each new situation has its gains and losses, and once more I'd had to let go of one life-phase to start another. In this new adventure, the loss of privacy and independence was as scary as being a student again, afraid the academic studies would defeat me.

God does not ask you to do something then leave you stranded. He equips you and you realise He's actually been preparing you for ages. Once you hear His call and choose to obey, it is amazing to see His guidance leading on towards the next part of His plan. No floodlight for the whole path ahead, exactly enough for the moment, no more.

Community living was not as bad as anticipated, in fact quite fun sometimes, and my first assignment earned an A grade. The two years raced by and really were great. What I gained could be summed up this way: a greater knowledge of God and a deeper relationship with Jesus; a better understanding of the Holy Spirit and the Bible, of myself, and others. Particularly seeing and understanding the Biblical truth of what God says about my true worth, my significance, security and acceptance: that none of it depends on anything I have done, not done, or will do, but on what Jesus has already done for me. That fact created a stronger desire to go out and talk to people about Jesus, to encourage and to teach as I had been encouraged and taught.

Well before graduation a suggestion was made which grew into a job offer: to remain at college and become part of the faculty. What a delightful privilege to continue living where I'd grown to feel so 'at home'. Here is part of what I read out as a graduate on June 16th 2001:

David said to Solomon his son:

Know the God of your father, have personal knowledge of Him, be acquainted with and understand Him, appreciate, heed and cherish Him, and serve Him with a blameless heart and willing mind. For the Lord searches all hearts and minds, and understands all the wanderings of the thoughts. If you seek Him, inquiring for and of Him, and requiring Him as your first and vital necessity, you will find Him; but if you forsake Him He will cast you off forever. Be strong and courageous and do it. Fear not, be not dismayed, for the Lord God, my God, is with you, He will not fail nor forsake you until you have finished all the work for the service of the house of the Lord (1 Chronicles 28:9, 20 AMP).

If any one of you is amazed that I'm standing here – like this, today – you are no more amazed than I am. Two years ago when I first heard God's call to put aside everything else and come here, He also assured me that if I would just trust and obey He would do the rest. He would get me through, and He has. It is a testimony to His grace and unfailing promises. It is proof that no one is too old to start again; no one is too bad or too stupid; no one need be held back by a shady past, or even dyslexia; no one is beyond redemption. Once redeemed, and forgiven, if we then make ourselves wholly available, God does the rest. He can even turn an old has-been into a rejuvenated going-to-be.

With only a week off between that very special cap and gown ceremony and my first morning in the office, it was another tricky adjustment. Even with my name on the door and a fancy sounding title of Dean of Women Students, it was still just me in there, getting to grips with all kinds of administrative work. Sue, the office manager, and I got on well and became firm friends. I learned so much from her. Quickly apparent was that my 'dean' part meant a combination of matron, pastor and counsellor. Whatever I was doing the students always took priority. Their needs were my work, not merely interruptions. I tried to be for them what I felt was missing in my student days, an intermediary outside the classroom. Most evenings my flat was open to any who wanted to chat. It was another haven of peace up on the top floor with wide views across fields to the South Downs, and filled with photos of my children and grandchildren. I was not the only one missing long-distance family; we were only a small college but sixteen nations were represented. I had received much wise counsel and valued being able to turn that around to offer the same to others. God was working His purpose out in each person He brought into that place, before sending them into the world with His good news.

Amongst many challenges and some really great times, several startling happenings kept me more fully occupied than expected that first year. Persistently heavy rain bringing freshly spread manure off the fields flooded the entire campus in a matter of hours. The insurance claims were lengthy and delayed. Soon afterwards a car parked overnight beside the chapel was arsoned, causing vehicles either side to incinerate with it. Mine was one of them. While housesitting for friends I experienced an allergic reaction requiring an ambulance.

Anaphylaxis is always shocking, especially when the cause is unknown. It was the first of six times over the next several years. In early summer I agreed to accompany Jo, a much younger staff member, on an adventure holiday to Switzerland. We had a lot of fun, survived the white water rafting and an arduous climb to see a glacier.

In June 2002 my first grandson, Henry, was born in Iowa. In October he flew over with his sisters and parents to join in the celebrations for Kate's wedding to Rob. Many of the students worked hard at The Rehearsal Dinner at College; the next day's ceremony was in Amberley church followed by a joyous reception in a magnificent Sussex barn. Other family and friends had come from the States, among them Ev and Tony. We three took a post-wedding drive up to Scotland and across to Northern Ireland.

Never had I dreamed of being a college lecturer, but that was how my job developed and I loved it. The prayerful, careful planning, re-writing my own notes and upgrading the syllabus for the class on Spiritual Authority took a great deal of time, but I thrived on it. I put heart and soul into each lesson and, judging by feedback and results, the students did too.

Two more years sped by with farewells to graduates and welcomes to newcomers. Naturally some students settled in easily and some struggled, and there were a few hiccups to sort out. Content and happy, I thought I would be there until retirement. However, underlying administrative issues had to be addressed and some valued staff members felt the need to leave, adding to the growing un-settlement. Then quite suddenly the building was up for sale and nearly everyone had to make other plans. With little enthusiasm I followed a few leads and filled out one application form. What was left of the college moved into a hotel for a seemingly unworkable merge, and I moved in with my aged mother, hopefully not for long enough to create anything similar, and to await developments. A situation did develop, slowly at first but gaining momentum along with amazement.

28

That one application resulted in an invitation. To 'preach with a view' anywhere is an honour, and terrifying; it means that a congregation wants to try you out. This was to conduct all of both Sunday services in a small church in small town in a northern part of the country. Much prayer, with urging on by dear friends, encouraged me to accept, fully aware it might not lead to anything. My goal was not to get there and 'strut my stuff' but simply to be the best possible ambassador for Jesus, particularly since it was surely His idea from the beginning. Not only did they survive, they asked me back to do the same again two months later, shortlisted from over forty applicants. When they called me to pastor that church it brought me to my knees, thanking God in wordless wonder, and a little trepidation.

Back in 1999 when He asked me to let go of my house plus much of the contents, I knew I had to trust and obey without knowing what would be next. Then the home unlike any other I'd had, for five years at Bible College, followed by another with all I needed, from many different sources, as part of the work He called me to do. I did not see that as my house or my church, but just given to me as one of His under-shepherds, to steward and oversee. He is the Good Shepherd, we are the sheep of His pasture, and it was only by His Holy Spirit enabling me that I was fit for the job. *Not by might nor by power but by My Spirit says the Lord Almighty* (Zechariah 4:6.)

Without the experiences, excellent teaching, training, and qualification, I would certainly not have been up to it. Lecture notes and reference books were made full use of, as well as necessities such as conflict resolution, and tackling difficult issues rather than burying them. The responsibilities were huge, as were the challenges but so were the joys and privileges too. My Induction Service weekend was memorable in many ways. Lots of friends and family made the long journey, new friends came from local churches, and my younger brother and his younger daughter sang a beautiful duet.

It seemed sensible to introduce myself to the local clergy. Churches of all sorts were prolific in the area and a good rapport with colleagues is always helpful. Two refused to converse with me at all due to their abhorrence of women in ministry. Not a great start. There were one or two similar surprises, but also some good friendships grew, two particularly would be a real support later. I was responsible for the fifty or so in the congregation, and a great many more in the neighbourhood. That soon included the elderly residents in nearby housing schemes; plus assemblies in infant and junior schools. It is said that a new pastor can do no wrong in the first six months, and no right afterwards. That is debatable. Frequently weary, and discouraged more often than is comfortable to admit, I battled disappointments, setbacks, and situations which appeared to be direct attacks. Wonderful things did happen, and some lovely surprises; so counting every blessing and keeping things in proportion with right boundaries and priorities was vital. Again and again I sensed the Lord was saying the same thing to me: *you do the business, leave the results up to Me.* Particularly so on the many Sundays I was nervous about delivering the sermon I knew He had given me. No rotten eggs were actually tossed, just verbal ones, but occasionally there would be applause. Unpredictable is one fitting adjective.

Geographically the whole area was truly beautiful. Hilltop views and deep valleys were close by, riverside marshlands and the sea. Whenever possible I walked, often with an adopted dog for companionship; very necessary exercise, and a great sanity-saver. Map in hand, I explored, frequently getting lost, and meeting new people along the way. One afternoon intensely loud bleating and baa-ing lead me to a field where two men were shearing sheep. The moment each ewe was grabbed and upended she became silent until turned loose with her new haircut. These words from Isaiah 53:7 came alive for me that day …*as a sheep before her shearers is silent.*

It was almost impossible to take a whole day off each week. There was enough work for at least two people, very little help available, far too many meetings to plan and chair, and many mid-week 'musts' to accomplish. That was just to keep things as they always had been, never mind attempting to implement any gradual changes and improvements. I did love preparing for the two-per-Sunday sermons because it required waiting for God to birth His plan in my mind and heart. It would start Sunday night and continue all week, far longer if it was to be a series to stretch over several weeks.

Time is no respecter of persons, and those persons were no respecters of my time. Phone calls and door-knocks would start as early as 6am or 7am and continue late into the night. Interruptions, especially people problems, were, as before, my work, but could be frustrating.

The more I learned about the history of the church and its people, questioning the brevity of each of my many predecessors' time at the helm, the more there was to question. In the final year at college it had been hard to be thankful for difficult things that, once discovered, had to be faced and dealt with. I knew God's guidance then, and now was so grateful for those experiences.

Surprisingly, there was a lot of joy too. Great friendships: what a blessing it is to get to know lovely people, to pray together and encourage one another wherever you are. I chatted with everyone I met and invited all and sundry to come and give church a try. Quite a few did, and stayed, despite the chilly unwelcome from 'the old guard', those few who made it clear I had no right to impose newcomers on them. Similar, perhaps, in some ways to the Vicar of Dibley's situation, minus the humour.

The upset was greatest of course when the neediest came in, and stayed: street people, known drug dealers or users, and a smelly drunk or two. The congregation gradually grew, especially when we put on potluck, or bring-and-share meals. Quite a few people living in the neighbourhood told me they didn't even realise there was a church. 'Barny' always thought it was a cult, Mr MacD only knew about the rats. Ah yes, the rats: from my earlier nightmare based on tortoise demise, to sharing house with them. Jake the exterminator said he'd seldom seen rats and mice together and their attic evidence told him they had lived there many decades. One of 'the old guard' said I must have brought them with me.

It was good that my autumn 2005 trip to Israel, pre-booked and paid for the previous year, received acceptance and caused no problems. I arranged guest speakers to take the services in my absence, and a colleague to be available if needed.

From Ben Gurion airport in Tel Aviv we were led by the Cuffs, a lovely couple full of knowledge and love for the Holy Land. We learned much and enjoyed their joy. Throughout the ages many churches, monasteries and basilicas have been built on top of excavations of 'holy sites' as memorials and protection from the elements. In some it is an effort to imagine the original life of the place. Up the Mount of Olives, amidst plenty of stunted trees, was the church of teardrop design, *Dominus Flavit – Jesus wept*. In a flower-filled, sun-dappled courtyard we shared communion with greedy wasps. The lofty cloisters held wall tile plaques of the Lord's Prayer in every language. Walking around the quiet Garden of Gethsemane affected me deeply (Luke 22:39-54). Olive trees never die; when cut down, the roots continue growing and producing new shoots. Beside the last gnarled twisted trunk was a plastic bucket of drying silvery-grey leaves, from which we were invited to take a handful. My leaves lasted well and several years later brought Good Friday alive for my youngest grandchildren. Gethsemane is pronounced Get-shemen, meaning oil press. Jesus allowed the life to be squeezed out of Him for us.

Looking down on the city, seeing the Golden Dome of the Rock, and the Gate Beautiful and later, walking around the Old City, we went through the Zion Gate. Walking beside those immense walls, touching the warm stone, imagining, jostled by crowds, I almost bumped into a shiny parking meter securely attached to that stone. At the lowest end of the wall is the Dung Gate and we proceeded on to the Western, or Wailing, Wall to undergo the police checks and gender separations. To pray, the men on their side of the dividing fence stand in their prayer shawls and hats; while the women stand, or sit in rows on white plastic garden chairs. Children are there too, reading from the Torah, memorising the prayers. The gaps between the wall's huge stones are stuffed with paper prayers, fluttering, faded, or flying away, nudged lose by the constantly bobbing foreheads of the faithful. I was mortified to be spoken to severely by a gun-toting female guard because my cardigan had slipped off my shoulder, rendering me uncovered. We had been warned. Multi-lingual signs shouted 'No Begging', so when an old woman held up her dirty, misshapen hands to me, I took them in mine to pray a brief blessing. She snatched them away only to re-shove them almost in my face, saying rudely, 'Money, money.'

We took a long time to explore Jerusalem, or Heru'shalom. The Abbey had a wonderful mosaic floor featuring three central circles for the Trinity in eternity and the God of Abraham, Isaac and Jacob. Then came the names of Old Testament prophets; and the third had the New Testament disciples and apostles. The outer encircling border held the zodiac star signs, the original biblical names of the stars and what they represented, as Abraham would have known them. King David's tomb and the rooms above it were impressive. If not the actual room, then similar to where the Last Supper took place and where, later, the disciples received the Holy Spirit. I saw a carved olive tree and carved pelicans. If all else fails those birds will cut their own bodies to feed their young; more reminders of Christ's sacrifice for us. It is said that He spent His last night alive where the church of St Peter in GalliCantu (Peter and the cockcrow) now stands. We climbed right down into its deep dry cistern or dungeon prison. Victims were let down by rope with no light and absolutely no way of escape. High ledges around the rim were for soldiers on guard duty to keep an eye on anyone incarcerated. We paused down there while Tim read Psalm 88.

From the Temple Mount and Citadel – David's Tower – we could look over the Kidron Valley, including Ghenna or Gehron (meaning 'hell') outside the City Walls. Here children used to be sacrificed to the god Molech. Amid the ruins of the pool of Bethesda, or pool of mercy, St Ann's church now stands, quite near the Sheep Gate.

The pool was built in five porticoes because both sheep and goats had to be thoroughly washed then checked for perfection by the rabbi before being sacrificed. The ritualistic cleansing was for the people too, prior to worshipping, which explains why the man in John 5:2-18 waited for thirty-eight years until he thought he'd be good enough. Then he met Jesus. 'Do you want to be well?' is the simple question He asked then, and He asks the same today, particularly of those who feel they must get it all together before they'll be anywhere near good enough.

The praetorium, or palace courtyard, mentioned in Mark 15:16, was underground due to the church built on top of the site, as usual. It was quiet, very sombre, and rather claustrophobic. Surely it must have felt that way to Jesus too, not because of buildings above but because He knew what was coming. Culture in His day decreed that prisoners were flogged to within an inch of their lives or crucified, not both. He was different. He was ridiculed and mocked within His own society as well as generally: total humiliation for Him to achieve total salvation for us. Standing on the stone paving slabs where He stood, I saw one had a worn engraving of a game like tic-tac-toe or noughts and crosses, possibly where the soldiers threw dice. In the domed ceiling of the church upstairs, the Monastery of Flagellation, hangs a huge metal crown of thorns, virtually pressing down its painful weight as those thorns dig in.

Outside the City Wall in what's called the land of Moriah we went from the highest point in the ancient quarry, past the 'field of stoning' where Stephen met his death, Acts 7:58, on to the Garden Tomb at Golgotha, the place of the skull. It is outside the city wall as in the old hymn, but it is not a green hill. It's right next to the main bus and coach station, with a constant noise of engines revving and idling, much hooting, and people shouting. Seemingly somewhat sacrilegious and yet how fitting that in today's world all Jerusalem transport starts and finishes right there, bringing people directly to Jesus' cross whether they see it or not. Roman law insisted that crucifixions must take place in busy public places for all to see. A long trough carved in the rock showed how the huge stone would have been rolled in to seal it shut, then rolled away on that first Easter Sunday morning

This is not just past history; Jesus did not linger in that tomb; He is the risen Lord and Saviour, our hope and eternal security!

How do you picture Bethlehem? It is definitely not like Christmas card artists would have us believe. Sometimes called simply Ephrat, from: '…But you Bethlehem Ephrathah…' (Micah 5:2). Five miles beyond Jerusalem is Palestinian territory, requiring us to navigate checkpoints and some serious security to enter and drive through The Wall, that solidly enormous dividing wall of control and angry hatred. There was no chatter on our coach, only quiet shock. We passed street after street of boarded-up houses and shops, new buildings left abandoned. Poverty was evident, plus astonishing quantities of litter, and sad people standing about, many faces covered with scarves. Then came more open spaces, called *Beit Sahour*, or Shepherds' Fields: just hill upon sloping hill of barren, stony wasteland. We sat a while in an open-sided 'church' with hens scratching in the dirt, a rooster repeatedly crowing, and a long-eared brown sheep that wandered down to say hello. It was good to stand briefly inside the Church of the Nativity, thick with crowds, ornate decor and heavy incense, reminiscent of Kiev's cathedral. Even better to leave, relishing the hot sun in Manger Square.

As we left poor desolate Bethlehem, prayer grew from deep within me:

O God, this dreadful mountain of hate is snaking its divisive way through hearts, destroying so much. You say Your Word is living and active, sharper than a two-edged sword dividing joints and marrow, discerning the thoughts of the heart. Surely this wall is doing the same but for all the wrong reasons. Your Word brings truth, peace and comfort; the wall brings lies, conflict and hardship. How can I pray for the peace of Jerusalem, and for all the Holy Land? By remembering You are the God of reconciliation and justice, in Your infinite love for all people.

In the twenty-four miles to Jericho, on extremely winding roads, we went from twelve hundred feet above sea level to an ear-popping eight hundred feet below, passing through desert wilderness and seeing the occasional nomadic family. Bedouins still live as they always have, under goatskin shelters with a few camels, donkeys, and small mixed flocks of sheep and goats. These are hard to distinguish as both are brownish with long ears like our Bethlehem visitor.

The coach driver needed a break, stopping on a desert ridge where we could look into a valley. Across that vast, inhospitable terrain Elijah ran to escape from Jezebel (1 Kings 19:3-8). I felt his exhaustion, the pain in his feet as the stones shredded his leather sandals. What a viewpoint to stand on, pondering the wisdom of God. He knows exactly what we are capable of, and so often still has work for us to do when we feel we've had enough and cannot do more. He provides time to rest, think things through, find support where none seems forthcoming, plus encouragement from unexpected quarters.

God knew what was awaiting my return to work and what would emerge during the following few years, and how I would need the confidence of His close companionship. I treasure the stone collected from that Elijah moment.

Jericho, or 'Yeriho', is, I believe, the oldest continuously inhabited city in the world. To get to it we traversed the same route as Joshua, Jesus, and the man who went down from Jerusalem to Jericho when he fell into the hands of robbers (Luke 10:30), and was rescued by the Good Samaritan. All that's left of the old city where Joshua entered, obeyed, 'and the walls came-a-tumblin'-down' is a disappointingly insignificant mound of rubble and a small excavation site with what looked like quad-bike trails around it. Cable cars whisked us up to a restaurant on the Mount of Temptation. The height presented stunning views of now fertile valley fruit farms and the 'new' city streets teaming with children enjoying the post-Ramadan festival of Eid with horse and camel races in amongst the traffic and blowing litter.

29

Initial efforts to cross into Jordon at the Allenby Bridge caused unexplained trouble and tension. Our infuriated driver turned boy racer and rushed us to a different crossing to change coaches, and driver, after a lengthy wait in a hot room full of flies and armed guards. It was somewhat unnerving. As was our new coach whose cheery pink paintwork could not conceal the bullet holes in the windscreen. Finally over the River Jordan, at that point no more than a mere trickle along a dry bed of scrubby bushes, we passed The Dead Sea. It is named well, and slightly eerie. It is, however, also impressive, with its pewter-like surface reflecting rumbling storm clouds, except where there were sun-silvered patches under fingered beams. Said to be the lowest place anywhere, with decreasing water levels and salt-encrusted rocky shoreline. Poor future prognosis seemed to be attributed to natural evaporation plus the greedy consumption by skincare manufacturers of the salty potash.

Climbing high into the wild Mountains of Moab was starkly beautiful as they were backlit with pinky-purple sunset. I thought of Ruth and Naomi travelling together (Ruth 1:16), returning to Bethlehem after their husbands had died. We continued in the other direction, on to Petra, staying at a fancy hotel for a couple of nights. November 5th was Guy Fawkes in UK, my granddaughter Catherine's fifth birthday in US, and I was exploring the ancient Jordanian city carved out of red sandstone rock. Suitably clad and prepared for intense heat, we nearly froze at the mercy of unseasonably cold winds, but nothing marred that day. We walked down and down along the *siq* or sandy ravine between towering rock walls. The path opened up into a central square, one side of which was the monumental Treasury building, columned and about five storeys tall, intricately carved doors and windows leading way back into the rock: an immense naturally fortified sanctuary. I accepted the option of a camel ride for the steep return: an interesting experience but one I do not intend to repeat. The lumpiest, bumpiest, rudest creature I've ever been within spitting distance of.

Many miles along the King's Highway, the ancient trade route through desert lands of the Edomites, Moabites and Ammonites, we came to a place I'd noted on the brochure months earlier: Mount Nebo, the very mountain where God took Moses to view the Promised Land (Deuteronomy 34:1-12). Our group shared a short communion service inside the simple stone church up there, but I was itching to get outside before the sun set. Managing to clamber down far enough to hear silence rather than the chattering crowds, I found a delightfully appropriate cleft in a rock to sit by; it even had a small windblown olive tree firmly rooted in its shelter. Communion with God, drinking in His stillness, remains wondrously private. Later, trying to achieve some order from my thoughts I jotted the following:

- that God had allowed me to see what Moses saw
- to realise afresh, as Moses surely did, the high cost of not obeying God
- the wonderful provision God planned for His people – and still does today
- that He doesn't only give us just enough, but so often more than we could ask or imagine
- looking down onto the distant Dead Sea, again silvered by cloud-piercing sunbeams, knowing that bitumen and pitch were shipped across – bitumen and pitch used to mummify bodies, coat boat hulls, Moses baskets, and anything else needing to be securely sealed, as in the Ark, sealed as a place of security – and now we have the Holy Spirit to do the same
- high above my head stood the famous sculpture, catching the glow

of last rays, of the Cross with a serpent wrapped around it (Numbers 21:8,9; John 3:14,15), very real to me for all they mean and because the same design is on the Medic Alert disc I have to wear.

The city of Amman could have been New York, London or Chicago: noisy, a permanent rush hour for irritated drivers, but still pretty amazing to be there. Our hotel was the epitome of elegance, but with comfort and welcome seriously compromised, partly due perhaps to a few too many unfriendly-looking men in long garments with daggers in their belts. Bethany-beyond-Jordon is the presumed place where John the Baptist lived, preached, and baptised Jesus. We spent an overcast morning there, walking a long way beside the river through olive and bamboo groves. At a deck where those who wanted could stand in the water and renew baptismal vows, it seemed overcast in a different way. Immediately across from us was high fencing with frequent guard lookout posts, making it abundantly clear nobody was meant to swim or wade over to Israel. A lazy spa afternoon followed back at the Dead Sea. Expecting a salty but warmly therapeutic dip from a sandy beach, the reality was very different: rocky pebbles, freezing cold, and surprisingly rough water. I did manage to float for a minute or two before accepting Penelope's help as we stumbled in unladylike exit with more than a mouthful of salt. That ranks up there with the camel ride – once was enough.

Hearing that the shallow, muddy river we were crossing was the Jabbok ford, I asked the driver to stop. There was a man wrestling a load of wood across the water; he did it twice and nearly overbalanced several times. I thought of Jacob wrestling with the Angel of the Lord (Genesis 32:22-32), ending up with a blessing, a new name and a limp.

I found it nearly impossible to be 'just a tourist' and received some good-natured teasing for wanting to linger at each place. My companions happily offered their backs when there was nowhere else on which to lean my notebook. I didn't want to miss any musings as I marvelled. For example, the dry, rough country surrounding Gilead, so famous for its balm made from resin. Walking along the main street of ancient Gadara, City of a Thousand Columns, noticing the ruts from chariot wheels and the original drainage system's 'manhole covers' every seventh paving slab. Later, peacefully sipping strong cardamom coffee, we had a stunning view towards the Golan Heights, and down to where Jesus met the man called Legion (Mark 5:9). Leaving Jordan was again full of officialdom and security.

Mountains have long been associated with closeness to God and readiness to hear from Him; Mount Tabor was no exception. A significant landmark because of its surprising height, rising abruptly from the surrounding plain, it is the most striking mountain in the Galilean area, visible for miles (Psalm 89:12). Another noteworthy Tabor happening is described in Judges 4:4-16. From the top we could see the town of Nain, or Na'een, where Jesus raised the widow's dead son back to life.

Nazareth, also known as Rose of the Desert, is maybe the biggest Galilean town, and probably has the biggest litter problem. After wandering along streets, alleys and souks, we greatly appreciated the warm welcome at St Margaret's Hostel with its stunning hibiscus courtyard. The Basilica of the Annunciation had magnificent bronze doors telling Christ's life in pictures. Deep inside, down at the lowest basement level, stood part of the original house where Mary had lived with her parents, where the angel Gabriel told her she was to be the mother of Jesus. According to the customs of her time Mary, being young, poor and female, would have been considered unsuitable for any great task. God chose her for one of the most important acts of obedience He's ever asked of anyone. Let nobody who reads this allow lack of status, confidence or education to become a label of unsuitability for God's service. He looks for availability rather than ability; He doesn't call the equipped, He equips the called. We were shown what was said to be one of the Holy Land's most authentic sites, Mary's Well. A shrine built up around a humble trickle, struggling to bubble up from a nearby underground spring. She certainly must have gone every day to a well as all women did; and she would probably have gone in the heat of noon wherever she was living, to avoid scorn from the others when she could no longer conceal her pregnancy.

Arriving at the Sea of Galilee was wonderful even in the dark. Hearing wavelets slapping against the stone walled edge and seeing twinkling lights of boats on the opposite shore beneath dimly silhouetted hills. How good it is when what your eyes see matches what was in your your mind's eye.

After a short night I was alone at the water's edge to watch a real treat. Hazy grey sea turned to molten silver then to rippling gold as the fiery sun appeared over the hilltops of Galilee. That day, our last, was deliciously hot, as I had imagined the entire time would be. The town of Magdala, or Migdal, named after Mary Magdalene, stood out as did so many buildings and ruins made of white limestone from the Jerusalem area mixed with black basalt from Tiberius. The Arabic border town of Capernaum, or Ca'far na'houm, where Jesus first began His ministry (Matthew 4:12-17) is all ruins, but nonetheless very moving. The bright bougainvillea flowers made shady patches for a gecko with its adhesive toes darting about on a vertical bit of wall. Incredible to me to be so many places where Jesus had been.

The excavations of what is believed to be Peter's house has, of course, had a memorial built over it, but this one is interestingly clever. On sturdy legs the eight-sided church hangs above the ruins like a hammock or a fishnet, almost like a boat hovering. I heard that the first fish carving was found here. Part of an inscription read: '... house of Jesus, house of Peter, cradle of Christianity.' On the lake, or sea, shore, one of the places where Jesus appeared to His disciples after His resurrection is called Mensa Christi, or Table of Christ. Here He cooked breakfast fish for them (John 21:9-13). The birdsong there beside the sparkling water was truly lovely. A little further along is Tabgha, or Tabrah, the tiny Church of the Multiplication, commemorating the feeding of the five thousand with just five loaves and two fish. We had that place to ourselves, except for a family of hyrax, a small hare-like creature, living in the boulders and inquisitively checking us out. It was the best afternoon. Sitting around on logs under a tall shady tree mingling its branches with the rough wooden cross, we prayerfully shared bread and wine to the liquid music of Galilee on shingle.

Being then able to stroll at will, shoes in hand, and gather an attractive pebble or two, was joyful. This was wading in waters which dazzled the heart as much as the eye. Simple moments, maybe, to write about, but powerful enough in the memory to re-live in awe and gratitude for having been there.

That evening provided a last chance to use up any remaining shekels in local craft shops while waiting to board a 'Jesus-boat' to sail right round the Sea of Galilee. A sailor obligingly demonstrated the art of throwing out a large fishing net and gathering it all back again. As the sun sank behind the surrounding hills we saw the v-shaped break between two, learning how the wind can roar through that gap to whip up sudden fierce storms. Hard to imagine on such a calm evening, but it certainly explained the water getting rough enough to frighten the disciples into waking Jesus Who was sleeping in their boat (Matthew 8:23-27). The next morning required us to be on the coach by 4am to check in at Ben Gurion Airport for the return flight to London, then back to work.

30

In December some loyal friends agreed to help me prepare and serve Christmas Dinner to any in the neighbourhood who would otherwise spend the day alone. We went to shops asking for donations of food, money or gifts: a few were generous, some gave grudgingly, some declined. Gladly making up any deficits we managed to serve over thirty people and give each one a gift. Many wept and all asked for a repeat next year.

A happy celebration of my sixtieth birthday was held at the home of a couple in the church. The summer of 2006 brought huge joy in various ways. Two people chose to become Christians, to follow Christ for the rest of their lives, and one wanted to be baptised right away in the sea. Several others gave their lives to Jesus and there were more baptisms.

I was able to go to Illinois for the birth of Kate's Leo, my fourth grandchild, who arrived late, just days before the end of my three-week visit. It would have been too awful to have had to leave without meeting him. Garth came from Iowa with his three so we had some wonderful family times together.

One dear couple became very special to me. He was so ill when we met I could only sit at his bedside. He could no longer speak so I asked him to squeeze my hand if he was at peace, if he trusted Jesus as his Saviour. Tears rolled down the wrinkled face as his fading eyes shone. He found the strength to grip my hand with conviction; a precious moment. It was an honour to take his funeral.

Tough meetings got even more difficult, progress almost impossible. The self-appointed 'secretary' refused to correct his version of any minutes taken, to reflect what actually happened; and the long-established 'treasurer' withheld all financial information, saying it was none of my business. The atmosphere intensified as tensions rose. My five-year plan was met with derision and hilarity: 'What makes you think you'll still be here in five years? We'll have got rid of you by then.' I sought help from other clergy as well as, of course, from the Lord. I planned what to say in my own defence, but His word in my spirit, several times, was to say nothing. Rather like those ewes, silent before their shearers. I was certainly being shorn. Warnings came that it was not wise to stay. The increasing hostility came from a only a few in the congregation encouraged by nearly all the 'old guard', who seemed bent on my destruction because I could not and would not bow to their demands.

One said to me, 'You just don't get it do you – we control the pastor.' My quiet reply of, 'Not this one you don't,' made them very angry. There were topics they allowed or tried to forbid me to preach; and their main complaints appeared to be that I used the Bible too much and would keep talking about Jesus. I never expected problems of that sort. In no way do I think I'm on a par with the patriarchs, but this description in Hebrews 3:5 AMP does sum up my intentions at least: 'And Moses certainly was faithful in the administration of all God's house but it was only as a ministering servant.'

It is said that good intentions pave the road to hell. Another word for hell is Godlessness, so it is true to say that much there was hellish. I was surrounded by attempts to silence God while pretending otherwise; to retain the long established cover of darkness by blatantly ignoring rotten foundations and skeletons in cupboards. Those included inter-family hate and unforgiveness, and full acceptance of diabolical behaviour. The 'old guard' had been in charge for so long, expecting total acquiescence. When these things are uncovered they have to be dealt with; it is impossible to overlook them and continue speaking about the good news of Jesus. Where freemasonry is established much good can be found, particularly in fundraising and generous help for charities in need. There can also be a lesser-known cloak of manipulation and control spreading throughout the community.

Again, in Isaiah 45, God promises treasures out of darkness. I'd seen several gems already in that place, and there were more to come despite appearances to the contrary. Having accumulated some time off, I went away briefly before coming back to prepare for Christmas. A letter greeted me with the blunt announcement of a meeting called in my absence in which I was voted out and given one week to vacate. It felt distinctly like a third divorce.

This seems to be the right moment to insert an anonymous quote:

God may lead me on paths which are not safe. He may throw me among strangers and take me to places where I recognise nothing. But He holds the map therefore I will trust Him. He may confuse me, let my spirits sink and hide my future from me. But He holds the map therefore I will trust Him. He may push me to question everything I used to be sure of; give me every indication of His plan for me then lead me abruptly to a closed door. He may put me through events whose significance will remain a mystery until I reach heaven. But He holds the map therefore I will trust Him.'

Dear and staunchly supportive friends helped to find me somewhere else to live, showering gifts of prayer, finances, food and even some fun, refreshing my true identity in Jesus. I took long walks, crying out to Him again to do something, to fight the injustices for me and show me how to vindicate myself. He did, oh so clearly. He highlighted, repeatedly, specific psalms where David asks for the same: *Listen to my words, O Lord; answer me when I call; give heed to my sighing and groaning; vindicate me, O Lord; judge and vindicate me, O God, plead and defend my cause; save me, O God, vindicate me by Your mighty strength.*

Not once did David say, 'Let me vindicate myself.' The message was obvious, if somewhat unwelcome. As previously, I was to do nothing, but continue to trust in Him Who had brought me to that place, in Him Who says in both the Old and New Testaments: 'Vengeance is Mine.' So I underlined the first verse of Psalm 94 AMP: *O Lord God, You to Whom vengeance belongs, shine forth.* He would, but I could not see it yet. Like the up-ended ewe, severely shorn, I needed to remain silent. There was no place to go, and no peace in the leaving, so I knew I had to stay put and wait for Him to open a new door. That was probably the hardest time of all. Some people I'd gotten to know refused to have anything to do with me: how quickly gossip spreads, both within and outside the church.

No human intervention ever spoiled the exquisite beauty of the murmurations of starlings. They would literally dance through the sunset, wheeling, twisting, turning as one, although each group held thousands of the aerial display artists. They never crashed into each other or even touched wingtips; I loved watching them, but in a few minutes each air show was over.

Already a primary school governor, I had to be out and about in town even when staying hidden indoors would have felt so much safer. With meetings to attend and opportunities to chat with parents, time with staff increased as did the small team who shared weekly assemblies, morning and lunchtime. Not only allowed, we were asked to use and promote the wonderfully age-appropriate Open-The-Book programme. Children loved hearing the Bible stories and watching as we acted them out, seeing how their Truth still applies today. Many little ones had only heard of Jesus as a swearword; some wrote us notes of happy amazement that they now knew He is a real Person – and alive. One shy young girl, tall for her age, had suffered considerable racial bullying. Before Easter she tremblingly asked to portray Jesus at His last supper and crucifixion. In the school hall that day there was utter silence as she powerfully completed her part, standing motionless with arms outstretched, tears dripping down her face. She was not bullied again. Each week we invited a different class to take part with us and before long lists were made so every child would have a turn, if they wanted one, to act, read, or mime. No one was excluded and eventually even the more sceptical staff offered to join in. Other schools invited us in to take assemblies for their children, then began making it part of their own weekly agendas too.

A different sort of rota was established when I asked all the other local clergy to join me at the grocery store. Having discovered a few of the big stores in large towns and cities had their own cleric on staff, available to listen and offer counsel and prayer when wanted, I felt compelled to visit local managers. I also felt terrified. A daunting task, and only one manager agreed, grudgingly, but that's all we needed. Six colleagues joined as we met to pray through the plan, so we each had to commit to just a few hours once every seven weeks. Given a table in the cafeteria, an identity badge, a sign on the table saying what we were there for, and more than a few hassles, we launched. Free to do more or less as we pleased and enjoy the generously offered coffees it was still quite a challenge. Weeks passed before anyone was brave enough to test this new phenomenon of un-Sunday un-church along with the groceries. I found the cafe staff to be the most interested and slowly some good conversations developed, while curious eyes stared and ears wagged. Brief chats with one or two ex-congregants were rare, but did take place, although each appeared afraid of being seen talking to me. Some 'shifts' dragged a bit and nothing happened, nothing evident that is, but other weeks a small queue formed, then one or two folk asked to be prayed for. Wow, what a delightful privilege, is all I can say to that. After a year it was difficult to obtain permission for a second year, and some of the team dropped out. After the second year the management changed and we were not able to continue.

With notice in hand, at what I intended to be my final school governors meeting, I was shocked to be asked to take over as Chair of Governors. Thinking I'd contributed little, quite sure I'd be useless as Chair, I declined. God seemed to be holding that door wide open, and they were very persuasive, so after a few prayerful days I accepted. Good things happened, enriched relationships with many in the school, permission to wander anywhere, join in classroom lessons and help with extra tuition for some strugglers. The school had gone through hard times, nearly foundering under frequent staff changes, poor results and reputation. Suddenly I was part of the selection panel interviewing prospective new head teachers. It was a lengthy process with a great result. The person in whom I had most confidence received the position, and her quiet comment to me later was that she knew she'd need someone to pray for her. Respect for her grew, then admiration, especially among those who had wanted someone else to fill the post. Within a couple of years she turned that school around. I'm so proud of her. We remain in touch and she sends me occasional updates on the school's growth. At retirement she will not be easy to replace.

Further gems came to light from the darkness. Instead of the earlier enforced reduction or possibly cessation of any ecclesiastical raison d'etre, gradually it was returning, and gaining the tiniest momentum. How good of God to allow small children to effect great restoration. Instead of cold-shouldered adult avoidance, I was quite often happily hailed in the streets by current or past primary students and sometimes their parents also. 'Oh, it's the Open- the-Book-lady' was a simple greeting, but so cherished.

Also cherished was the request to take the funeral of a friend's father. That meant the long drive back to Sussex for a few days, but I was glad to do it. Apart from visiting friends and some of my family on that trip, the bereaved son asked me to speak clearly about Jesus during the twenty-minute slot in the large crematorium. Many of those who would gather to pay their last respects to the departed had paid little or no respect to his Creator.

Then came the exciting news of another long awaited birth in August 2008. Annie arrived, Kate's daughter and my third granddaughter. What joy, what a gift of pure blessing.

Then something quite unexpected. We had all watched the large new grocery store take shape on the outskirts of town, but the surprise was reading in the local paper that they were advertising for an in-store chaplain. *Lord? Do You mean this for me?* The door, both literally and metaphorically, was opened wide. Warmly received, I was shown around the whole premises and, once it was understood that I would not actually hit people over the head with a Bible, or pray embarrassingly loudly, the 'job' was mine. Given identification and access to the staff door, cafeteria, lockers and office, I started right away, several hours one day a week, at my convenience. Mostly I walked the aisles talking with any staff or customers who could take the time.

Warehouse staff seldom entered the shop floor and seemed really grateful for the chance of a chat amongst all the hi-vis jackets. Similarly, the till staff welcomed some attention. There was no discount on my shopping, but I seldom paid for café snacks. There were usually a few people eking out a coffee, or eating alone; some wanted it that way, but others welcomed the company.

Regular chats with a girl in the bakery had built her confidence, enabling her to put a request in the staffroom prayer-box. She asked for an hour off and we sat in an empty office while she poured out her heart, fearing she was too wicked to be prayed for. She told me later she was going to commit suicide that morning. *Thank You, God, for saving that girl.*

The idea of the prayer-box came to a dear friend, Sandra, while we were praying together. My boss asked many questions, but then approved the installation. He also gave me permission to use one of the staff notice boards.

Sometimes other notices were pinned over mine, or mine disappeared altogether. Unlocking the prayer-box was interesting since written requests were infrequent whereas other items were not, sweet wrappers being the least troublesome.

One of the office workers was continually caustic, as unhelpful as she could be. It was only by God's grace that I did not respond in kind. Incredibly, after many months, she suddenly asked to be prayed for. Two more lovely God-instances stand out: a beauty rep quietly wept while arranging make-up selections; she told me her troubles then asked how she could become a Christian – what a great question to answer. And two sweet boys on the produce aisle, both so enthusiastic about keeping the greens and the fruit neatly displayed. After some weeks they asked for advice and prayer, so we stood beside the broccoli and talked to the Lord. Much later I heard that one of them had decided to follow Jesus.

Occasionally I'd see someone from the church and either they would scuttle off down another aisle or, if we came face to face, there'd be a blank stare or perhaps a chilly hello. One woman did agree to a coffee in the café, a tricky but encouraging half-hour. One store staff member on the tills loved to chat about his dear wife, family, and his elderly, ailing mother. One day I received a message to contact him because she had died. He and his wife ushered me into their enviable cottage to ask if I would take her funeral. Really touched, I made sure to get all the information details correct, and prayed that Jesus would shine through into the hearts of the grieving family who 'did not want much religion in the service'. An easier request to comply with than some; they heard no religion, just the simple good news of the gospel. One of the small crematorium's officials said afterwards he wished more services could be real like that. *Thank You, God. I could never have done it without You.*

Unfortunately, my health continued to decline. Walking was painful, standing around virtually impossible. The initial diagnosis of arthritis was changed to polymyalgia rheumatica and I was told it only lasts two years. By that reckoning I should have been fit again, having known the stiffening pains in muscles and joints for several years already. Then it was thought I must have lupus. I hated to give my notice in to the store manager, and was quite overcome by his response. He said: 'I don't know how we'll carry on without you; we'll always have to have a chaplain here now. You must find us a replacement and train 'em well before you go.'

On a bright summer day as I walked across the park, a church couple headed straight for me. Expecting trouble, I was surprised to see she was in tears and he promptly joined in. When they could speak, and I understood, my tears flowed freely also. Abject apologies kept coming from them both. They admitted to being part of the plan, more than three years earlier, to oust me because they simply believed what they'd been told. Gradually they saw what was going on in that little church, and spoke up. Remaining there then became intolerable for them as well, so they left. They told me many others had also left, now happily worshipping God elsewhere, just as I was. Once they had realised the extent of the damage and understood more of what I'd been put through, they decided to find me. What joy and release forgiveness brings. From an unexpected source, what a sudden gift of divine vindication. Oft repeated maybe, but always so true: His timing is perfect.

Very shortly after that, quite early one morning, another surprise delighted me. Sitting quietly with a coffee, I was not in fact praying or journaling, or thinking of anything particular, when I heard, unmistakably clearly: 'There is peace in the leaving.' *Lord, is that You? It must be. It's You Who has given me no peace in the leaving all this time. Are You now telling me I can leave?* What a marvellously humbling thing it is to hear God, whether in the silence of your own spirit, or audibly in your own ears. I am so grateful to have been blessed with this more than once. Knowing I had heard the voice of God, knowing I could now return home to Sussex, it was some time before I could move, or bother about the cold coffee. Then the enemy barged in with doubt and fear: but where will I live, what will I live on, how will it work out, where do I start?

The friend who had guided me through the benefit application process several years earlier now found contact addresses for various rental agencies and housing associations. Driving back to Sussex, the conversations with the Lord bubbled on about where He wanted me to live, and how I would know where to start looking. I asked for just one flat in one town to be available because physically I was not able to traipse around very much. Once again, my sister kindly offered her spare room as a base for as long as necessary. Remarkably quickly I was contacted about one vacancy. I did go to see two others which were in hopelessly bad condition, but I knew what I had asked of the Lord. To double check with Him, I got more specific by asking three things for that one as yet unseen flat: that it would not be on the ground floor, that it would be light and airy, and have a balcony. It only took a moment, when called in to look around the tiny studio flat, to say a resounding Yes please. Small maybe, but all else was perfect, plus a view of the South Downs. Not quite perfect, for the carpet was old and horribly stained, but before I moved in a brand new neutral carpet had been laid throughout, with thick underlay, and a new shower installed. Perfect. This is my God, my Heavenly Father, Who promises to sustain and provide for His children: *Thank You, Lord.*

31

A great blessing was being invited to preach now and then at a small church in a nearby Sussex village. I didn't think I could do that ever again, but The Lord – and the people – reckoned I could. It was reassuring, a great blessing. Much of that winter and spring was taken up with visiting my mother and having to make other arrangements for her care. It was good to have my brother's help with that, and all four of us in agreement. Her new home was within walking distance of me so we saw a lot of each other in what was to prove her final months. Before every visit I had to pray for grace, patience, and the ability not to react to her jibes and negativity. I confess I no longer held much hope for any peace between us. In the autumn my sister moved away to be nearer to her expected grandchild and in early December nearly the whole family met together in Amberley for Mother's funeral. Nearly at the end, bedridden and helpless, she startled me one morning as I entered her room. Instead of the customary complaining and turning her head away, she reached out a skeletal hand to hold mine. Then a bigger surprise: looking directly at me she whispered how sorry she was. Instinctively I knew it was a huge coverall apology and that I needed to respond in kind. I take no credit for that, it was purely God's grace in action: the God of Reconciliation. After drying our tears I just heard her asking me to stay holding her hand, which of course I did. Three weeks later she died, without having spoken any more. At her service, after reading out tributes from my children in absentia, I felt I had to speak briefly on God's ability and desire to reconcile and redeem even the most unlikely situation, and the importance of forgiveness.

Some say there is no obligation to forgive unless or until the perpetrator apologises. That is not what God's Word says. What if the damage-maker sees no need to apologise, or flatly refuses to, or is dead? Where does that leave the damaged one? Angry. In pieces. Holding onto the damage as it grows year by year; becoming an impossibly heavy burden, far bigger than the original injury or insult. Possibly well camouflaged, that unforgiven issue will always be ready to surprise and embarrass as it surfaces waving the flag of bitterness. Surrender all the damage, and all the perpetrators: *For if you forgive men when they sin against you, your heavenly Father will also forgive you. But if you do not forgive men their sins, your Father will not forgive your sins.* Matthew 6:14,15.

A great delight was catching up with old friends in and around Lewes, now being able to spend time with them in person and not just by email. Also, wanting to put something back into this welcoming community, I found additional venues for volunteering and made new friends. Trying to lose weight and exercise more, I joined the GP recommended gym programme. In March, with the doctor's approval, I started horseback riding again. It was far nicer to exercise out in the fresh air than in a stuffy gym. I loved it, and yes, felt pretty chuffed that I could still mount up, at least from a helpfully placed box, and stay up and not roll right off the other side. Most of my joints complained, but not much worse than in the gym. The countryside and woodland available to riders was beautiful even in late winter bareness, and neither deer nor a family of foxes bothered to hide from us. Often seen was a pair of buzzards wheeling high above us, but not so high we couldn't hear their mewing calls. We also heard occasional gunfire. Usually about six of us went out each time. It was good getting to know new people, and different horses. Quite quickly I earned promotion to join those who veered off for a genteel canter. After the fifth ride it was time to purchase my own fetchingly elegant hardhat, and leather-palmed gloves. Was I trying to recreate my youth? Honestly, no; I was simply enjoying a healthy outdoor hobby and the amazement that I still could. April 30th 2010 was my sixth, and last, ride: I broke my back.

Cantering through a bluebell wood I thought I must have been shot. The pain in my lower spine was sudden and severe. My limbs went numb, mercifully only temporarily, and I remained in the saddle, but useless. That faithful steed knew something was wrong – my crying probably a bit of a giveaway – and slowed herself down to a gentle walk. Everyone kindly slowed to walking pace with me all the way back to the stables where the leader thoughtfully helped me dismount into the manure heap for the softest landing. Somehow I got into the car and drove home leaning only on the front edge and rear shoulder part of the seat.

With a cup of tea, painkillers and a hot-water-bottle surely it would ease if I sat still. I did, but it didn't. It was a bank holiday weekend so not till Tuesday morning could I drag myself to the surgery. They sent me to the hospital, thanks to a kindly neighbour who drove up the very moment I'd been praying for help, and came back to collect me. Certainly no bullet, but the diagnosis was a vertebral fracture of the L1, clearly visible on the x-ray, even to me. Then they asked why I was riding with spinal osteoporosis and arthritis, also evident on the film. The answer was my spine had been the only part of me that didn't hurt, and I was unaware of any osteoporosis. Given a prescription for four weeks of morphine patches with instruction to go home and lie down for eight weeks, I left. Many times since I've wondered why I did not question this. Pain does funny things in your head, and opiates make it very woolly, but who's complaining as long as it dulls the hurt?

Ancient Aunt lives nearby and brushed up her nursing skills to spoil me for a week. Her house has a lovely sunny guest room plus a stair lift. There, and once again home in my flat, I was overwhelmed by kindness. Sweet people, old friends and new, popped in regularly bringing food, treats, flowers, plus offers of laundry, vacuuming, and transport to and from medical appointments, for which the drivers brought cushions. The church had set up a list so I had a meal every day, sometimes from folk I had not met, but it made great introductions and some treasured friendships have resulted.

At the eight week hospital check I was told I'd done well, but not well enough, and to go home and lie flat for another eight weeks. Contrary to expectation that summer flew by, and boredom never got a look in. I felt so blessed, so thankful not to be paralysed, and that week by week I could move a bit better, though turning over continued to be the most awful. The walls of that tiny abode did occasionally press in on me, but the view from the little kitchen window always restored a sense of space. Hours went by reading, enjoying enriching radio from United Christian Broadcasting, and plenty of peaceful thinking and praying. It felt as if Jesus were chatting right beside me – no, not morphine-induced hallucinations. I bless that drug, but came off it before running out of it.

Impressive care was provided, and greatly appreciated, at the hospital in the form of physio- and hydrotherapy. It was wonderful, too, to keep up with my gradually increasing family, as Kate's third pregnancy progressed. Doctors disagreed about the advisability of what I hoped to do, which was to get to the States for the December birth. Just in time I was pronounced well enough, so with walking stick plus airport wheelchair assistance, I got there to welcome little Isla. A wonderful shared Christmas followed, with a January visit from Garth and his three, blessing me with all six grandchildren together under one roof – how delicious.

Before I left for the States the housing association decided I should be on the ground floor to make future wheelchair use more convenient. The negative of that was so wonderfully outweighed by positive gain and so many lovely people carried everything downstairs so I didn't have to lift a finger. In exchange for my balcony and view I was given a real bedroom, plus a tiny garden; and I don't need a wheelchair. Blessings galore, *thank You, Lord*. Unscathed from the travels, if rather tired, I was able to settle into my newly decorated spaciousness, resume driving and most of the various volunteer jobs, while being all too aware of increasing arthritis pain and stiffness.

In September the wider family met up for a few days in Scotland, by the only lake not called a loch. Reports of Isla's health, fine initially, went downhill a bit, worryingly so in the late autumn. By her first birthday she was very poorly and I was asked to go. Putting everything on hold and marvelling again at God-given generosity as my church – the church in action again – gave me my ticket money, I flew to Chicago on Christmas Day, not knowing what I'd find. *He holds the map, therefore I will trust Him.*

Isla and her mum had been in hospital for eight days already, but discharged in time for us to have a rather muted celebration on Boxing Day. Of course, so good to be together again, but not easy because the baby was far from well. We saw lots of medical people, and enjoyed another special weekend visit from Garth and his three. Eventually the undiagnosed hole in the heart was discovered and little Isla was surgically repaired just in time: *Thank You, Lord.*

Once back in England, huge anticipation grew at the prospect of Kate and family being here long-term. Huge disappointment overtook when that was not possible. Sometimes when things look like they're falling apart they may actually be falling into place. Now I have started on a new, two-year bone treatment and am already feeling better and able to walk more. I'm enjoying plenty of transatlantic communication, and looking forward to continually improving health, and maybe some new challenges and opportunities.

One recent challenge has been getting to grips with the computer programme to complete the final editing of this manuscript. To state whether I agreed with the suggested improvements, all I had to do was click the Accept or Reject button. Jesus is ready to make improvements in your life. The choice is yours: will you reject or accept Him?

I have tried hard to keep this magnum opus within right biblical boundaries: as stated in Titus 2:8 AMP, 'And let your [writing] be sound and fit and wise and wholesome, vigorous and irrefutable and above censure, so that the opponent may be put to shame, finding nothing discrediting or evil to say about us.' Amen. Be it so.

In acknowledgement of two other great hymn writers, Henry Lyte and Frances van Alstyne: Praise, my soul, the King of heaven; to His feet my tribute bring; ransomed, healed restored forgiven, who like me His praise should sing?

Blessed assurance, Jesus is mine: oh what a foretaste of glory divine!

Only when my citizenship and residence become permanent in heaven, and I see Jesus face to face, can this book at last be called **Renewed** instead of *Renewing*.

THE AUTHOR

Ruth Magdala, a late bloomer in every sense, was born and raised in England but, soon after her fortieth birthday, had been living in the States for half her life. Frightened of much, secure in little, she was good at making do, although quite unable to prevent a second marriage also ending in divorce. A scary way to live. Discovering Who Christianity is all about and getting to know Him did not smooth away her troubles, but did turn everything upside down and inside out, adding exciting to scary. Her two children were born and raised in the States and have now, thirty years on, made her a proud grandmother of six. She has settled peacefully back into the UK, is loving retirement, thankful for technology making possible frequent communications with them all, plus the wider family and many dear friends dotted around the globe.

Magdala's book has had a long gestation: many years stuck in the back of a drawer. She too has spent many years stuck in dark places, not all of her own making. She found hope and began to understand forgiveness, which gave her the courage to finish what she started writing in the 80s. Still amazed that Jesus found her worth bothering with, sorting out, and using in His service, she therefore believes that not one person is beyond redemption. She is also certain that He allowed her to struggle through so many bad experiences in order to let her grow, finally, into some wisdom. There *is* hope, and His name is Jesus. Magdala offers her story as encouragement to those still stuck in the dark, captives in all kinds of chains.

Lightning Source UK Ltd.
Milton Keynes UK
UKOW05f1242210114

224941UK00002B/48/P